Author
Cung Thị Lan

Two Sisters

A story that gives us hope even though there are sad elements

To my dear friend Marylee

Diem Tran
March 26, 2022

Translator
Diem-Tran Kratzke

Cover Picture by Lan Augustus
Cover Design by Minh Thanh Pham
Prepared by Hiep Quang Pham
Published in Washington DC
C T Printings & Graphics, Silver Spring, MD
Copyright ©2014 by Author and Translator
U.S Library of Congress Cataloging
Library of Congress Control Number: 2014909469
ISBN 978-0-9838040-3-1

Acknowledgments

I would like to thank the following persons who took time to read the manuscript and provide valuable editorial comments and encouragement: Marsha Collins, Jane Cruz, Mike Leali, Hiep Pham, and Tom Kratzke.

I would like to thank Minh Pham for the book cover design and to Lan Augustus for the artwork.

I would like to thank Cung Thi Lan for being a friend and for entrusting me with the translation of her book.

I would like to thank Jane Cruz for A Reader's Review.

—Diem-Tran Kratzke

A Reader's Review

What happens to children caught in the tight corner at the juncture of the working class and the educated class? The engaging novel *Two Sisters* explores that question by beckoning you to enter the world of two young girls growing up in the 1950's and 60's in Vietnam. We veritably hear their poignant stories as the narrator follows Ha and Vy from their tiny cottage on the grounds of the mansion their father's family owns through neighborhood friendships, trials at school, rocky relationships with their father's family, a visit to their mother's humble birth home, and on into the broader society.

Ha's and Vy's father passed away a few years ago. Although he was from an educated family, he fell in love with a beautiful woman from a rural and uneducated family. The relatives of their father had never accepted his marriage to their humble mother and were frustrated that she and her daughters were now part of their family. To accommodate them, their father's parents and siblings afforded them a small cottage without electricity and allowed the mother to work as a servant for the food and home they received. At the beginning of the novel, we picture the young girls in their dark cottage, doing all chores and homework before night fell. As the story progresses, that actual darkness in their environment is mirrored in the experiences of their lives.

The trajectory of their lives is foretold in the first pages of the book, when at Christmas time instead of quivering with excitement, they "dejectedly sit down on the porch to swallow their sorrow, blending in with the surroundings, taking in their solitude and familiarity." At the same time, their Young Aunt wears her Vietnamese dress with two long panels, "separated at the waist, flowing gracefully in the gentle breeze. Young Aunt wears her hair high up in a bun, exposing her elegant white neck and the pearl necklace that shines like a string of tiny glass ornaments." That dichotomy weaves its way through the whole novel, underscoring the timeless tale of the haves and the have-nots, the in-group and the out-group, the bullies and the bullied, the oppressors and the oppressed.

However, in this tale we see and feel not only the pain and anguish of the mother and her daughters, but also of their relatives, the ones who inhabit the "big house." The reader may believe that we need to be cheerleaders for the sisters, but in the intricate interplay of this family, we need to support each character in some manner. Each has his or her own pathos. It is that interplay that moves the girls into adolescence, the aunts into maturity, and the family into a realization. In the final pages of the book, Ha queries, "Don't you think [we] should be helped and loved, rather than despised and hated?... Is it true that we cannot love each other if we don't understand each other?"

Between the first and last pages lie poignant and profound experiences that define the lives of Ha, Vy, their mother and relatives. And in that definition, we have an intricate glimpse into Vietnamese society, culture, mores, and history.

The power of the novel lies in the author's deep understanding of the norms that governed Vietnam society in the 50's and 60's as well as the emotional development of young girls in that environment. She implants us into a city teeming with all of its pretentiousness and privilege coupled with the pain of poverty, takes us into rural Vietnam and introduces us to a more humble and modest life, and injects us deeply into the passions, desires, agonies, fears, resourcefulness, and ingenuity of the two sisters. The altering and developing relationships of the family members

Two Sisters

are mesmerizing, ensuring the book will seldom rest for long on a bedside table.

This is one of many books written in Vietnamese by Cung Thi Lan. It is the second book Diem-Tran Kratzke has translated into English. Together the two authors paint a vivid picture of the landscape, society, social system, and culture that defined Vietnam fifty years ago.

It's a place worth the visit through the pages of *Two Sisters*.

—Jane Cruz

CHAPTER ONE

Christmas is a busy time for Catholics, a time brimming with expectations for rich kids, a time of wonder for the two sisters. Ha and Vy are not Catholic, nor are they rich, but they look forward to Christmas because on that special day, in their uncle's big house, they get to see the green Christmas tree sparkled with silvery tinsel and colorful glass ornaments. Moreover, they get to witness the exciting gift exchange or perhaps even receive a few small gifts and taste a few morsels of exquisite food such as ragout chicken or yule log.

This year, the days leading to Christmas were not the same for Ha and Vy. Something really bad had happened between one of their aunts and Mother. One morning a few weeks back, when the leaves in the garden were still wet with dew, Mother walked out from the little house to start her cleanup routine. When she saw a brand new broom next to the old blunt one, at the corner of the storage room, near the lucuma tree, she took it to sweep the patio. Alas, she had no idea that this action would aggravate the ongoing conflict between her and her youngest sister-in-law.

Two Sisters

At the first sweeping sound that broke the morning's silence, Young Aunt, as Ha and Vy call her, immediately walked out the back door of the big house to investigate. Angry that her new broom was being used without her permission, she quickly yanked it away while berating Mother. She said something about Mother being too inconsiderate and full of herself. Then she pointed the broom at poor Mother's face and screamed invectives. It was unfortunate for Young Aunt that her fiancé, a mild and handsome man, entered the estate at that moment and, as he stood on the pebbled path connecting the front gate to the tiled patio, clearly witnessed the diatribe of his bride-to-be against the pitiful widow.

It is unclear why he happened to be in the garden of the Hoang extended family at such an early hour when the sun was not yet up. The two sisters' mother and aunt were equally astonished and stupefied when they saw him, becoming silent, unsure, and embarrassed. He also remained silent. He simply turned his back and walked away. Even after the front gate had closed behind him and his tall, thin figure had disappeared on the other side of the wall that separates the estate from the outside world, his silence pervaded the garden's atmosphere. His strange behavior disrupted Young Aunt's angry tirade. She put the new broom back in the corner of the storage room and went back to the big house. Young Aunt's sudden retreat, along with the unexpected appearance and disappearance of her fiancé, made Mother nervous as though she had committed a crime. Mother stared at the fallen yellow leaves covering the patio for some time before resuming her chore, but this time she swept the garden with the old blunt broom.

No one has seen Young Aunt's groom-to-be in the Hoang family garden since. People speculate that he left the beach city of Nha-Trang in Central Vietnam to forget the

Two Sisters

promise of marriage he made to Young Aunt. She has been waiting for him to return, only to end up going to mass by herself on Christmas Day. Ha and Vy have been counting the days to Christmas while reminiscing about wonderful Christmases past and they are so engrossed in reliving the good old days that they almost forget this day is the special day they have been waiting for, until Young Aunt returns from mass. They figure she goes to mass on Christmas Day not for any religious or other reasons but for the hope of seeing her fiancé there.

The extended Hoang family is split between two faiths. Elder Uncle[1], his wife, and Young Aunt follow the Christian faith while Sixth Aunt[2], Grandmother, and Mother follow the Buddhist faith. Young Aunt has been baptized Catholic at the behest of her fiancé who is a devout Christian. Since the Buddhists in the family do not pay attention to Christmas activities and the Christians keep their distance, Ha and Vy did not know if they would witness the Christmas party or taste the special Christmas food, even after they heard Elder Aunt tell Mother that she and her husband were going to have Christmas dinner at another relative's house and that Mother would not have to serve them dinner as usual.

Normally Ha and Vy have the leftover food after Mother cooks and serves dinner to Elder Uncle and Aunt and the rest of the family. But on this Christmas Day they have freshly cooked food because Elder Uncle and Aunt do not eat at home. However, they have more important things on their mind and do not care for dinner. They reluctantly put something in their bowls just to please Mother and quickly

---

[1] Elder Uncle is Mother's oldest brother-in-law.
[2] Sixth Aunt is a younger sister of Elder Uncle and a big sister of Young Aunt.

Two Sisters

excuse themselves, then run breathlessly to the front porch of the big house. Climbing the porch with quickened steps, they hold their breath, hoping to see a Christmas tree surrounded with colorful packages in the living room. Wouldn't it be grand if some of the gifts were for them!

Finding the double door to the living room tightly shut, they flutter their eyelids and slow their steps. Inching their way to the open window, they lean forward against the iron bars to take a peep inside – only to find no Christmas tree and no gifts. Everything is in its familiar place in the room, with no signs of Christmas. It is not clear to Ha and Vy whether it is a coincidence, or it has to do with the disappearance of Young Aunt's fiancé, that the patriarch of the extended family did not put up a Christmas tree in his living room and no one has mentioned a word about celebrating what had once been a wonderful time. They dejectedly sit down on the porch to swallow their sorrow, blending in with the surroundings, taking in their solitude and familiarity.

Between the little house where they live with Mother and the big house where they sit is a large garden with fruit trees they know so well. Without looking, they can envision the branches from the bent trunks of the coconut trees lean down and touch the roof of the little house as if threatening to fall down any moment. In the middle of the garden near the well, the star apple tree with its gigantic branches and dense leaves gives shade to almost the entire garden, serving as a haven for Ha and Vy, under which they have played countless games and confided innumerable secrets in one another. Along the back wall, the symmetrical branches of the soursop and green wax jambu trees add beauty to the garden. Lining a path from the well to the big house's kitchen are the carambola, sapoche, and lucuma trees. Along the pebbled path on the right side of the big house, the

Two Sisters

Western hibiscus plants stretch high toward the sun and wave their glorious blooms triumphantly in the air, while the Chinese hibiscus plants stay low but display their beautiful deep red flowers waving long yellow pistils gracefully under the sky.

Usually the appealing fruit trees call to Ha and Vy, especially when they are hungry, but as they sit on the porch of the big house, they want a Christmas tree so badly and none of the fruit trees they knew so well is it. The trees bear only leaves and fruit. They bear no lights, no ornaments, no sparkling tinsel. They know only how to dance and play with the wind and sunlight. They wear only the one color green which is so ordinary compared with the fanciful colors of a well-trimmed Christmas tree. And most importantly, they bear no gifts. Neither the garden trees nor the showy flower bushes can emotionally move Ha and Vy. Nothing in the garden can take the place of a Christmas tree they fervently wish for.

As they lean on each other in the quiet early evening, Ha, the big sister, comes up with an idea. As it takes shape in her mind, she jumps up. "We have a Christmas tree!"

"Where, where?" Vy asks, both dubious and hopeful.

Ha points to the Chinese hibiscus bush. "Don't you see? These green leaves have the same color as a Christmas tree and the red flowers are the small red lights."

Looking at the flower bush, Vy claps her hands. "We have our own Christmas tree with so many red lights! It is the most beautiful Christmas tree in the whole world! But what about gifts? Where are our gifts, Sister Ha?"

Two Sisters

Ha walks around the bush. "Look! There are many gifts under the Christmas tree. Now we'll play opening Christmas gifts. Okay, Vy?"

Vy nods and immerses herself in Ha's fantasy. "Let me open my gift first."

"Okay. What do you want?"

"I want a doll!"

"A doll? I know there is a doll somewhere. Let's look… Here it is!" Ha bends down and reaches under the bush, mimicking a motion of getting a gift box from under a tree to give to Vy. "Open it."

Vy pretends just the same, making a motion of opening a gift box. She spreads her arms as if holding a baby and rocks them as if lulling the baby to sleep. Ha closely watches Vy's every action. "Do you like it? Is it pretty?"

"Yes. All dolls are pretty."

Ha nods and changes the subject so that Vy will not describe a doll that may be different from the one in her own imagination. "Do you want to open more gifts?"

"No. It's your turn. You should open yours."

"I don't want presents anymore," Ha hesitates.

"So what do you want?"

"I also want a doll but there are not any more dolls."

"But you said that there are many gifts."

Two Sisters

"There are many but they are not dolls."

"So pick something else."

"I don't know what to pick. And I don't want anything anymore."

"What do you like?"

"I like a shiny ornament."

"Go get it."

"There are no shiny ornaments."

"I get a doll, so you can get a shiny ornament!"

"But this Christmas tree only has lights. It doesn't have shiny ornaments or tinsel."

While Ha and Vy go back and forth, Young Aunt, wearing a white Vietnamese dress, walks in through the front gate. The two long panels of her dress, separated at the waist, flow gracefully in the gentle breeze. Young Aunt wears her hair high up in a bun, exposing her elegant white neck and the pearl necklace that shines like a string of tiny glass ornaments. Ha stands aside, willing Young Aunt to stop so she could look at the pearls in detail. Ha wants the pearls in her own hands so that she can touch them, feel them roll around her fingers, and see her own reflection in them. Ha always enjoyed looking at her own reflection in the glass ornaments of the Christmas tree in the living room of the big house whenever she had a chance. Ha considers saying hello to Young Aunt so she can look at the pearls a while longer, but before she does so, Young Aunt has hurried by. Young Aunt walks fast and appears distant and uncaring as though she did not see her nieces or her dogs, Kiki and Yellow, who wag their tails nonstop at the excitement of seeing her.

Young Aunt used to wear her best dress and jewelry to attend church with her fiancé on a Sunday evening or a Christian holiday. She would be cheerful on those occasions as she walked with her future husband, and stopped to talk to Ha and Vy if they were in the garden and from where they stood, they could smell her perfume. Sometimes Young Aunt patted their heads and asked them to take care of the dogs so her dress would not get soiled. But Young Aunt acts strangely on this Christmas Day, making them nervous and scared. They sense something terrible is about to happen…to Mother. They immediately run home to find the front door ajar and the large oil lamp – the sole source of light for their household activities – already lit, but Mother is not there. She apparently has returned to the big house to finish up her chores after giving them dinner. Unsure of what to do, they stand at their front door, looking at the big house in search of anything unusual. They want to call out to Mother to come home early before something bad happens, but they remain silent.

A loud curse breaks the silence. "Bitch, are you happy now that you've ruined me? Damn you, mean spirit!" Ha and Vy stand still as Young Aunt repeats the epithets again and again as though she wants them remembered word-for-word. She continues with a stream of more curses. "Bitch, I wish you dead! You've ruined me! So you want to ruin me, huh? May you be torn to shreds. You think you're good and fine? God has punished you. You're a husband killer. You deserve what you get. You try to ruin me now just because you were punished and ruined by God."

Ha and Vy are too scared to move. They do not understand all the words, but they know from her tone that

Two Sisters

Young Aunt is furious. Now and then they hear Mother's quiet and timid voice drifting from the back patio of the big house. She probably pleads to be understood, but no understanding comes forth from Young Aunt. Young Aunt taunts Mother by mimicking her country accent. She repeats Mother's words in a drawn-out manner. When she finishes taunting Mother, she challenges Mother to a fight. "Idiot! Country girl! My brother was blind to marry you. Your kind does not deserve to live in my house, to be in my family!"

The more Young Aunt spews charges, the more perplexed and scared Ha and Vy become. Her words are strange to their ears. They do not understand the nature of the conflict between their mother and aunt. They try to comfort each other by anxiously leaning against one another. They want Mother home, but she cannot find a way out of the conflict just yet. She cries softly, trying to explain her innocence. Her cries in the otherwise quiet evening unnerve Ha. She stands up, pulling Vy with her, wanting to go to Mother, but stops when Young Aunt raises her voice again. Ha and Vy feel paralyzed as if their feet were glued to the ground.

Vy sobs. "Why doesn't Mom come home, Sister Ha?"

"She has to finish her chores," Ha answers, trying to look and sound calm. "Don't worry about it, Vy. Mom is used to being scolded."

Vy cannot stop crying. "I'm scared,"

Ha worries too. She knows that Grandmother and Sixth Aunt often take Young Aunt's side and Mother has suffered the consequences. Ha and Vy already lost their father, so Mother is their only source of comfort. The spiteful actions and condescending words directed to Mother from the family members living in the big house show them that Mother is despised because of her low social rank and lack of education. The disparaging words and hostile actions do not lessen the value of Mother's presence in their hearts. They love Mother as she is their only source of safety and comfort in the world. Mother is going through a terrible time and they cannot do anything about it, especially at their tender ages of six and eight. Their anxiety increases as they remember the harsh way Young Aunt has treated Mother in the past. They pull close to each other and their eyes are glued to the back patio of the big house. Thoughts of Christmas gifts and delicious food have vanished.

They are momentarily distracted by the new voices of Grandmother and Sixth Aunt. The regular rhythm of their voices suggests that Grandmother and Sixth Aunt are trying to pacify Young Aunt who has become louder. Ha and Vy listen closely, but they cannot discern everything being said, nor do they understand why Young Aunt stays angry for so long. They only know that Young Aunt uses terms that Mother never lets them use with each other, terms they often hear from Young Aunt's frequent and harsh tirades against Mother, terms that certainly are not endearing.

The back-and-forth dialogue is altogether one-sided, for Mother's quiet sobbing and muttering cannot balance Young Aunt's loud screaming and scolding. It continues until midnight. Ha stubbornly ignores the mosquito bites and steadfastly stays at their front door waiting for Mother's return.

As darkness descends, the garden takes on the savage coat of the wilderness, and Young Aunt's anger still has not subsided. The otherwise quiet night is alternately interrupted by Young Aunt's loud ranting, Mother's whispered explanation, Grandmother's murmured appeasement, and

Two Sisters

Sixth Aunt's quiet advice. The sound of the nocturnal birds feeding in the night becomes background music to the human woes in the garden. A shrill scream of Young Aunt tears through the midnight air. "I'm going to beat you to death! Go to hell!"

Mother's sudden loud cry comes amid Young Aunt's screaming and Grandmother's and Sixth Aunt's pleading. The cacophony of screaming, scolding, muttering, and crying disturbs Ha who decides that enough is enough. She boldly stands up and pulls Vy with her. "Get up, Vy. Let's go see if Mom is being beaten." The little one, startled, opens her eyes, grasps her big sister's hand, and runs with her toward the big house. They slow down when they get to its side and walk cautiously toward the patio. As they tentatively land their feet near a hibiscus bush, they hear the front gate being opened. They freeze while Kiki and Yellow bark loudly and happily to greet the two people walking in. The dogs run wildly in circles around Elder Uncle and Aunt who have just come home from their Christmas dinner. Elder Uncle and Aunt do not go into the big house through its front door but walk along the pebbled path to the patio. Ha and Vy step back. "Hello Uncle and Aunt," they mutter in tiny voices.

Elder Aunt busily waves the dogs aside so that they will not jump up and soil her beautiful dress while Elder Uncle furrows his brows. "Why aren't the two of you in bed at this hour?"

They do not answer but let their uncle and aunt pass by, walking quietly behind and cautiously stopping at a flower bush. From there, they witness a pitiful happening on the tiled patio. Young Aunt, Grandmother, and Sixth Aunt stand around the shadow of a miserable woman who sits on the ground with her head bowed almost all the way down.

Two Sisters

Young Aunt screams while pointing her finger at the miserable woman's face. The woman leans one way and then the other, trying to avoid the pointing finger that is continually fired at her face. Grandmother and Sixth Aunt try to pull Young Aunt back whenever she attacks the figure on the ground. As Elder Uncle and Aunt approach, Young Aunt ignores them and continues hurling derogatory insults. Ha's face turns red with anger. She wants to run in between Mother and Young Aunt to push away the accusing finger and take Mother's frail body home. She wants to shout "Don't you bully Mom," or "That's enough." But her thoughts do not translate into actions. As in countless times past, she stands still with feet glued to the ground.

"You should not be so rude, do you hear?"

Everyone stands agape at hearing Elder Uncle's words except for Young Aunt. She reacts as though he has thrown more fuel on the fire. She flings her body over his, determined to hit the pitiful woman in revenge. But before she can do so, he kicks her twice in the chest.

"You can kick her some more," Grandmother says, exasperated. "I told her to stop but she didn't listen."

Elder Uncle disregards Grandmother's words, taking them as a complaint rather than a command. He grunts and walks away. Tired from struggling to separate Young Aunt from Mother, Grandmother breathes heavily. "Sisters and brothers! You won't be satisfied until someone dies."

Sixth Aunt pulls Young Aunt away, appearing irritated. "I've been trying to stop you, but you didn't listen to me."

Elder Aunt calmly walks toward Mother and speaks in a clear and dignified manner. "You go home to sleep and come

Two Sisters

back tomorrow. There's no reason for you to stay here." Then she heaves a heavy sigh. "There's no dignity in arguing so loudly at night. What a shame that you did not respect the neighbors!"

Elder Uncle does not pay attention to the women. He quietly walks into the big house through the back door. Elder Aunt follows his footsteps, but not without looking back one last time to throw a despising look at everyone. Perhaps Young Aunt is physically hurt by the kicks and emotionally wounded by the words; she stays silent. Grandmother and Sixth Aunt guide her into Sixth Aunt's little house while soothing her. Mother is left alone on the patio, surrounded by the big house, its kitchen, Sixth Aunt's little house, the garden, and the path to the front gate. She cries softly. From the darkness of the hibiscus bushes, Vy pulls away from Ha, runs to Mother, and holds her. "Mom! Let's go home and sleep with me."

Mother holds Vy tight, puts her head on Vy's shoulder, and lets loose with an audible cry, a heartfelt cry she has been suppressing throughout the ordeal. Ha stays put, quietly observes her mother and sister, and patiently waits for Mother to take them home. Mother continues to cry on Vy's shoulder and stays glued to the patio as though it were a shelter that could protect her from Young Aunt's anger.

"Let's go home, Mom," Ha finally says, tears falling down her face. "Don't stay *here* anymore!" Ha does not like the fact that they stay "here," at the Hoang estate. She pours out her anger. "Why do we stay here? Young Aunt always gets mad at us."

She wants to say much more to show her grandmother and aunts the anger she feels. But she is only eight years old. She does not know what to say and only sputters a few

Two Sisters

random statements. "Scream at us all you want. You are all bullies. Would you yell at us if Dad is alive?"

Vy is so surprised at Ha's loud and big words that she stops crying while Mother sits stupefied. Mother at last pulls herself up and covers Ha's mouth with her hands. "Hush! You can't be rude! I am taking you home." She pulls her children to her. "We are going home right now."

Together they walk toward the little house. At the well, Mother washes Vy's feet and urges Ha to do the same.

Vy snores as soon as she lies down. Ha's eyes stay wide open as she ponders things. She hears Mother's sighs and sobs amid Vy's snores. She waits for Mother to say something until her patience runs out. "Were you beaten?"

Mother is not surprised that Ha is still awake. She confides, "From the beginning, I understood my lowly background and did not want to marry your father."

Ha is surprised. "Why didn't you want to marry Dad?"

"Because he was the teacher in my village. I was a thousand times beneath him in knowledge and education." Mother pauses, and then continues when she receives no immediate feedback. "He was from Hue[3], an affluent city. I was afraid of the Hue people, especially the educated and the rich. I figured that your father's family held high positions and was conservative, so I said no to him. And yet in the end I could not avoid my fate."

---

[3]Hue is the former imperial capital of Vietnam during the Nguyen dynasty.

Two Sisters

"So what happened?" Ha asks, dying to know more.

"Your father tried to commit suicide several times. That's why my father ordered me to marry him."

Ha is dismayed to know this about her father. "Dad tried to kill himself? Why?"

"Because I said no to him."

Ha has loving memories of Father and does not like the direction of the story, but she wants to know more. "You said you didn't want to marry him. Why did you change your mind?"

"After your father tried to kill himself the third time, your grandfather took Fourth Aunt to the hospital to pretend to be me and accept your father's proposal. When your father was discharged from the hospital, your grandfather told me to marry him."

Ha does not know what a proposal is but guesses that it is related to "accept" and "marry." She surmises that "accept" is responsible for the terrible ordeal that Mother goes through. Ha wants to ask a thousand questions that begin with "why," but she cannot keep her eyes open. She yawns and soon falls asleep.

Mother stays awake, feeling trapped in a fate she had tried to avoid long ago. In her mind back then, the fate she tried to avoid by not marrying up consisted solely of minor cultural conflicts with her husband's family. She could not have imagined the depth of her hardship, especially now with no husband to support her, emotionally or financially.

Two Sisters

Thinking back to what happened earlier in the day, Mother feels traumatized. If it were only verbal abuse as it had always been, she figures she can still go into the big house to do chores for her late husband's brother and sister-in-law. But the problem has become much more serious – so serious that her brother-in-law has hit his own sister! It was clearly an intolerable event that had never happened before. She feels guilty and unsure of the best course of action to take when she faces her mother- and sisters-in-law the next day. She is terrified when she thinks about walking across the tiled patio, entering the big house, and interacting with the people who were involved in the conflict. She considers quitting being a maid for her brother-in-law and his wife, but is not sure how else to earn money.

Since her husband's death, Mother has been empty-handed. All the money she and her husband managed to save from his modest salary as a civil servant was spent on his hospitalization. The gift of money from friends and relatives after his death went toward the funeral. Afterwards, she had nothing in her name but a three-year-old toddler and a baby just learning to walk. At that time, her husband's sister-in-law was frank to her. "If you are unable to raise the children, give them to us. If you wish, you could walk another step and remarry but you'll have to leave the children here. They belong to this extended family."

With no income, no money, no education, and no job, there was nothing else she could do but accept the proposal and become Elder Uncle and Aunt's maid, performing all their household chores. She could not stand the thought of leaving to others the children she had born. Being a maid for her brother-in-law's family would allow her to keep and raise her children until they were grown.

Two Sisters

After years of being a single mother, working hard and barely having enough to eat, Mother has not saved enough money to quit the job to which she is accustomed. She wonders if she will have to return to the maid job after all. She wonders if she will be able to endure the curses and the abuses heaped on her almost daily and if there really is no way out of this kind of life for her and her children.

With no plan and no solution, the trapped mother feels totally hopeless. The darkness enveloping her tiny abode reflects the bleak future she envisions for her little family.

CHAPTER TWO

•

The clash of the pot lid on the cement floor wakes Ha up. The sunlight, through the open door, casts a rectangle on the floor of the area they call the "dining room," where Vy picks up the fallen lid. Ha knits her brows, thinking hard. Each morning when she and Vy wake up, they linger in bed for a while to ponder their dreams in the "bedroom" where it stays semi-dark because the sunlight is blocked by the dresser. They like it that way since the soft diffused light gives them a calm and peaceful feeling as they prepare for a new day. Mother would light the incense sticks on Father's altar and close the front door behind her as she goes to the big house to begin her work day. When Ha and Vy wake up, they can smell the sweet fragrance of the incense while still in bed.

This morning, Vy has gotten up before Ha. When Ha sees sunlight on the dining room floor, she figures she has overslept. She quickly jumps out of bed, thinking they are late for school. While she gathers the sides of the mosquito net into a bundle to be tied at the top, she has time to remember that it is not a school day. After heaving a sigh of relief, anxiety returns as she realizes that it is the day after

Christmas. Recalling the events of the previous evening, she asks Vy, "Where's Mom?"

"She's home," Vy replies, covering the rice pot with the lid.

"Where?"

"In the altar room."

Their one-room house is divided into functional areas that are loosely called "rooms" by the occupants. The altar room is in the front, separated from the back by a large sheet hung on the ceiling beam by Mother, and has two windows that are usually open during the day. Next to the window that faces the South side of the estate are two altars, one for worshipping Buddha and one for commemorating Father. The little oil lamp on Father's altar is always lit in his remembrance. A wood table and chairs are set at the window that looks out to the front gate and the garden. The back part of the house consists of the dining room and bedroom, separated by a dresser. The bedroom has two beds, the larger one is Ha and Vy's, the smaller one is Mother's. The dining room where they eat their meals receives the first rays of sunlight when Mother opens the "front door," the only accessible door to the outside. The bedroom has no windows and therefore does not receive direct daylight. The door originally meant to be the front door is blocked by the West wall of the estate and is forever locked shut. The four long, tall, and white walls enclosing the entire estate impose an air of importance and lend the small house the appearance of a status equal to that of the big house.

Ha runs to the altar room to find Mother sitting in front of Father's altar, staring vacantly at the dancing smoke of the incense sticks. Unlike other days, the room is dark with its

Two Sisters

windows closed. Mother stays put when Ha enters. Ha stands there for a long time waiting for Mother to speak. Finally, defeated, she walks back to the dining room and checks on Vy. "Did you brush your teeth and wash your face?"

"Not yet."

"Why not?"

"I am looking for food."

"You can't eat before brushing your teeth."

"But I'm very hungry."

Ha suddenly realizes that she is also hungry. Neither of them ate much at dinner the day before because their minds were occupied with Christmas things. "What are you looking for in the rice box?"

"I want to see if there is anything to eat."

Ha feels pity toward her little sister. They often gather soursops or sapoches from the garden when Young Aunt is away, and hide them in the rice box so they would have food to eat when they are hungry. The days before Christmas were too exciting for them to think about storing food.

"There's nothing to eat. I'll give you something else. Let's brush our teeth first."

Ha walks to the kitchen, a lean-to attached to the left side of the little house. Vy follows. This is where they store their toiletries. Ha takes out some salt pieces from a clay pot to use as toothpaste. Vy puts the salt pieces on the bent and worn bristles of her toothbrush and uses water from a bucket

Two Sisters

next to the well to brush her teeth. Ha does the same. After brushing and washing themselves, they sit at the front door contemplating a plan for the day. The quiet and peaceful garden lacks a sense of excitement and even seems dull without Young Aunt or any other adults. Vy does not hide her unhappiness at being hungry. She has been waiting and Ha has not given her anything to eat as promised.

Ha cannot think of a way to obtain food, but she is excited with a new idea. "Hurry up and follow me, Vy." Vy hurries after Ha, trusting that she is going to be fed at last. She recalls numerous times in the past when Young Aunt was away, Ha would pick fruit from the garden and let her eat whatever she wanted. But to her surprise, Ha is not heading toward any fruit-bearing trees. Vy is even more perplexed when Ha sits down at the star apple tree, shakes off the plastic flip-flops from her feet, and uses them to scrape the dirt on the ground. Ha heaps the dirt into a pile and pats it down to flatten it. Vy watches Ha closely and cannot fathom the kind of food she is about to have. Ha is delighted to see that Vy is wide-eyed and earnestly anticipating. She orders Vy to sit and wait while she gathers materials. First Ha runs to the kitchen, then to the water barrel, then to the sweet carambola tree, and finally to the Western hibiscus bush. Ha arranges the items gathered around the flat dirt. With flying hands and nonstop talking, she explains, "The hibiscus buds are red peppers and the water is fish sauce. I'll cut up the buds and add them to water to make spiced fish sauce. The carambola leaves are fried green onions and this bowl is rice flour."

Vy cannot imagine the food Ha describes, nor does she understand how the phantom food can relieve her hunger, but she is too stunned to say anything. Ha takes Vy's silence as her being up to the game. "Watch, I'll make rice cakes." Ha spoons water from the bowl onto the dirt, creating dark circles of wet dirt so they look like little ramekins. Ha is pleased with her creation. She imagines the flat dirt a baking oven to cook the ramekins of rice cake dough. Vy watches Ha in silence. Although Vy does not show any enthusiasm, Ha feels completely confident that Vy will like her made-up game. Ha laughs heartily. "The rice cakes are ready. I'll get you some."

Plucking two star apple leaves from a growth near the ground, Ha uses the smaller leaf as a ladle to spoon the "rice cakes" onto the bigger leaf used as a plate. She uses twigs for chopsticks and tops the five rice cakes with fried green onions. She spoons spiced fish sauce into a small tin can lid. "Have some rice cakes, Vy." Vy reluctantly receives the strange breakfast food and stares at it with a long, sad face. She sits still as a stone. Ha silently observes her little sister, patiently waiting for a reaction. Ha's eyes searchingly move from Vy's face to the food, up and down, back and forth; and as if she knows what the problem is, she cheerfully sets two tiny star apple twigs on the plate. "I forgot. You need chopsticks to eat."

Vy's face elongates some more and tears form in her big sad eyes. She sulkily lowers the plate. "How can I eat the dirt cakes?" She throws the content of the plate and bowl on the ground. "This is not food!"

Ha raises her brows. "How can you throw things away? If you don't want to play, you should just give everything back to me." Vy does not dare to talk back; Ha is upset nevertheless. She intends to give Vy a lecture, but before she can open her mouth, she hears a laugh coming from behind.

"This is strange. How can anyone eat dirt cakes?"

Two Sisters

Turning around, Ha sees the three granddaughters of Elder Uncle and Aunt staring at the two of them. These are three of the six children of their cousin Trinh, the only daughter of Elder Uncle and Aunt. Perhaps the little ones have been watching the breakfast game for a while, but Ha has been immersed in it and was not aware of their presence. They wear pink lace dresses with matching pink shoes and white socks. Their hair is neatly combed and tied into ponytails with matching hair ties. Their fancy clothing is in stark contrast to the dirt ground they stand on. They carry coloring books and dolls – the kind of dolls with eyes that can open and close. Ha is still mad at Vy and does not appreciate being teased. She twitches her eyebrows and tries to think of something to say as a comeback to release her anger, but she cannot come up with anything appropriate to the occasion.

The littlest girl, who is about three years old, stops her thumb-sucking and walks toward Ha. She sits down next to the flat dirt, holding a doll on her lap, and innocently asks, "Can I play?"

Ha calms down and nods. "Do you want to eat or to make rice cakes, Phi?"

"I want to make rice cakes."

"Sure. I'll let you make rice cakes," Ha happily says. She gives the spoon to Phi and tells her how to pour dough into the ramekin. Phi laughs out loud when she sees how water seeps into the dirt and darkens it. Phi's older sisters, Phong and Phuong, become interested. They plop down next to Phi, spreading their clean lace dresses on the dirt ground. Seeing the little ones having so much fun, Vy forgets her hunger. She squeezes in the middle to participate in the game she did not care for at first.

Two Sisters

"It's my turn," Vy protests. "Let me pour the dough."

"Everyone will get to pour the dough," Ha solemnly says. "But this oven is not the same as what you see in the market. If it collapses, we'll have to rebuild it. You'll have to wait until I build a new one right now."

Again Ha uses her worn plastic flip-flops to scrape and gather and flatten the dirt to build a new oven. The little girls watch until Ha finishes, and then they all talk at once.

"Let me do it first."

"No, me first."

"No, you already did it. It's my turn."

While Ha has not decided whom she should give the turn to, she is startled by Elder Aunt's booming voice from behind. "You three go inside right now. What are you doing over there?"

Immediately Phi, Phong, and Phuong scramble up and run away. Feeling guilty and scared, Vy moves closer to Ha as if for protection. Ha, whether being too scared or pushed by Vy, cannot move. Her eyes glance back and forth from her aunt to the dirt of disarray. Ha feels lucky that Elder Aunt does not question her about the game. She simply pushes her grandchildren away from the star apple tree and toward the big house. Ha and Vy, left by themselves in the middle of the garden, absentmindedly watch the little girls go away until the three hair bows disappear behind the hibiscus bushes. Their aunt's voice, although not directed to Ha and Vy, is loud and clear. "Who let you play with the dirty girls? Look at this. Your dresses are filthy. Your great uncle Giu's children always play with dirt in a low-life way.

Two Sisters

Why do you have to play with them and get dirt all over you like this?"

Elder Aunt speaks so loudly that Mother, who has fallen asleep sitting on a chair in the altar room, wakes up. Mother runs to the garden and quickly helps her daughters clean up. She orders them to go back inside to do homework. Ha and Vy open the window next to the table for light, but they do not read or do homework. They longingly look at the big house through the window. They daydream about playing with the little girls and touching and holding the beautiful dolls. A feeling of regret fills their beings and lingers on the window bars – the perceived barriers through which their yearning lies.

In the evening, Mother uses up all of the rice they have to cook congee. Ha does not care much for this kind of food. This is a problem whenever she is sick because Mother always makes her eat congee before giving her medicine. But right now Ha is not sick, so she feels justified in complaining. "We are not sick. Why do we have to eat congee?"

"We do not have enough rice," Mother calmly replies. "We're lucky that we still have any left." After a brief silence, she continues, "You should feel lucky that we have congee today. We may not have anything to eat tomorrow. Eat what you have, do not wish for more. If you don't eat and get sick, I do not have money to buy medicine."

Ha does not contradict Mother because she senses dejection in Mother's voice and posture. Vy does not complain. She is happy to eat congee with salt. It is better than nothing. She has not had anything to eat since she got up this morning. She greedily gobbles up the congee as though it were gourmet food, without stopping to see if she

Two Sisters

should share it with anyone else. Ha tries to eat, too, but after two spoonfuls, she lets go of the bowl. Vy opens her eyes wide in amazement. "You don't want to eat?"

Ha shakes her head. "No."

"You want to eat the fake flour cakes instead of the real congee?"

"The fake flour cakes were for pretending."

"So eat the real congee."

"I don't like congee."

Vy wipes her mouth with her hands. "You just like flour cakes?"

"No."

"So why did you make them?"

"Because we did not have anything to eat and there was no other game to play."

"Why didn't you pick fruit?"

"Because Young Aunt is still at home. We were lucky that she did not come out and scold us."

Vy eats up every grain of the rice congee before putting her bowl down. "I am full. I do not want any fruit now. Congee is good. You should eat."

Ha shakes her head. "I won't eat. I don't like congee."

Two Sisters

Vy eyes Ha's congee bowl, hesitating. "So...can I have your bowl?"

Ha leaves her congee bowl with Vy and walks out to the garden to look for Mother. She finds Mother and Elder Aunt talking under a coconut tree. From where she stands, she can hear their conversation.

"I cannot continue to work for you. I will feel strange walking in there and seeing her. I can't go in there anymore."

"She was punished for her rudeness. There's no reason you can't work for me anymore. I had many relatives over today and I didn't have anyone to help me. How could you have left me high and dry like this?"

"Please try to understand. I can't work for you anymore. I just need some money to start a business."

Elder Aunt raises her voice. "Business? Do you think it's easy to run a business? There are people who are shrewder than you and yet fail in business."

Mother bends her head. Elder Aunt looks intensely at her sister-in-law, waiting for a reply. A long silence follows, which makes Elder Aunt angrier. "I've spoken my words. You can quit if you want. But do not ask me for money. How long have you worked for me that you think I owe you money? Where are the thanks and grace? Now I will have to go look for a maid and I need to pay her, I have nothing left for you."

Mother blinks her eyes and bows her head. "Yes."

Elder Aunt is furious at the persistent refusal. She widens her eyes and walks back to the big house in a huff.

Two Sisters

Ha has a surge of pity for Mother, though she is not sure if Mother is right in refusing work. She approaches Mother tentatively. "Mom, can I ask you something? You're not working for Elder Uncle and Aunt anymore?"

"No."

"What are you going to do?"

"I will be a vendor and sell things."

Ha brightens up at the prospect of Mother selling things. "Really? What will you sell?"

"I don't know yet. I don't have any principal."

"What is principal?"

"Principal is the money I need to buy things to sell."

Ha is disappointed. "So how can you sell without principal?"

"I thought I earned some money working for Elder Aunt these past few years, but I have nothing."

"Why?"

"Apparently she pays me with the food we've already eaten."

"So will you still sell things?"

"I don't know."

Two Sisters

Ha cannot stay quiet, even when she sees that fatigue is written all over Mother's face. "Do you own anything you can sell for principal?"

"I had my lock of hair, but I've sold it. What I have now is too short to sell."

Ha shrieks in surprise. "You sold your lock of hair?"

Mother's voice is full of sadness. "When you were sick last year, I sold it to buy medicine. I got sixty dongs[4] for it. The medicine cost me forty dongs. I used the rest of the money to buy good food for the two of you so you'd stay healthy."

Ha is saddened upon hearing that the long and smooth black lock of hair that Mother had saved is gone. She remembers well that each time Mother combed her hair, she would carefully gather the fallen strands to add to the shiny, soft bundle and tie it with a rubber band. Mother held the lock of hair with the love and care reserved for her most precious asset. Mother knew that the lock of hair would fetch money because many women had approached her, wanting to buy it. She often looked at her beautiful hair with tenderness and pride. Ha did not know that Mother had sold the hair she treasured so much and is moved by this big secret. She never thought Mother would part with her precious possession. Ha feels overwhelmed with love for Mother and wants so much to express this undying love to her. But, as often, she remains quiet and is unable to express her feelings through words or actions. She feels guilty when she thinks of Mother's sacrifice and her own rejection of the congee. When she looks up and reads hopelessness and

---

[4] Dong is the Vietnamese monetary unit.

Two Sisters

despair on Mother's face, she prays to Father that she will never get sick again. She prays that Father will move his extended family members so that they will have pity on Mother and lend her a small amount of money to start her business. Ha's mind comes alive with images of a cozy store where Mother sells hundreds of different types of general merchandise, a crowd of people pushing and shoving to buy the best merchandise from Mother, Mother's coming home with a bag full of money, and the stack of cash from the money bag filling the whole house from floor to roof. Mother will have so much principal that she can buy expensive jewelry to adorn her ears, her neck, her wrists, and her fingers – just as the rich female relatives do.

Then Ha remembers that Mother has given her and Vy gold chains and bracelets to wear on New Year's Day and has said, "I am saving these gold chains and bracelets for the two of you for when you get married. You can wear them only on New Year's Day, not on regular school days."

"Can I ask you another question, Mom?" Ha asks.

Mother is somewhat surprised at Ha's persistent interest. "Yes, go ahead."

"You said that the gold chains and bracelets are for us when we get married, right?"

"Yes. But those are gifts from your grandmother and aunts. I am only keeping them for you, I can't sell them." Mother pauses. "I do have a gold necklace that your father gave me as a gift. But since it holds sentimental value, I can't sell it either."

"I think Dad would want us to sell them if we do not have enough to eat," Ha insists.

Two Sisters

Mother turns pale. "I can't sell it," she mutters to herself. "It is carved with our initials G. and H." Mother continues to mutter to herself. "Keep the pendant. Sell the chain. When I have enough profit, I'll buy another chain."

Ha is so happy to hear Mother talk about doing business. She does not dare to say anything lest it interrupt Mother's thoughts. Mother looks at Ha. "Tomorrow I will sell the chain. I will go to the market to talk to others to see how vendors work, and then I'll decide what to sell. I will need to go to the market very early. Can you take care of Vy in the morning and walk her to school?"

"Yes, Mom, I can," Ha eagerly replies, "but only if..." She was going to add "...you will not be a maid for Elder Uncle and Aunt," but she stops because she is afraid that the word "maid" will humiliate Mother.

The image of Mother's independence and success in the new endeavor fills Ha with happiness and hope. She begins to form plans in her head of all the things she can do to help Mother. She smiles as she thinks of a day when Mother will associate and interact with her paternal relatives on an equal basis.

CHAPTER THREE

Ever since Young Aunt was kicked by Elder Uncle, she no longer harassed Mother, especially now when Mother works at the market and is often not around. Ha and Vy are at peace without having to endure vicious words from Young Aunt.

On this hot afternoon as soon as Ha and Vy get home from school, Vy asks for lunch. Vy sits at the door, holding an empty bowl in one hand and a spoon in the other, impatiently waiting for Ha who takes her sweet time at the well. Ha has lowered the bucket but has not pulled it up. She is keenly observing Young Aunt who squats among a pile of dirty dishes. Young Aunt is not there to wash dishes; her hands are up on her chest as she has a terrible coughing fit, interrupted by sporadic phlegm spitting. Ha is alarmed to see that the phlegm is mixed with bright red blood. She momentarily forgets her anger at the way Young Aunt unfairly treated Mother. A different image of Young Aunt emerges. It is no longer an image of a mean and angry person that Ha often associates with Young Aunt, but one of a sickly person suffering from a terrible coughing fit, making Ha wonder if it is the result of her being kicked in the chest by Elder Uncle. Compassion wells up in Ha's heart,

Two Sisters

replacing bitterness with tenderness and anger with...love. Ha allows the tender feeling toward Young Aunt to stay within, for certainly Young Aunt and Father were related by blood. Young Aunt was Father's own sister, just as Vy is Ha's own. Since Ha does not want to see Vy in pain, surely Father would not want to see Young Aunt in pain. Ha wonders if Father ever hit Young Aunt, but decides that Father would never do such a thing; he would perhaps only scold and correct his sister if she did something wrong. On the one hand, the image of a kind man that Ha associates with her late father tells her that Father would never hit anyone. On the other hand, the image of a mean Young Aunt allows the possibility that Father could have acted the way Elder Uncle did if he happened to witness a vengeful act by his sister. Conflicting thoughts fill Ha's mind and she still has not pulled up the water bucket.

Ha hesitates because she does not know how Young Aunt will react if she wants to help. "Let me...rinse it off with water?" As soon as Young Aunt nods in agreement, Ha pulls up the bucket and pours water over the bloody phlegm. Pleased with her accomplishment, Ha is filled with confidence. "How are you? Does your chest hurt?"

Young Aunt shakes her head and continues to cough, bending her head even lower. Ha is perplexed and unsure of what to do next. She draws up some more water to rinse her feet and is about to walk away when Young Aunt speaks up. "Have you had lunch?"

"Not yet. We just got home from school. We're going to eat now."

Ha quickly walks away for she is afraid that her tears will show. From the time Mother started her business, Ha and Vy have not been eating regularly. Mother is gone from

Two Sisters

early morning until late in the evening. Ha helps out by waking Vy up in the morning, making sure Vy is clean and ready for school, and walking Vy to school. Partly because Ha is picky with food and partly because they do not have much time before school, the two of them often go to school hungry, even though Mother cooks and leaves food for them. After walking home from school during the noon hour when the sun is at its highest, Ha is usually tired and just wants to drink a glass of water and take a nap. She does not really care for the food that Mother cooks early in the morning. She would rather sleep than eat the soggy rice with a few small fish lying in a pool of sauce that has gotten cold.

Vy clangs her bowl with a metal spoon. "I want lunch, Sister Ha."

"Okay," Ha says reluctantly. "In a moment."

Walking into the kitchen, Ha sighs at the sight of the pot of rice. She has already assumed that the rice would be cold and dense as usual since Mother is often in a hurry and does not puff up the rice as she should. Ha is even more disappointed upon opening the lid and seeing that the cold, dense rice is covered with red fire ants.

"Give me food, Sister Ha," Vy says impatiently.

"We can't eat. Ants are all over the rice."

The ants, which cover the rice completely in one corner, start to move en masse. The ants have formed a line from the floor, where there are three pieces of brick holding up the pot, to the top of the pot and down inside the pot to their "meeting place." Ha looks at Vy, expecting and waiting for Vy to decline lunch. Vy stares at the rice pot, speechless. Ha is not sure if Vy is more mesmerized by the ants or the rice.

Two Sisters

Ha shakes her head. "Don't eat, Vy. The ants will bite your mouth."

"But I'm hungry."

Ha musters all the authority she has over her little sister. "How can we eat rice with so many ants? You want to eat the ants, too?"

Vy's mouth twists in anguish. "I want to eat."

"The ants will bite you! Your lips will swell up and your friends will laugh at you. They will say ants bite you because you're too greedy for food."

"How will they know that ants bite me? How will they know I'm greedy for food? If my lips swell up, that does not mean I'm greedy."

"Oh sure, oh sure," Ha taunts. "They will not call you greedy. They will say you're a bad girl and Mom gives you a beating for being bad."

"I just want some food," Vy insists in tears. "I'm hungry."

Ha is fired up as though Vy just dumped fuel on her. She points to the floor and inside and under the pot while giving Vy a lesson in hygiene. "You're a bad girl if you don't listen to me. Don't you see that these ants crawl from the dirty ash? You'll get sick if you eat this rice."

"I'll shake the ants away," Vy cries loudly. "I want to eat."

Two Sisters

At Vy's insistence, Ha reluctantly tries to find a compromise. "Okay, go away. Let me take the pot out to shake the ants away and then I'll give you food." She tentatively extends her hands to pick up the pot by its handles, walks out to the garden, and quickly throws it hard on the ground. Dust blows up from the uneven dirt, from which the imbedded pebbles scatter in the air. Ha furiously wipes ants away from her arms and legs while keeping her eyes on the pot. Some ants fall out while those remaining in the pot run wild. Seeing that her method gets rid of some of the ants, Ha picks up the pot and repeatedly bangs it on the ground. But in so doing, some of the ants that have already climbed to the rim of the pot fall back down into the rice. The ants seem confused, not knowing which way to turn. Soon Ha gets impatient with her method – it seems the more she bangs the pot, the more ants remain in it.

Under the merciless sun, its harsh rays weave through the coconut leaves and land directly on Ha's back, Ha feels miserable with the heat and the seemingly impossible task of getting rid of the ants. Wiping the sweat off her face, she relishes a vengeful idea that momentarily pops into her head. Telling Vy to go sit at the doorstep to wait, Ha places the pot directly under the bright sun. Ha and Vy are delighted to see that the intense heat causes the ants to climb out of the pot.

"Sister Ha, use this spoon to get the ants away."

Ha takes the spoon from Vy and bangs it against the side of the pot where there are not as many ants left. As the ants move away, the white rice shows up.

"Quick. Give me your bowl." Wasting no time, Ha spoons the white rice into the bowl. "Now I'll get you fish." Vy follows Ha back into the kitchen. But as soon as Ha lifts the lid off the fish pot, they face an unbelievable sight.

Two Sisters

Vy cries and runs out of the kitchen. "I don't want to eat any more!" The fish pot holds an army of dead ants lying in a sauce among three pieces of cooked fish. It looks as though someone had carelessly dumped a jar of black pepper in it. The few ants that are still alive struggle to swim toward the pieces of fish, appearing as victims of a sea voyage accident, nearly drowned, and trying to survive by reaching out for the solid rocks of nearby islands.

After recovering from shock, Ha puts the lid back on the fish pot and walks out to the garden to talk to Vy, intending to ask if Vy prefers to eat rice with salt or fish sauce. There, Ha chokes up at the sight of Vy trying to find the edible part of a piece of Indian almond she has found on the ground, apparently already bitten off and discarded by bats. Vy is startled by Ha's footsteps. "I only bite where it's clean," she exclaims, embarrassed. "I don't eat the part bats ate. It's dirty there, right, Sister Ha?"

"Don't eat it. It's still green. I have some dry almonds in my school knapsack."

Vy throws away her bat-eaten Indian almond and runs inside to fetch Ha's worn and faded school knapsack. Ha pulls out some light gray nuts and orders Vy to get a rock. Vy pries a piece of brick from the ground. Ha holds the nut in her left hand and the piece of brick in her right hand. She hits the nut with the brick and removes its rough outer shell. Then she hits the smooth, hard inside cover until it breaks open to reveal the edible soft part covered by a layer of thin brown skin.

"My sister Ha is the best nut cracker in the whole world," Vy gushes. She swallows hard while buttering up her big sister. "You did not break the almond nut!"

Two Sisters

Ha is completely flattered. "It's for you. Eat it."

Vy eagerly pops the nut in her mouth. Then, on second thought, she spits it out, bites off half of it, and pushes the other half toward Ha's mouth. "This almond is so crunchy. Try it."

Ha wipes her hand on her trousers, takes the half piece of nut, and twirls it around. A whole nut is oval and has pointed ends and looks like a tiny loom shuttle. She smiles at the idea of having Indian almonds as their food source.

"It's really good, Sister Ha," Vy says. "Eat it."

Ha decides to give it back. "You eat it. I'll eat something else."

"Where did you get it?" Vy asks.

"At school. The almonds in our garden are not dry because the bats drop them after eating the green ones. The nuts on the school ground dry out under the sun."

"So pick a lot for me tomorrow."

"If the other kids see us, they will laugh at us. We need to go to school early. Can you get up early?"

Just then Young Aunt appears, walking toward them with a food tray in her hands. Kiki and Yellow are right at her heels, eagerly eying the tray while wagging their tails and jumping up and down. Young Aunt shoos the dogs away. "Are you two hungry?"

"Yes, thank you." Ha automatically takes the tray from Young Aunt without thinking. Young Aunt turns wordlessly

49

Two Sisters

away and goes back to the big house with Kiki and Yellow at her heels. As Young Aunt disappears behind the tiled patio, Ha realizes that she will have to walk across *that* patio to return the empty dishes. The patio reminds her of the incident on Christmas Day when Mother suffered from Young Aunt's vicious words, and the promise Ha made to herself that day. She had vowed to dissociate herself with the relatives in the big house.

As the painful event replays in her mind, Ha has an urge to run after Young Aunt to return the food tray, but Vy's voice brings her back to reality. "Let's eat inside, Sister Ha."

Ha is momentarily distracted by Vy's pleading. She tries to block it out of her mind so she can decide what to do. But her indecision causes her to stay rooted to one spot as if she were a soulless statue with no awareness of her surroundings. She looks at the food Young Aunt brought, feeling torn and regretful. She wants to be able to stand firm in her resolve and let her relatives know that she is on Mother's side, that she would do anything for Mother, and that she does not want to receive any pity or handouts. But now as she has accepted the tray, she faces a dilemma. She has only herself to blame. What reason would she give to Young Aunt if she returned the food? How would she say what she needed to say? But if she accepted the food, then she would have to be grateful to her relatives, and she would not be able to indicate to the adults in the extended Hoang family that she disapproves of the spiteful words and condescending actions they reserve for Mother.

Vy pulls Ha's hand. "Give me food, Sister Ha. I'm very hungry."

Two Sisters

Ha is startled. She moves her eyes from the food to Vy's dirty face, then nods and tries to stop tormenting herself. "Let's go inside."

"Give me lots of rice to eat with the fish," Vy says happily. "It will be so good!"

Ha knows that the fried fish is good, not because Vy is easily satisfied, but because their aunts have cooked it. She knows it will be so delicious, especially when eaten with the dipping fish sauce. In fact, the sauce alone is so good that she can eat the rice with just the sauce.

It is true that their aunts are good cooks and make tasty specialties from Hue. Even Mother has conceded that she cannot make fancy dishes the way her sisters-in-law do. They know how to mix the right proportion of garlic, chili, sugar, and lime for the dipping fish sauce; how to combine sugar water and fried lard as a marinade for the fish; and how to complement stir-fry dishes with green onions and parsley.

Ha and Vy like to rate the food they eat and they have come to the consensus that their aunts are better cooks than Mother. They do this only for fun, for as far as Vy is concerned, the quality of the food is not nearly as important as the quantity, especially when she is hungry. Ha, on the other hand, has delicate taste buds and is very picky with her food. She would rather stay hungry if the food is not to her liking. Since she is used to not eating enough, she is tall and skinny like a bamboo tree. Sometimes her paternal relatives give her leftover food in private, out of concern for her health. When they do, Ha's mind would fill with conflicting thoughts. Her pride does not allow her to accept handouts from her relatives, but her taste buds do. To ease her

Two Sisters

conscience, she argues with herself that it is better to have tasty leftovers than bland home-cooked meals.

Vy bends all the way down to the tray, shoves food into her mouth, and chews in earnest as if she had never tasted this kind of food before. She excitedly verbalizes her plans to get up early to go pick dry almond nuts in the morning. Ha hems and haws an agreement. Her nose puffs up and her eyes turn red as she is filled with self-pity. Ha often daydreams about having an "ideal" family, one that includes both a father and a mother, who shares hot meals around a dining table. In reality, her dining experience does not include a father because he is no longer with them, nor a mother because she is working, nor does it include a dining table and chairs. Ha and Vy sit on the floor and eat from the metal tray that is set between them. It contains a small fried fish, dipping fish sauce, a small dish of stir-fry vegetables, and a bowl of cold broth.

Ha cries silently because the two of them now often eat without Mother. Ha imagines possible misfortunes that could befall them. Images of these misfortunes play out in her mind, one after another, as if they were recorded in a book whose pages are turning in front of her. A phantasmagoria plays out Mother's death due to a fatal illness, their being orphans among the rich relatives, and being all alone – just the two of them – eating, sleeping, walking to and from school. Ha's mind is numb with the obsessed thought of losing her beloved mother. She assesses her survival skills. How would she and Vy live without Mother? What would she do to earn a living for the two of them? Would she have to work for Elder Uncle and Aunt or some other paternal relatives?

Tears fall down Ha's face when she imagines having to work for her relatives. She wonders if she will eventually share Mother's fate. She remembers an old saying she has learned from Mother, which conveys the idea that a person can never depend on his or her rich relatives. Her nose puffs up as she feels bitter and depressed, thinking of the contrast between the rich, fancy relatives and themselves. She tries to imagine working for people other than her paternal relatives. She racks her brain trying to think of Mother's friends who may be able to help, but she cannot think of any. She shakes her head in disappointment. Mother does not have friends. There is one sole person that Mother has mentioned, but that person is someone who comes to the kitchen of the Hoang family to fetch leftover food to feed pigs. This woman wears ragged clothes. She must be as poor as they are and would not be in a position to hire anyone.

Ha sighs while taking stock of their possessions: a food pantry whose torn screen is covered by pieces of old newspapers, two old wood beds, a worn-out dresser, a set of wobbly table and chairs full of peeling-paint flakes. These are items that would not sell, but at the same time, she would not want to sell them. The thought of having to part with anything in the little house twists her heart. Each item holds precious memories that are an integral part of their lives as cells are to a body. Ha resolves in her mind that as long as they live in their little house, they will not part with any of their belongings. These are the things that Father bought before he died – souvenirs that hold his love and care. Thoughts of Father calm Ha down. She makes a silent promise to always live in this house and keep everything they own, no matter what happens. She tries to think of ways to earn enough money to take care of themselves without having to sell things. Begging comes to mind. She sees themselves as beggars – each carrying a cloth bag, wearing an old hat, bowing their head, stretching their arms, and repeating phrases similar to what she often hears from other street beggars: "*I bow down before you, sirs and madams.*

Two Sisters

Please give me a dong. I am poor, without money or rice. Please take pity on me." Tears fall down her cheeks again as her imagination runs wild and she recalls verses from a folksong: *"One without a father eats rice and fish. One without a mother starves on the street corner."*

Vy is confused. "Why are you crying? Why are you not eating?"

Ha shakes her head while wiping away her tears.

"Don't cry, Sister Ha," Vy says. "I'll leave the rest of the fish for you."

Ha cries even harder. She keeps shaking her head no. Vy is perplexed and scared. She puts her chopsticks down. The two of them stay silent for a long time until they hear Grandmother's call from the well.

"Ha, come get dessert."

"Grandma is calling you," Vy says.

"I'm here, Grandma." Ha runs out to greet Grandmother who is holding a china bowl painted with green dragons. Ha is surprised to also see Mother who has come home earlier than usual. Mother sets the two baskets down and leans the carrying pole against a coconut tree. Ha hesitantly looks at the food tray that Grandmother offers while stammering a greeting to Mother. "You have sold everything?" Ha asks.

Grandmother says, "This bowl of sweet royal bean pudding is just for you. Make sure you eat it. You're getting thinner every day."

Two Sisters

As she takes the bowl and walks back inside, Ha hears Mother question Vy. "Why didn't you eat the food I cooked?"

Ha feels the need to answer for Vy. "Well...both the rice and the fish have ants... Vy is eating the food that Young Aunt gave us."

While Mother wordlessly goes into the kitchen to verify things, Vy fixes her eyes on the pudding bowl. "What kind of pudding is that, Sister Ha?"

"It's royal beans."

"Do royal beans taste good?"

"I think so. People used to serve these beans to kings only, so they must be good."

"How do you know kings ate these beans?"

"Grandma and Young Aunt say they're called 'royal' because kings ate them."

"So these beans are for rich people?"

"I think so."

"So Grandma wants you to be rich and be king."

Ha shakes her head. "I don't think so. I think it's because she wants me to get fat."

Vy swallows hard. "Can I have king beans too?"

"Sure, but it's called royal beans, not king beans."

Two Sisters

"Okay, can I have royal beans?"

"Vy, you may not have the pudding," Mother coldly interjects. "That is for your sister Ha. Your grandmother gave it to her, not you." Vy pouts while Ha does not know what to say. Mother's voice has an edge. "Vy, you should not want something that *they* don't want you to have. To your grandmother and aunts, Ha is the only person related to them."

Ha recoils to hear Mother stress the word "they." She lowers her head in pain. She often hears that her face looks just like Father's and that is why she is favored by her paternal relatives. She is aware of the disparity in the way Vy and she are treated, but she never imagined that Mother would try to separate them with that fact. She inwardly blames Grandmother for giving her only one bowl of pudding and insisting that it be just for her, and blames Mother for uttering words that could tear apart the sisterly love she shares with Vy. Without knowing why, she feels guilty. She half-heartedly starts to clean up and is relieved to see that Vy appears oblivious to Mother's remark. Vy follows Ha to the garden and when they are far away from Mother's hearing, Vy whispers, "Let me have some royal bean pudding, Sister Ha."

They sit under the coconut tree next to the water barrel, passing the bowl of pudding back and forth while savoring the moment. Vy puts a spoonful of pudding into her mouth, holding in its sweetness while closing her eyes and inhaling its aroma, before swallowing. Ha gathers all her senses to enjoy each piece of the sweet, soft, and flavorful beans whose taste lingers on her tongue and teeth. They eat until there is nothing left. They do not leave even a drop of water or a fleck of uncooked flour at the bottom of the bowl. After

Two Sisters

eating, they sit and share with each other everything that sisters often do, including matters of school and friends.

Ignoring the dirty bowl carelessly left on the ground, Ha and Vy enjoy the late afternoon sunlight weaving around and through the coconut leaves to rest on their hair and shoulders. Above them, on the tree branches, the birds open up in song. It seems as if the birds, just as they, are confiding secrets to each other.

CHAPTER FOUR

Ha repeatedly calls until Vy stirs. "Vy, Vy. Let's get up." Vy reluctantly opens her eyes but closes them again when she sees it is still dark. "Vy, get up!" Ha calls more loudly. Vy grunts and turns to her other side, intending to go back to sleep.

"You want to pick almonds but you don't want to get up!" Ha grumbles. "Get up later and you can forget about picking!"

Seeing no movement from the lump on the bed, Ha climbs on it and shakes its shoulders. "Vy! Do you want to pick almond nuts? Yes or no?"

"Almond nuts?... Okay, I'll...go," the lump finally speaks.

"Then you have to get up right now."

Vy sits up, looking around. "Now? Is Mom still home?"

Two Sisters

"She's gone. I tried to wake you up as soon as Mom called me to lock the door. Go brush your teeth and wash up. Quick."

"It's still dark. Can I sleep some more?"

"No. It looks dark because I didn't open the door. It's light outside. Hurry up so we can pick almonds without being laughed at."

Vy slowly climbs out of bed. "Okay, I'll get ready."

After Vy finishes washing, Ha combs Vy's hair and puts a rubber band on it. They hurry out of the little house in silence. Under the dimly lit sky, the big house and the garden seem to join in a conspiracy with Ha and Vy to stay quiet. Stealthily closing the gate behind them, Ha and Vy almost run as if being chased by spirits. Without speaking, they walk fast along streets that are mostly empty, save for a few cars now and then. Beyond the horizon, blocks of dark multi-colored clouds float in the sky, visible by the street lamps from the sleepy city below.

Vy squeals in delight. "The sun is coming up over there, Sister Ha."

"That's the ocean," Ha replies.

Vy is surprised. "How do you know? Did you go there?"

"No, but my classmates said so."

Vy looks longingly at the sunrise where the ocean is supposed to be. "Let's go there some day."

Two Sisters

Ha slows her steps and shakes her head. She tries to be as responsible as an older sister should be. "No, we can't go to strange places without adults."

"You are the adult. You take me."

"I can't."

"Yes, you can."

"No, I can't."

"Yes, you can."

"How can you argue with me? Don't be sassy."

"I'm not sassy. It's true."

"How can we? I'm not an adult."

"But you take me to school."

Ha speaks slowly and emphatically. "That's different. I take you to school because Mom tells me to. Also, I do not know how to get to the ocean." She wants her words to settle with Vy that it is impossible for her to do what Vy requests.

There are no other students walking to school and there are just a few vehicles on the street: a car going toward the ocean, a horse carriage full of people and merchandise heading toward the market, two bicycles, and a cyclo[5] full of

---

[5] A cyclo is a three-wheeled vehicle similar to a rickshaw that can transport people or merchandise. The driver sits at the back and pedals while the passengers (or merchandise) are in front.

Two Sisters

fruit. Waiting until the street is clear, Ha takes Vy's hand before crossing. Vy's mind is still preoccupied with the mystical ocean. She resumes her inquiry, "If we go to the ocean early in the morning like right now, Mom does not know."

Ha resolutely shakes her head. "No."

"Why not? What about today? Mom does not know we go to school early."

"Going to school is not the same thing as going to the ocean."

"We are walking. It's the same."

"We go to school early to pick dry almonds to eat. What do we go to the ocean for?"

"I just want to know what it's like," Vy sadly says. "I think it will be fun. I am tired of the same old games we always play."

Ha's curiosity is aroused. She also wishes to know the ocean. At the age of eight, she does not have a clear concept of what an ocean is because she has never seen one. She supposes Father might have taken them there when they were little, but she does not remember. After thinking it over, she says, "I think I want to go once, but I don't know the way. I'm afraid we'll get lost and then we'll be in big trouble. My classmates said the ocean is over there but I never went."

Vy regretfully follows the purple clouds with her eyes, watching them turn pink by the sun's rays and drift away in the horizon, before turning back toward the direction of school. The wind starts blowing hard, making the tall trees shake their leaves as in a fury. At the main road, the air darkles and the temperature drops. Ha and Vy walk faster and stay close to each other for warmth. When they arrive at the side school entrance, the school ground is empty and the classrooms look dark. Fumbling to find the gate latch, Ha discovers a big lock.

"This gate is locked, Vy. We need to go to the main gate."

The wind picks up in velocity, chases itself, playfully strips leaves from the trees, and mischievously stirs up the already-fallen leaves. The leaves gracefully dance in circles before landing all over the ground, on the sidewalks, and on the road. Ha and Vy waste no time. They run to the main gate which is made of iron and painted brown just like the side gate. Vy shivers. She tries to find a warm spot under the brick column that holds the plaque engraved with "Nha-Trang Girls' Elementary School."

"This gate is also locked, Vy."

A strange voice comes from behind. "Obviously it has to be locked because it's not time for school yet."

Ha turns around to see a girl in a ponytail, about her own age, wearing white clothes and holding Indian almond leaves in her hand. Ha is not sure what to say.

"You didn't know the caretaker only opens the gate fifteen minutes before school starts?" The same strange voice comes from this girl who is curiously staring at them. "Why...do you go to school so early?" she asks.

Two Sisters

Ha tries to think of a white lie, but she cannot think of any, especially when the girl looks straight at her. So she speaks the truth. "We came early to pick almonds."

"You go early because you don't want to be teased, right?" the girl observes. "But it's too early. The caretaker opens the gate at seven." The girl feels sorry for them. "You don't need to go inside. There are plenty of almonds out here."

"Where?"

The girl points to a tree in an island in the middle of the street. "See that big almond tree?"

"But it is right in the middle of the road."

"There is not much traffic this early in the morning. You can go when there are no cars. Just stay right next to the tree and out of traffic."

"Li, come quick," someone calls. "There are so many leaves here and you dawdle! What are you doing?"

The voice comes from one side of the almond tree. There stands a woman, in dark clothes and hat, who has trouble keeping her balance in the strong wind. Leaves are being blown in a whirlwind as though the wind wanted to strip the tree of all of its leaves. Both wind and leaves seem to have a blast.

The woman calls again. "Are you coming, Li?"

"Ma, I *am* picking leaves," the girl says. Then, turning to Ha, she asks, "You want to pick nuts? I'll take you over there. There are lots and lots."

Two Sisters

Ha is unconvinced. "Yeah? If so, why don't you pick them? Why do you tell us?"

"I need leaves, not nuts. I pick from both sides of the road and don't worry about cars. You just have to be careful to watch out for them. Hurry! My ma's calling, I have to go."

Ha cannot make up her mind.

"It's a shame that you are wasting time," Li says. "You're already here."

Ha is taken aback with Li's honest assessment. She pulls Vy. "Let's go." The three of them run together across the road, through the wind, to the Indian almond tree.

"Who are these girls?" Li's mother asks.

Li has to shout to be louder than the wind. "They're students from my school. They want to pick almonds."

Li's mother points. "Plenty over here. There, there. Pick as much as you like."

Ha politely thanks Li's mother. Ha and Vy are happy to see dry nuts all over the ground and completely forget about their apprehension of traffic. No exposed roots are spared as they step over every one of them; their hands are quick in a rhythmic up-and-down motion, picking and squirreling nuts away. So engrossed in their task, they do not pay attention to Li's mother's mumbling to herself. "What parents let their children out so early? I bet these girls act on their own without permission."

Li seems to be efficient in catching almond leaves that swirl in the wind. She puts the leaves she catches in a basket,

Two Sisters

and stops to pick up nuts from the ground once in a while to give to Ha and Vy.

"Why...don't you keep the nuts?" Ha asks.

"Take them. I just want leaves."

"What do you use the leaves for?"

"My ma wraps the glutinous rice with them."

"But they are dirty."

"I have to clean the leaves, of course. My ma is very careful. She wraps the rice in my notebook paper first, then the leaves. If you want glutinous rice for breakfast, buy it from my ma. She sells it in front of school."

Ha is about to say that she has no money to buy breakfast and that she often goes to school hungry, but she decides against telling her sad story to someone she just met. Instead she says, "Sometimes the glutinous rice is stained with ink."

"So you ate my ma's glutinous rice? The ink is from my notebook paper."

"No, I did not. But if you eat the rice, you also eat the ink... You...go to this school?"

"Yes."

"What grade?"

"Third grade, class 3A."

Two Sisters

"I'm in class 3C, same grade."

"I'm the class leader of 3A."

"That's why I don't know you. I don't play with class leaders."

"Why? You are jealous?"

"No. My class leader is selfish and snobby. I don't like her."

"I've been class leader for two years, but I'm not snobby. I help others with homework. I don't like being selfish. Do you think all class leaders are selfish?"

Ha does not know what to say.

"No one works harder than me," Li continues. "I help my ma sell glutinous rice before school each morning and I don't care if the other kids laugh at me. If I want to pick almonds, I do it during recess. Other kids do it, too, so you should not feel bad."

Ha cannot argue with that. She feigns disinterest and looks elsewhere.

Li does not seem to want to drop the subject. "You still think class leaders are selfish? Do you think I am?"

Ha shakes her head. She is a little dazed with admiration for the newly acquainted girl. Ha has not met any girl her age who is as lovely, open, and straightforward as Li. Li not only shows Ha and Vy where to pick almonds, she even does it for them.

Two Sisters

"Can we be friends, Sister[6] Li?" Vy asks.

"I don't know," Li hesitates.

"Where do you live?"

"At Ong-Choi Village. Do you want to visit?"

"I want to go after school is over," Vy excitedly says. "Okay, Sister Ha?"

Ha shakes her head and scrunches up her face. "I don't know how to get there. We may get lost."

"If you want to come, I'll show you," Li says. "No worry about getting lost."

"I don't know," Ha hesitates. "I think Ong-Choi Village is far away because I never heard of it." She turns to Vy. "We can follow Sister Li but I won't know how to get back home. And don't you remember that Grandma and Elder Uncle say we cannot play with people we don't know?"

"But we don't have any friends," Vy reasons. "Sometimes we can't even play with our cousins."

"You can play with your classmates," Ha replies.

"Please! Please! Please, Sister Ha! Let's be friends with Sister Li and go to her house."

---

[6] Because Li is as old as Ha, Vy shows respect to Li by addressing her "Sister" as she does Ha.

Two Sisters

Ha is thoughtful. "No, we can't. I don't know where her house is. I won't dare to take you there. I won't bring you to school so early anymore either."

"Students start coming now, so I have to go to help my ma," Li says. "Bye. Be careful crossing the street."

As Ha takes Vy's hand to cross the street, Vy whines, "I don't have any toys. I am not allowed to go to the beach. I don't have any friends. I don't have anything. I hate you. I hate you."

CHAPTER FIVE

The drum has been beaten three times to announce the end of school, but the teacher of class 3C waits until all grammar notebooks have been distributed to students before giving a signal for them to leave in an orderly fashion.

The school ground is full of students walking, running, hollering, calling, talking, and laughing with the released energy that has been suppressed during class time. The students are cheerful and talkative as if they were a flock of birds basking in the sun. They walk en masse toward the two wide-open gates. Cars, motorcycles, bicycles, cyclos, and people are already lined up outside waiting. Parents stare at both gates in search of the familiar faces of their children. In contrast to the quiet morning, the afternoon is noisy with loud honking amid talking.

As soon as her teacher allows the class to leave, Ha walks quickly past her classmates, down the hall, to Vy's classroom. When she gets there, she sees no one but Vy's teacher who is collecting notebooks from students' desks.

"Teacher, where is my sister Vy?"

Two Sisters

"My class lined up and left after the first drum beat. She is probably waiting for you outside."

Ha hurries back to her own classroom, but it is empty. She runs to the back of the school, thinking Vy may be picking dry almonds there. No luck. Disappointed, she runs to the front of the school, looking into each classroom as she passes it, but there is still no sight of Vy. The crowd has thinned out and Vy is nowhere to be found. Ha breathes heavily in annoyance and worry. She leans against a column in the hallway to collect herself and think hard. She remembers that Vy put on a white dress in the morning and she tied Vy's hair in a ponytail. Not seeing Vy's familiar face among the last group of students leaving, Ha cups her hands together and calls out loudly, "Vy, Vy!"

A few heads turn. Feeling embarrassed, Ha stops calling, but follows the last group of students outside, walking fast, hoping to find Vy among the crowd. Seeing no Vy, Ha walks home by herself. When she gets to Phan-Chu-Trinh Street, she hears anxious calling from a few neighbor kids.

"Ha, Ha, your sister was hit by a car."

"I saw it with my own eyes. A car hit your sister!"

"They took her away already."

"Where is she?" Ha screams. "Where was she hit?"

A few kids gather around her. They try to talk over each other.

"She was hit right over there."

"That's because she crossed the street without looking."

Two Sisters

"I think it is serious."

Ha pushes the kids aside and tries to get through a crowd in the middle of the street, but it is almost impossible. Adults, children, and cars have formed a big mass with hardly any space to get through. Presently, two adults push her and a few other curious children back onto the sidewalk.

"Are you not scared? Do you want to get hurt? Get back!"

Ha chokes up. "Where was the accident? Where is my sister?"

The big man who pushed Ha stops in his tracks. "So the girl in the accident is your sister?"

Tears run down Ha's face. "Yes. Where is she?"

A woman squeezes her own daughter's hand. "Your sister? Oh my God. Why did you let her go by herself? The car driver who hit her took her away. We do not know how she is."

"Did my sister die?" Ha screams.

People surround her and freely dole out opinions.

"Oh dear. Where were you? Why did you leave your sister alone?"

"That's what happens when parents do not take care of their children. Sooner or later something bad will happen. How can you leave children this age to be latchkey kids?"

Two Sisters

"The car driver took her to the hospital, where else? How could she cross the road so carelessly and not see the car?"

"Oh my God, my sister is dead, isn't she?" Ha wails. The adults do not answer, but look at her with pity.

"Poor girl! I don't think she can survive."

"I pray that the doctor can fix her. I did not see any movements from the little girl after the accident."

"I wonder if the driver would take her to the hospital in time. Traffic is bad now that school just let out."

The cacophony of different opinions confuses Ha. She runs home in tears. *Vy, why do you have to die? Please live.* Images of a bloody Vy and her suffering tear Ha's heart apart and prompt her to pray out loud in anguish. "My dear God, please do not let my sister die. Vy, do not die." Ha feels scared and hopeless and slows her steps when she is almost home, not wanting to go inside. Leaning against a pole outside the estate wall, she allows her body to slowly sink to the ground. She calls out to Vy in sobs, "Why did you go by yourself? Why didn't you wait for me?" She stays at the pole for a long time, ignoring the rising temperature as the sun rises overhead. She does not go into her house because she does not want to be interrogated by the relatives if they hear her cry, and besides, she does not think anyone would understand and share her sadness.

When a movement catches her eyes, Ha notices a group of women proceed toward her while holding a person up. The person being supported is slumped over like a piece of soft meat. Ha is astonished when she realizes that the piece of soft meat is Mother. There is no life left in Mother's pale face and no strength left in her body. Mother looks pitiful as a ragged crazy woman in disheveled clothing whose babbles are unintelligible at times.

"Let me die. Let me die...right now...no reason...to live...daughter has died...don't want to live anymore."

Ha stands up in alarm. Her fears and worries are replaced with self-pity and shock. She is confused to hear Mother speak nonsense. She feels utterly lost with the thought of the deaths of both sister and mother, one after another, and of being abandoned and alone in the world she does not understand. Would she live in Grandmother's estate without the two most important people in her life? She is unsure whether she is living or dreaming. If dreaming, it is so different from her usual sweet peaceful dreams that help her forget reality, but is more like a nightmare that causes suffering and misery. *I already lost a parent, how could Mom want to die and leave me behind all alone in this world? Why does Mom have to die if Vy dies? Doesn't Mom think of me? How can Mom forget that she has another daughter? Can it be that Mom does not think of me as a true daughter, but as someone belonging to Grandma's family? Does Mom consider me an outsider? Does Mom want me to live a rich life in the big house of my roots? Do I belong to Dad because I look like him, and Vy belongs to Mom?*

It is true that the Hoang family pays attention to Ha and pampers her more because she looks like Father. They rarely scold her because they cannot bring themselves to do so when she reminds them of their beloved son and brother. And they have no lack of unkind words when they talk about Vy, even when Vy is innocent or her offense is slight. "You're just like your mother!" they'd say. But Ha did not think Mother shared the view of her paternal relatives – until now.

Two Sisters

Ha follows the women inside the estate, still crying, half worrying about Vy and half feeling sorry for herself. Grandmother and Sixth Aunt throw out questions in a fury. "Have you found Vy? People say she was hit by a car but they do not say where she is." "Do you know where she is?"

"She does not know where Vy is," a woman speaks for Mother. "When she heard that Vy was hit by a car, she jumped onto the street and said she wanted to die. We took her home."

All eyes are on Mother, but she does not pay attention to the women. Her red eyes search for Ha. "Why did you let her go home by herself? What do we do? You do not have a sister now."

Feeling guilty, Ha justifies, "I did not let her go by herself. She did it on her own. I looked for her everywhere. I heard about the accident on the way home."

Ha wants to ask Mother why she wanted to die and leave her older daughter all alone, but words do not come. She tries to comfort herself with the thought that Mother would act the same way if an accident happened to her; perhaps Mother would say to Vy the same thing Mother says to her now. Ha wipes away tears while trying to conjure up a loving image of Mother and to stop feeling sorry for herself.

"Sister Giu[7], they are bringing Vy home!" The welcome news is announced by Elder Aunt from the garden.

A middle-aged man, carrying Vy in his arms, follows Elder Aunt to the little house. "May I ask who the mother of

---

[7] Mother is called here by her late husband's first name.

this little girl is?" he hesitantly asks the group of women who have walked out of the little house when they heard the news.

Mother reaches out her arms. "It's me. Oh my God. Thanks to God. My daughter is alive."

Vy reaches out to Mother. "Mom! Mom!"

Mother is about to take Vy when the man stops her. "Let me bring her into the house."

Mother walks ahead to show the way. "Please bring her in here."

People immediately question both the man and Vy.

"Did you bring her home from the hospital?"

"How is she?"

"How are you, Vy?"

"How do you feel?"

The man puts Vy down on her bed. "We are lucky that she is okay."

Mother strokes Vy's body all over as if to verify that Vy is indeed her physical flesh and blood. She turns to the man. "What happened?"

"I was driving when your daughter suddenly ran across the street. It's good that I was driving slowly because students were just let out. She's lucky that she fell underneath the car right in the middle. She probably lost consciousness just because she was scared. I took her to the hospital and asked the adults to leave word with you."

"Thank you. Thank you very much. I do not know how and when I can repay you. I will remember your deeds forever."

People offer remarks and advice.

"It's a miracle that she's alive."

"Hit by a car, went unconscious underneath it, and survived! Someone above is looking out for her. It's her fate to live."

"Fifth Sister[8], you should buy fruit and flowers to offer to Heaven."

"Thank you for taking care of her," Grandmother says to the man.

Sixth Aunt adds, "If you did not bring her home, we would not know how to find her."

"It is my duty as a driver, whether it was my fault or not." He turns to leave, then pauses. "Oh, your daughter's knapsack is still in my car. I'll return it to you."

"I can go get it," Mother quickly says. "I do not want to bother you."

---

[8]Mother is called here by the order of birth of her late husband. He was the fifth son of his parents.

Two Sisters

Mother follows the man outside. The women bid goodbye. Grandmother, Elder Aunt, and Sixth Aunt return to their big house. With just the two of them at last, Ha asks Vy, "Did the car run over you?"

"No, but I was scared."

"Why did you go by yourself?"

"I saw Sister Li. I thought you were with her, I ran after her."

"Sister Li is not in the same class with me. Don't tell Mom about Sister Li. She will not be happy to hear we went to school so early. Next time wait for me. I'm so happy that you're okay. If you died, Mom and I would be very sad."

"Did you cry?"

"Yes, of course, I was so worried. I thought you were dead."

"I did not die."

"Now that I see you, I know. But everyone cried because we thought you were dead."

Ha cries some more, but it is for herself. She has not forgotten about Mother's wish to die and leave her all alone in the world.

"I'm alive," Vy says. "Don't cry anymore."

"I will stop crying." Ha wipes away her tears. "But you have to promise you won't follow anyone else. You have to wait for me from now on."

Two Sisters

Vy nods in agreement and asks for her knapsack. Mother comes in just then and hands her the knapsack. "You did not lose it. Do not worry. Stay still."

"Are the almonds still in there?"

Mother knits her brows. "What almonds?"

"Did I lose my almonds, Sister Ha?"

Before Ha could say anything, Grandmother, Sixth Aunt, and Young Aunt walk in and save her from having to answer. "This orange is for you," Grandmother says to Vy. "The jambus and dates are also for you. Your sister had her things. These are for you this time."

"Rest well," Sixth Aunt says. She puts her hand on Vy's forehead to check the temperature. "You can't run out right away, you hear?"

"O gives you this box of candy," Young Aunt says. "But you have to eat congee before you can have any."

Ha smiles and steals a glance at Young Aunt. It is the first time she hears Young Aunt speak in her native accent and uses "O," an endearing term for "I," when speaking to Vy. Young Aunt has never used her native tongue when speaking to the three of them before. Mother looks relieved and happy, even though Young Aunt did not look directly at her or say a word to her. Still, Young Aunt's presence allows her to hope that their conflict will end. Vy is happy to receive gifts from Young Aunt. She shakes the cylindrical carton imprinted with colorful pictures of chocolates on it. "This is a box of chocolates," she squeals.

Two Sisters

Somehow the car accident has caused everyone to behave differently. Vy is pampered as an important member of the family. Ha is happy that the family members get along, but she cannot stop feeling envious toward Vy. She is sure that Vy will share the chocolate if asked, but she knows she will not have the empty box. This is the same box from which Young Aunt sometimes retrieved a piece of chocolate to give to Ha. Ha had hoped to ask Young Aunt for this box when it becomes empty. Now it belongs to Vy and she will never have it.

Mother says, "Your grandmother and aunts give your sister gifts because she is not well. Do not be sad."

"I am not sad," Ha says. "I am not jealous of my little sister." Ha quickly retreats into the altar room so that Mother does not see the tears she wipes away. She does not want Mother to misunderstand her feelings for jealousy. Although still feeling sorry for herself, she is at the same time happy about their relationship with the relatives in the big house. She never dreamed that her aunts and grandmother could be so sweet to them and actually set foot inside their little house and even bear gifts. They do care after all! She holds high hopes that the chasm separating them will magically disappear, all of the adults in the extended family will get along and love each other, and Vy and she will be treated equally. She fervently hopes and believes that the hurt will lessen with time, the curses will be forgotten, and the separation between the little house and the big house will be just a physical garden and a tiled patio.

CHAPTER SIX

•

The intermittent insults from Young Aunt come fast and furious at times, echo in the garden, and form a cacophony when combined with the soft cries from Mother. Ha and Vy exchange sad glances. They steal a look Mother's way when they want to tell her to stop crying, but they do not know how. Quietly sitting at the table at the window, they find comfort staying close together. Despite Young Aunt's antics, she cannot entice Mother to walk out into the garden to face her and that makes her more furious. Her diatribes are long and even sound rhythmic at times, but many words are lost on Ha and Vy. Now and then, Young Aunt points her finger at the little house, waving it around as if she were casting a terrible curse. Ha and Vy tremble inside, too scared to move, even though they would dearly love to walk out of the house to escape the situation and stop hearing Mother's cries.

After the car accident, people in the little house had hoped that everything would be fine and the extended family members would get along at last. Ha and Vy long to be embraced with love and happiness in the extended Hoang family. Their hope is now like a broken dream. Lately, Mother has been home more often and Young Aunt finds

Two Sisters

reasons to denounce her sister-in-law whenever she has a chance. Young Aunt is angry perhaps because Mother's presence reminds her of the disappearance of the man she was about to marry, or perhaps because the task of sweeping the patio in early dawn has fallen to her. Ha and Vy do not know why else Young Aunt likes to hurl insults at Mother with no immediate cause or provocation. Other family members seem to be used to her rants and raves. They ignore and consider them background noise – as merchant calls from the street or blaring music from public places – that has become too familiar and banal. No one cares to figure out the real reason of Young Aunt's outbursts, nor do they have time to dwell on her odd behavior. Perhaps no one is even aware when each outburst begins and when it ends. Ha and Vy are also used to Young Aunt's tirades, but unlike the relatives in the big house, they do not have the means to escape them. They have to endure her rants from the beginning to the end, and not until she withdraws into the big house do they retreat to the star apple tree, their favorite haven and playground.

The two sisters' fate is tied to their staying home and witnessing Young Aunt's angry fits. Often they wish for an opportunity to go out, but they have no one to take them to town or anywhere else. Whenever Ha hears the neighbor children happily and noisily play beyond the confinement of the estate wall, she is tempted to join in the fun, but dares not. She is still obsessed with the time Elder Uncle caught her red-handed climbing the estate wall. He gave her a stern warning and forbade her to ever climb it again or play with children she does not know, and she gave him a promise to never violate his rules.

Ha has been thinking hard for a way out of their little house since Young Aunt started hurling insults at Mother, but she has no solutions. She has nothing else to do but sit and stare at her surroundings and redraw the image of the

Hoang estate in her mind. She can envision the front white estate wall covered with yellow golden trumpets and the left side of the big house adorned with red Western and Chinese hibiscus blooms. In Ha's mind, the estate has the appearance of an old castle in the middle of the forest as in a fairytale. In the garden between the kitchen and the well, the carambola, sapoche, and lucuma trees quietly bask under the sunlight. The coconut leaves droop and twist around the two electrical lines that run between the two houses, cutting the electrical circuit from the big house to the little house, bringing perpetual darkness to the little house's every nook and cranny where sunlight does not reach. Along the back wall, the wax jambu and soursop trees, heavy with fruit, hang their branches low, cruelly teasing, tempting, beckoning, and daring Ha and Vy to come out. But they dare not as long as Young Aunt is still there. The song birds string their melodies along their flying path from one tree branch to the next. Alas, their sweet music is muffled in the air by Young Aunt's loud voice.

Ha and Vy are accustomed to their situation and have accepted their fate of limited resources. They do not take anything, including play time, for granted. Play time is a precious commodity regardless of the time of the day or the season of the year, whether it is summer or winter, day or night, vacation or school time.

They welcome a change when someone opens the estate gate and they hear laughter and dogs' barking. They curiously press their faces against the window bar.

"Elder Aunt has guests!"

"I think Phi, Phong, and Phuong are here."

Two Sisters

"No, I don't think so. Look at the suitcases. These are visitors from far away."

"Let's go look," Vy suggests. She drags her body onto the table while her face maintains contact with the window bar. Ha hesitates, looking for cues from Mother.

"You can't go if there are guests," Mother says. Her eyes are still red from crying.

"Please, Mom," Vy pleads, climbing down from the table, "just for a little while."

To their delight, Sixth Aunt's voice calls out to them from the garden. "Fifth Sister! Fourth Brother and his family are home. Bring the girls over to say hello."

Mother jumps and runs to the door. "I hear you. I'll bring the girls over."

Turning to Ha and Vy, Mother says, "You can go say hello to Fourth Uncle." Then she takes them by their hands and walks them to the big house while giving them instructions for proper behavior. "You'll have to fold your arms and bow your head in front of each adult and say 'We are here to greet you, Uncle and Aunt, who just arrived.' Do you understand?" Being forever careful, she corrects herself. "No, you'll have to say 'We are here to greet you, Uncle and Aunt, who just came home.'"

Ha and Vy say yes to whatever Mother tells them, but they do not worry too much about the exact words to use. They are curious about the people called Fourth Uncle and Aunt and want to know what they look like. Mother hesitates and slows her steps when they are at the patio of the big house. Relieved that no one is around, she regains her composure and moves forward. To reach the living room from the back door, they pass Grandmother's parlor, the dining room, Grandmother's bedroom, Young Aunt's bedroom, Elder Uncle and Aunt's bedroom, and the altar room. Each bedroom has a large heavy door with a glass panel. They all look imposing and solemn as though being proud to befit the house's richness and elegance. Mother stops at the entrance to the living room, bends down, and whispers her last command. "Bow in front of each adult and speak in a clear voice, not too loud and not too quiet, you hear?"

"We know. You already told us," Ha and Vy impatiently reply and eagerly enter the living room. As their hands are still being held in Mother's, they pull her with them into a roomful of people. The laughter and lively conversation abruptly stop.

"There! Those are Brother Giu's children."

Mother pushes them forward. "Go say hello to Grandma and Aunts and Uncles."

Ha and Vy obediently cross their arms and bow their heads, reciting the greeting they already know so well to each adult. They begin with people they already know: Grandmother, Elder Uncle and Aunt, Sixth Aunt, and Young Aunt.

"Go say hello to Fourth Uncle and Aunt and Sister Lily who just came back from Saigon," the relatives from the big house say giddily. "You don't need to say hello to us."

Ha and Vy walk over to the sofa next to the television. They are somewhat nervous when they come face-to-face with a serious-looking man in a gray suit.

Two Sisters

"Fourth Uncle, we welcome you home."

The man pulls them close and strokes their hair. "Very good. Are you two good students?"

They nod their heads slightly.

Mother reminds them, "You have to say 'Yes.' You cannot just nod your heads."

The lady in a flowery Vietnamese dress who sits next to Fourth Uncle speaks in a sweet voice. "That's okay. Come over here, I have something for each of you."

Ha and Vy come to the lady, waiting expectantly. Placing a shiny black purse on her lap, the lady pulls out a wad of bills, separates it into two, and gives half to each of them. "This is your snack money."

Ha and Vy are as stunned and happy as if they had won a big lottery. This is the first time in their life that they have such a large sum of money. Even one bill would be enough to buy them so much, and yet Fourth Aunt tells them all of it is snack money. Vy excitedly hands Mother the money. "Save this to buy me snacks, Mom."

Mother reminds them. "Say thank you to your aunt."

"Thank you, Fourth Aunt," Vy gushes.

"Thank you, Fourth Uncle and Aunt, for the money," Ha says.

Fourth Uncle smiles gently. "That's okay. Now go say hi to Sister Lily."

Two Sisters

Ha and Vy follow the direction of his pointed finger and walk to a round rattan chair on which sits a well-dressed young lady who is about twenty years old. The fluffy white dress she wears drapes over the two red cushions of the chair, creating a pleasing contrast of colors. The dress falls all the way to her ankle, where it meets a pair of white shoes and white lace socks – enhancing the air of elegance and everything else about her. Ha and Vy subtly move a little away to allow a comfortable distance between them and their newfound cousin. They sense a day-and-night difference. They are painfully aware that the clothes on their backs have not only gone from white to grey, but also are blotched with dark spots, an evidence of the many times they have played on the dirt ground and the many evenings they hovered around the oil lamp, the sole source of light for their daily activities in the little house when sunlight is not available. Mother has tried to scrub the dark spots with soap to no avail. They bend down in shame and stand as close to each other as possible.

Lily bursts out laughing. "These two kids are so cute, Maman!"

"I don't think they're that cute." Elder Aunt smacks her lips. "They play in the dirt all day long and get dirty."

"I think they are very cute, Tata!" the girl counters. "The little one has such red lips as if wearing lipstick. And look at the big girl's eyes. Her lashes are so long and so curly as if they weren't real."

Vy's big eyes look up at Lily in stupor. Her mouth hangs open as though she wanted to be fed some delicacy by her older cousin's beautiful white hands. Ha is ashamed and full of self-pity. She looks down at her blackened toes that rest on a pair of plastic flip-flops on the fancy tiled floor. She suddenly wishes the meet-and-greet would end right then so she does not have to witness the contrast between the high-class relatives and the three of them. Fourth Uncle's voice is full of pity. "It's so sad for the two girls. They are too young to be orphaned." Ha tries to hide the tears that start falling and control to keep her cries from becoming audible.

Ha dearly wants to go back to the little house so that she does not have to watch Mother be subservient and awkward while their relatives sit on nice sofas and have a good time. She cannot help but compare Mother's simple language to the elegant foreign terms spoken by their relatives, terms such as Maman, Tata, and Tonton. The gap in social status, education, and rank within the extended family widens as the disadvantages of being a member of the pitiful little family are so painfully palpable. The dream Ha had of being welcomed in the big house's living room falls apart when she is slapped by the harsh reality.

Whereas Ha feels bitter and wishes for things to be different, Mother seems to have accepted her place within the social setting of the extended family. The living room where they are standing is the very place she used to sweep and mop and serve food and drink to the owners. Now she brings her children here to greet the close relatives of her late husband. She is able to take it all – a furious glare from Young Aunt, the contempt for her low social ranking, the showing of wealth – while trying to forge a bond between her daughters and their paternal relatives. Presently, she's awkwardly trying to explain her situation to the brother-in-law who is visiting from afar.

"Yes... That's right... I no longer work for Elder Brother. I am a vendor now."

"Really? What do you sell?"

Two Sisters

"I sell fruit."

"How do you do that?"

"I leave the house very early in the morning to go to the horse carriage station to buy fruit from the country people and then resell them at the market."

Fourth Aunt is interested. "Really? I know many fruit merchants in the Saigon market who are doing very well. The guavas are this big." She makes a circling motion with her hands. "Oranges and tangerines, too. Everyone wants to buy them. People always buy nice big round pieces of fruit to put on their altars. If you buy fruit from the Saigon market, you'll make a handsome profit."

"Yes, I know," Mother replies. "But I do not have enough money to buy fruit from Saigon."

Fourth Aunt opens up her shiny black purse again. "Here, take this. This is a gift from both of us. I feel for you, having two daughters to take care of."

Fourth Aunt's generosity seems to surprise other family members who are rendered speechless, until Elder Uncle manages to say to Mother, "Even if you have to work hard, you need to reserve time to raise the girls properly."

• "Yes," Mother mutters timidly.

Fourth Aunt says, "If you ever do not have the strength or ability to take care of the girls, send one of them to Saigon to live with us. I see that Vy is a very charming girl. We'll be able to take care of her very well. When she grows up, we'll return her to you."

Two Sisters

"Yes," Mother replies in a barely audible voice.

Ha cannot control her tears anymore. She runs to the front porch, wanting to put Mother's subservient *yes* and the possibility of being separated from her own sister out of her mind. Vy runs after Ha. "Wait for me, Sister Ha." Together they walk to the star apple tree where they could be in their own little world by themselves.

"Let's play hop-scotch, Sister Ha."

Ha shakes her head.

"What about baking cakes?" Vy asks.

Ha shakes her head again.

"*Man-eating Crocodiles* game then?" Vy insists.

Ha keeps shaking her head.

Vy is exasperated. "So what do you want to play? Why don't you say anything?"

Ha leans against the star apple tree. Its numerous branches are dense with green leaves woven together to form a canopy in the middle of the garden. Grandmother teasingly calls this tree "male" because it provided only a few pieces of fruit at the beginning and has been barren since then. Ha and Vy are glad that no one wants to remove it even though it takes up so much space and is useless in terms of fruit production. Under this tree, they have their own world to themselves when they need it.

"I want to play something," Vy says.

Two Sisters

Ha starts from her day dream. Picking up a dry branch on the ground, she uses it to draw a line in the dirt from the tree to the wall in one direction, and from the tree to the well in the other direction.

"What are we playing?"

Ha writes "Happy Rich" in the dirt on the side of the big house and "Unhappy Poor" on the side of the little house.

Vy follows Ha around. "Are we playing *Happy Rich Unhappy Poor*, Sister Ha?"

"Yes," Ha answers impetuously.

"How do we play it?"

Ha tries to think. "Uh...uh... At the beginning you have to stand at the tree."

Vy walks over to the tree and stands on its exposed roots. "And then?"

"And then, you have to walk on the line."

"How?"

"You walk on it, how else? If you walk the whole line without falling over then you'll have as much education as our aunts and uncles. If you fall on the side that says Unhappy Poor then you'll grow up poor. Don't fall on that side."

They walk on tiptoe on the drawn line and try hard to keep their balance, but both of them fall on the Unhappy Poor side.

Two Sisters

"We'll both be poor when we grow up," Ha grumbles.

Vy jumps from the Unhappy Poor side to the Happy Rich side. "I'll be happy and rich," she yells. She jumps back and forth between the two sides, saying "Unhappy Poor" and "Happy Rich" alternately. Ha follows and joins in the fun. The dirt swirls up from under their feet, filling the air with tiny dust particles, sticking to their clothes, and turning them from "faded white" and "gray" into "grayer."

Out of the corner of their eyes, they catch a glimpse of Lily's white dress over at the big house's front porch. Lily throws her big curious eyes toward the two sisters who are playing a silly game in the dirt. She shakes her head, ignoring the alluring calls of their laughter that echo throughout the garden, and walks back inside.

CHAPTER SEVEN

Now that summer is over and another school year has begun, Mother, Vy, and Ha have settled into a routine. Their life is fairly stable at the moment. Mother sells fruit at the market. Ha and Vy move up a grade, fourth for Ha and second for Vy. They walk home from school together, eat the lunch Mother has cooked and left for them, do their homework without adult supervision, and clean up after themselves before Mother gets home.

Mother no longer leaves early in the morning to go to the horse carriage station to buy fruit. She now has enough principal to go in with other fruit vendors to contract with local orchards in the area. She has a number of female business partners and has formed a strong bond with five of them. They often gather at the little house to plan their next move, do accounting, and split their profits. In so doing, they bring some joy into the otherwise lonely little house. Mother's business partners treat Ha and Vy as nieces and the two sisters, in turn, call them aunts. Although it is customary to address adults as aunts or uncles, Ha and Vy do have a warm feeling toward the five ladies as though they were relatives. Ha and Vy call these ladies Third Aunt, Third Aunt

Two Sisters

Ro, Fourth Aunt, Fifth Aunt, and Ninth Aunt. Each lady is called by a name that is indicative of her birth order within her own family. Since there are two ladies who are third-born, there are two Third Aunts. To distinguish between the two, one is called Third Aunt and the other is called Third Aunt Ro, Ro being the first name of the latter. Ha and Vy do not worry about confusing Fourth Aunt who is Mother's business partner and their own Fourth Aunt who sometimes visits from Saigon because these two aunts are not likely to be together. The business partners Third Aunt and Fifth Aunt live outside of the city. They often bring fruit from the country to sell to the four partners who live in the city. The city women resell the fruit at the Dam market. Sometimes all six women pool their resources together to contract a large orchard, such as the time when Third Aunt and Fifth Aunt did not have enough money to enter a contract themselves.

Ha and Vy enjoy their interaction with these women. While the adults gather what is left after a day at the market and divide profits, the two sisters get to taste the "face fruit" that were used for display and have been sliced off for customers. They love to eat whatever is left after throwing out bruised parts. At the beginning, they get to taste familiar local fruit such as oranges, grapefruits, sweet mangos, green mangos, sour gooseberries, sweet gooseberries, and star apples. Then later, they also get to taste fruit from faraway places bearing exotic names such as Saigon oranges, Saigon tangerines, Saigon mangos, Saigon star apples, Bien-Hoa grapefruits, and Indian mangos. The firm and sweet fruits from the capital city of Saigon give them the impression of a glamorous and trendy city. Although the word "Saigon" brings back the "yes" Mother uttered as a reply to Fourth Aunt's suggestion to send Vy to live there, Ha and Vy do not dwell on it. The memory is like a breeze that blows through gently and fleetingly, and then is forgotten. The success of

Two Sisters

Mother's business is an assurance for the three of them to live together under one roof until the two sisters are grown.

Ha and Vy look forward to Tet[9] which is celebrated in a series of festivals and prepared for weeks in advance. People don new clothes, visit relatives and friends, wish each other happiness and prosperity, and buy fruit to put on altars to make offerings to God and Buddha and to commemorate ancestors. The adults give money in red envelopes to children to wish them luck.

Some weeks before Tet, Ha and Vy get excited when Mother and her business partners laboriously carry two wood boxes inside the house. The two sisters are enthralled of the sweet aroma these two boxes emit. They bombard the women with questions, but the adults do not care to answer questions while they are busy.

"Go away. We are working."

"Don't come near. This is expensive stuff."

"Did you hear us? Scat!"

But this only makes Ha and Vy more curious than ever.

"Why don't you store the fruit in baskets? Why in boxes?"

"What are they called?"

"Why are they all wrapped up?"

---

[9] Tet is the Vietnamese New Year according to the lunar calendar. The term can also include its celebration, lasting several days.

Two Sisters

"Where are the fruit from? Are they from Saigon?"

Mother is not pleased because she thinks her daughters act like pests. "Are you going to leave us alone? Do not ask so many questions."

"They will only ask more questions," Fourth Aunt intervenes. "Just answer them."

"These are bomes and pears," Ninth Aunt calmly explains.

Fourth Aunt corrects Ninth Aunt by carefully pursing her lips together to make the "p" sound. "It's pome, not bome."

"I thought I heard bome,'" Ninth Aunt says. "No matter. It's just an apple. Why do we call it pome? It is so tiring to have to pucker your lips."

"No, it's not an apple," Third Aunt Ro contradicts. "Apples are tiny. This fruit looks like an apple, but two or three times as big and so red and shiny. That's why we call it pome."

"Then why don't we just call it Western apple?" Ninth Aunt smacks her lips. "Call it anything you want, the name alone is already so complicated. I agreed to buy it just because you all wanted to, but I'm afraid we won't be able to sell it."

"Why not?" Fourth Aunt remains optimistic. "I wanted to taste it as soon as I smelled it. Customers will like it."

Another partner chimes in, "Because Ninth Sister is afraid to try something new, we have lost several opportunities. If we don't sell new kinds of fruit, someone else will and we will lose customers."

Seeing Ha and Vy look curiously at the two boxes of red and yellow fruit wrapped in soft white tissue paper, Ninth Aunt throws them a warning. "Don't you take any of this fruit. It is expensive."

"Will you use any for face fruit, Ninth Aunt?"

"This fruit is not cheap," Fourth Aunt replies for Ninth Aunt, indirectly setting a policy at the same time. "We will not use it as face fruit. The customers will just have to decide to buy or not without tasting."

Vy presses for more information. "Which one do you call pome, the red or the yellow, Fourth Aunt?"

"The red is pome and the yellow is pear, but how can you tell their colors? Did you snitch one already?"

"No, I did not," Vy protests. "The tissue paper is so thin that I can see through."

Mother volunteers that the fruit is from America. When Ha asks where America is, Mother just says, "I don't know – probably very far away."

Ha excitedly shares the interesting fact she learns with Vy. "Did you know where these are from? They're from America!"

"Where is America?"

"It's far away."

Two Sisters

"Far away where?"

"Farther from here than Saigon."

"Is it bigger than Saigon?"

Ha stretches out her arms and waves them up and down to demonstrate the largeness of a certain place called America. "Of course. It is the biggest in the world, the whole wide world, the entire planet!"

"Is America pretty?"

"Of course."

"Is the food there good?"

"No doubt," Ha adds for good measure. "You don't have to ask. Just smell the pomes and pears and you know."

That evening, the business partners decide to sleep over at the little house so they could take the exotic fruit to market at early dawn. Mother lights incense sticks for Buddha and Father, as she does every night before going to sleep. She spreads mats and blankets on the altar floor for the guests. After making sure that Ha and Vy are in bed, Mother turns off the oil lamp and stays up to discuss business with her partners. The women begin discussing business and end with talking about children and personal matters. Ha and Vy listen in, but because children are to be seen and not heard, they do not interrupt the adults when they are not clear on something. Besides, the women's personal stories do not interest them much. They are preoccupied with the exotic fruit whose aroma eclipses the scent of the incense sticks. Vy tosses and turns, taking up space and pushing Ha aside. Taking a deep breath to inhale as much air as she can and with her nose puffed out, Vy whispers, "The pomes and pears still smell so good, Sister Ha."

"Uh huh."

"I wish I could taste them."

"Me too."

"I don't think Mom will let us."

"Mom needs to sell the fruit so that she can buy rice for us. Stop thinking about eating them," Ha scolds Vy.

Even though Ha tells Vy not to think about it, she also wishes she could taste the alluring fruit. She wishes she had enough money to buy a whole fruit. She would cut it in half and share it with Vy. They would eat it under the star apple tree.

When the conversation among the women from the altar room dies down, the aroma still emanates from the boxes. Ha inhales slowly to gather its sweetness into her lungs. She is thankful that the walls keep the aroma inside. As she slips into a deep sleep, she finds Vy and herself lost in an orchard, suspended in the clouds as in a fairyland. There, in the middle of the orchard, a pome and a pear tree stand tall; their branches droop down from the heavy load of juicy red and yellow fruit. Alluring and inviting, the pomes and pears beckon them to come near. Together they pick fruit to their hearts' content – until their arms are so full that they cannot carry any more.

- When Ha and Vy wake up in the morning, Mother and her business partners are long gone. The boxes of pomes and pears are no longer there, but a faint scent still lingers in the

Two Sisters

air. Ha and Vy regret not seeing the wonderful fruit one last time. Vy asks, "Is it true that pomes and pears are from America, Sister Ha?"

"It's true. We have never seen them before."

"How is America different from Nha-Trang and Saigon?"

"America is a lot bigger."

"Is America pretty?"

"Yes. A big place has to be pretty."

"Were you ever there?"

"No."

"Then how do you know?"

Ha is annoyed, but she does not want to lose the war of knowledge. She must be more knowledgeable than her little sister. While she cannot think of a more satisfactory answer yet, she counters, "Why not?"

"Why?"

"Everyone knows."

"Who knows? How do you know everyone knows?"

"Who doesn't know? Only you don't know America."

"Who knows?"

Two Sisters

"Grandma knows. If Grandma knows then everyone knows. The whole world knows."

"When did Grandma know?"

"For a long time. If she didn't know, why did she name Seventh Aunt *My*[10] which means America? She knows that America is very big and pretty, that's why she chose that name."

Vy figures that makes sense. She no longer has doubts about a big and beautiful America and she stops questioning Ha about it. Ha silently thanks Grandmother for having given their aunt a useful name so that she could defend her logic. She does not know that "My" is actually the name of her aunt's husband and by custom, a woman is called by her husband's name. The fact that Seventh Aunt has an elegant air about her helps solidify Ha's assertion. Ha and Vy are lost in their own thoughts about the connection between their aunt's name and the new fruit that they did not get to taste. They think about the fruit from the time they walk to school, to the time they are in class, to the time they play at recess, and to the time they come home from school. Their minds are filled with curiosity about the mystery of the strange new fruit.

---

[10] My is a person's name, and it also means "America."

CHAPTER EIGHT

Each day as Ha and Vy walk home from school, they pass by the nice multi-level houses on Phan-Chu-Trinh Street. Today, the guard sitting in a small booth in this neighborhood calls out to all the girls walking home from school on the same route. "Come here, girls. These two Americans want to give you gifts."

The students stop and stare at two white-skinned, blue-eyed American men in soldier uniforms who are smiling at them. The men speak to each other in a foreign language as they beckon the girls with their fingers. At first, the students are unsure and no one moves toward these men who look suspicious for they have too many boxes and bags in their hands. The men give two boxes and two bags to two girls who stand the closest to them. These girls are excited when they realize they were given chocolates and raisins. This makes other students think that the men must be harmless. They begin jostling each other to get close to the two Americans. "Me too," they gush as they push and shove. Ha is easily pushed because she is as thin as a toothpick, but even the plump Vy is forced all the way back. Vy looks longingly at the brown boxes given out, wanting them, but

Two Sisters

not knowing how to ask. Ha shouts in Vy's ear. "They are Americans, Vy. So now you can say you've seen one."

Vy is annoyed. "I know. I just want candy."

The commotion causes some confusion to the Americans who do not give out things in a fair manner. They hand things out to some girls more than once and none to others. The guard does not like the chaos created by the girls. "Stop shoving each other. Don't you mind that the Americans will laugh at our people?"

The students ignore him and continue to encircle the two Americans shamelessly. The guard cannot stand their unruliness; he puts himself in the middle of the crowd and pushes the girls away. "Go home now. No more candy." The Americans, as though understanding the guard, give what is left to the girls standing nearest to them and wave their empty hands in the air to indicate there are no more gifts. The students disperse, leaving Ha and the stunned Vy behind. Vy stares at the two Americans without speaking, ignoring Ha's urging to leave. The two men confer with each other in their own language before walking back to the nice houses. When they return, they give something to the guard who calls out to Ha and Vy. "The American men saw that you didn't get anything. They give you some food, and also two dresses for the little one." He hands the dresses to Vy and the food to Ha.

Ha is excited. "Let's hurry home to tell Mom. She will be so happy."

Ha and Vy take off as fast as they can, almost running. As soon as they get home, they dump their flip-flops at the door, throw their hats and knapsacks on the floor, and pull

Two Sisters

out the food. "Candy! Sister Ha." Vy brings the bag of candy to her nose, inhaling gently. "They smell so good."

Ha shakes the food cans, listens to the sound they make, and reads the labels aloud. "This can is B1, this can is B2."

"I wonder what is in each can," Vy says. "How can we open it?"

"I don't know."

"So let's eat the candy first."

"No, let's look at the dresses first."

They carefully take the dresses out from the plastic bags. The dresses are the same size but in different colors, one yellow and one pink. There are two layers of fabric from the waist down, and the outside layer is sheer. Vy tries on the pink dress and it fits her perfectly. The yellow dress is too short on Ha and is tight around her armpits. Ha is sorely disappointed because she had hoped they could wear matching dresses to school.

Vy gets in front of Ha, holding her dress' ribbon. "Can you tie my dress, Sister Ha?"

"Okay. Turn around."

"It's so pretty, isn't it, Sister Ha?" Vy cannot help but talking non-stop. "The ribbon makes it even prettier, right? I wish the yellow dress fits you so we could wear them to school together."

Ha thinks of her own simple wishes that are not about fairies or magic or princesses of fairytales, but about the two

Two Sisters

of them being with both parents. She often daydreams about getting pretty dresses and modern toys from Father, hopscotching with the rich kids in school, being clean and wearing clean clothes, and standing next to teachers and friends with no inferiority complex.

"Am I pretty?" Vy repeats. "Why don't you answer me?"

Ha comes back to reality. "Yes, you're very pretty. You're pretty no matter what you wear."

"But you're not even looking at me."

Ha is not looking at Vy for her eyes are up at the ceiling and around the house. There are holes in the spider-web-covered ceiling so that they can see through to the roof. The sheet that divides the room into functional areas, their clothes, and everything else in the house are stained with smoke from the oil lamp. Ha figures that the new dress Vy wears will darken with time, just as everything else. She wants to cry just thinking about it. Her wish of having Father back and receiving little gifts from him when he gets home from work or shopping is as elusive as fairies who grant wishes to good kids in the fairytales Mother recites at bedtime. Ha is old enough to know that fairytales are illusory and will never really happen, but that does not prevent her from daydreaming.

The dogs' barking brings Ha back to reality. She looks out to see Mother come in through the gate. Vy runs out to greet Mother. "Mom, look, am I pretty? Do you like my dress? I have two!"

Mother does not sound pleased. "Who gave you the dresses?"

Two Sisters

"Two American men."

Mother takes off the cone hat; her forehead is glistened with sweat. Her face that was already red from the sun is now turning even redder upon hearing "American." She frowns. "Which two *American* men? Where are they from?"

Vy talks fast, wanting to be the first to tell Mother. "The two American soldiers at the nice big houses. They gave out candy and gave me dresses because I cried. No one but me has the pretty dresses."

"Who told you to beg for things?" Mother demands. "Who gave you the idea?"

Vy stops in her tracks with her mouth hanging wide open. She cannot take back her words and does not know how to alleviate Mother's anger. Mother puts down the carrying pole against the coconut tree. "Go lie on your bed to learn your lessons."

Vy timidly follows Mother inside. Mother becomes more agitated when she sees food cans on the floor. "You begged for all of this, didn't you? Ha, go lie down on the bed also." Tossing her bag and hat on the floor as she walks out to the garden, Mother mumbles to herself. "How dare they beg Americans for things!"

Ha has not seen Mother this angry before. As Vy, she is surprised and scared. When the sound of leaves being stripped off a tree branch is heard, she knows what Mother is doing. No one is fond of getting lashes from a rod of a star apple tree branch. Ha's immediate plan is to lie down next to the wall, to be as far away from Mother and the rod as possible. When Ha climbs across Vy who is already lying

Two Sisters

facedown on the bed, Vy protests, "You have to be on the outside. Mom told me to go lie down first."

Ha can be stubborn at times. "But Mom didn't say where to lie on the bed. I can lie where I want to." Vy pushes close to Ha. The two of them lie as close to the wall as possible, leaving a large gap on the bed. They are as stiff as two pieces of wood planks, waiting for Mother to come back from the garden, as they nervously listen to the sound of leaves being stripped off their branch and Mother's grumbling. With their faces down, there is not a lot of room between their noses and the pillows. Their heavy breathings sound like whispered prayers.

When Mother comes back, she startles them by striking repeatedly on the hard bed with her rod. "Come closer to me."

They move one inch toward the outer edge of the bed.

"Some more!"

They move another inch in the same direction; their bodies synchronize as one solid unit.

"Some more. You hear?"

Vy nervously separates herself a bit from Ha.

Mother speaks sternly. "Which one of you started this business of begging the Americans?"

"I don't know," Ha says.

"Not us," Vy says.

Two Sisters

"So why do we have strange things in the house?"

"They gave the stuff to us."

"Who are they?... Vy, be quiet, I want to hear from Ha."

"A Vietnamese guard and two American soldiers."

"Where are they from?"

"They live in the big houses on Phan-Chu-Trinh Street."

"Did you have permission to accept gifts from strangers?" Mother leans forward to strike on Ha's bottom. "Why do you think you can receive gifts from strangers without permission?"

Ha sobs, stroking her buttocks. "I don't know."

Mother gives her another lash. "Move your hands away or else I'll break them."

Ha sobs on her pillow. She does not think it is fair because Mother has told them only not to steal or rummage through things that do not belong to them, but she never told them not to accept gifts from people.

Mother turns to Vy. "Who gave you this dress?"

Vy is unsure of the best way to avoid punishment. "From...that man."

"Who is that man?"

"That man...is...that man," Vy stutters.

Two Sisters

"That man is American?"

"Yes."

It is Vy's turn to get a lash on her bottom. The puffed-up two-layered dress must have lessened the effect of the strike. Ha figures Vy cries from being scared rather than being hurt. After a while, Vy's cry turns into a whimper, matching with Ha's own.

Mother is not moved. "You cannot accept gifts from anyone when you do not have permission. Do you understand? When you go to school, go straight there and don't look East or West. Lately I hear that many children beg from Americans. If their parents know, they will not permit it. We are Vietnamese. Even if we're poor, we have to live within our means, we cannot beg from foreigners. Do you hear?"

They both say "Yes" even though they do not retain what Mother just said because they did not listen. When the rod comes down on the mat, they stop their whimpers and utter more yeses to make sure the rod stay on the mat and not land on their buttocks. Mother gives Vy another lash. "Get up. Vy, take off your dress and come here."

Vy gets up on all four. Her cries are a bit louder because she doesn't want to part with the dress. Standing in front of Mother with arms folded, Ha feels sorry for Vy. In her mind, Vy is like the character Tam in the familiar fairytale *Tam and Cam*. In the story, a fairy gives Tam a new dress, but alas, Tam's big sister Cam steals the dress before Tam has a chance to wear it. Ha thinks of Vy as Tam, and Mother as a stern fairy, who looks at them straight in the eyes without a smile and speaks to them in a serious tone, not the nurturing fairy as in the fairytale.

Two Sisters

"What do you say now? Ha, you can speak first."

Ha has memorized what to say in situations like this. "Mother, next time I will not..." She stops mid-sentence, trying to think of a word to substitute for "beg" because she did not beg. The gifts were freely given to her. She decides to say, "Mother, next time I will not take gifts from the Americans."

Mother nods with satisfaction. "That's good." Her voice softens. "But it's not just from the Americans. You cannot take gifts from anyone. We have to accept our lot in life. We cannot covet, steal, or beg from anyone."

Ha bows her head low. "I understand. It will not happen again."

Mother turns to Vy. "What do you say?"

Vy looks pale. Her face is smudged with snot and tears. She repeats what Ha just said in whimpers. "Mother, I will not take dresses from the Americans anymore."

"Not just dresses," Mother emphasizes. "You can't take any kind of gift from anyone, not just from the Americans."

Vy wipes her smeared face with the back of her hand. "Yes, Mom."

"Will you beg and take things from strangers anymore?"

"No, I will not."

"Remember what you promise me today. This time I gave each of you two lashes. Next time I'll double the punishment. Now go return everything."

Two Sisters

Tears fall down Vy's face again, this time from the pain of having to part with the dresses. She looks imploringly at Mother, hoping for mercy, but Mother is steadfast. "Ha, help Vy put everything back into the bags and return them. Then come home for dinner."

Ha and Vy reluctantly gather the dresses, the food cans, and the candy bag. They slowly and carefully put each item back in the same bag from which it came. They drag out their actions, lengthening the time they have with the precious things. They linger a while before putting on their flip-flops and hats in hope that Mother will change her mind at the last minute.

On the way back to the neighborhood of nice houses, Ha tries to comfort Vy who cannot stop crying. "Don't be too sad. When we grow up, I'll have money and I'll buy you pretty dresses."

Vy shakes her head. "I don't want you to buy me dresses. I want these dresses."

Ha schemes to hide the dresses so that Vy can wear them to school. She is dying to tell the other kids that the American men gave the dresses to them and not to anyone else. She wants to show the other kids that Vy has pretty clothes just as they do.

"We'll hide these two dresses. Okay, Vy?" Ha says.

Vy looks at Ha in alarm. "No, not okay. Mom will beat us."

Ha shudders, thinking of the star apple rod and the beating they just received. "You're right. Let's return them." While waiting for traffic to clear at an intersection, Ha

Two Sisters

shakes the paper bag. The sound it makes reminds her that the candy bag is inside it. She mischievously pulls the candy bag out, tears it open, gives a piece of candy to Vy, and takes one for herself.

Vy pops the piece of candy into her mouth. "So delicious, Sister Ha," she gushes. "American candy is so good. Is it a waste to return it?"

"Yes, it tastes and smells so good."

"Should we return it?"

Ha hesitates. "The candy bag is already torn. They'll know we ate some."

"Can we keep it?"

"Where do we keep it?" Ha asks.

They are almost at the nice houses and there is no way they can eat up the candy. Vy tries to chew the piece in her mouth as fast as she can. "Stop," Ha exclaims. "I know where we can hide the candy." Ha pulls up her shirt and puts the candy bag inside the elastic waist of her pants. Vy is ecstatic. She urges Ha to return everything else quickly.

The guard smiles sympathetically at them. "Your parents do not allow you to accept the gifts, right? I know. No one wants their children to beg."

On their way home, the sun is high above their heads and beats down mercilessly, but the two sisters are happy and proud of their cleverness. They do not mind the heat. They cheerfully talk and laugh all the way home. They do not pay attention to the shiny cars, elegant shoppers, busy

Two Sisters

walkers, or children playing on the sidewalks, and they do not see two little shadows following them home. If they had looked, they would have seen that the taller shadow wore pants with uneven legs.

CHAPTER NINE

•

Ever since Mother and her business partners contracted with the orchards for their right to fruit trees, Ha and Vy have been going to the orchards with them. The two sisters are simply happy to be together and go places with Mother. They no longer dream of pretty dresses or exotic gifts and have pushed these out of their minds.

The trips to the various orchards usually occur on Sunday afternoons either by van or by horse-drawn carriage. Neither the van nor the carriage is big enough to fit everyone comfortably, but Ha and Vy are used to discomfort and they do not mind it. Because the roads to the orchards are not paved and therefore rough, the passengers often get tossed around for anywhere from thirty minutes to two hours, depending on the orchard location and the mode of transportation. Ha and Vy are familiar with their routine of first stopping at the owner's residence to say hello before exploring the orchard on their own while the adults do their business. Some orchards are so big that it can take Ha and Vy awhile to find Mother and her business partners once they are done exploring.

Two Sisters

Today the windowless wagon-like van takes them to a rather large orchard. The adults lead Ha and Vy to the orange and tangerine area without first stopping at the owner's residence. When Ha asks about it, the adults say, "This orchard is very big and we may not have enough time."

"But don't we have to ask for permission?"

"The owner already asked us to come several times, but we couldn't until today." Ninth Aunt laughs heartily. "She'll be very happy to see us here."

Third Aunt Ro climbs up an orange tree. "These oranges are ripe. If we don't pick soon, they'll fall to the ground. We can't sell fruit with no stems and leaves."

Fourth Aunt pulls out baskets from her bag. "Go pick something for yourselves. Get away from here."

Ha hesitates. "We...do not have permission yet."

"I give you permission," Fourth Aunt says forcefully. "I am the owner."

"But we did not have permission from the real owner."

"Oh my God," Fourth Aunt says to Mother. "Fifth Sister, give them permission. They are only in the way here."

"We are now the owners," Ninth Aunt says while handing Third Aunt Ro a basket to put the fruit in. "We bought the right to all the fruit in this orchard. We already paid for this back when the trees just had buds."

"So can we pick anything, Mom?" Ha excitedly asks.

Two Sisters

Mother smiles. "Go ahead and pick anything you want as long as your aunts agree."

"That's okay, Fifth Sister. How big are their stomachs that we can't let them pick and eat as much as they want?" Ninth Aunt says. She then kindly turns to Ha and Vy. "Eat anything you want, but make sure to leave the ones with stems and leaves for us." She adds, "If you want to taste something, ask me and I'll cut it with my knife."

"Don't be too easy on them," Mother says. "They are here to help us gather fruit, not just to play and eat."

"Don't worry, Fifth Sister," Fourth Aunt says. "Let them have fun. They don't need to help us."

Mother is grateful. "Thank you, Sisters."

Ha and Vy thank the adults before turning away. Ha points to the direction of quacking sounds. "Let's go over there where the ducks are, Vy."

"Be careful," Mother says. "There is a pond over there."

"The fish pond is fenced," Third Aunt Ro says. "They'll be okay."

Ha and Vy walk away until they no longer hear the women's voices. They enjoy their freedom and take their time strolling and listening to the sounds of birds singing and leaves rustling in the breeze. Ha cannot decide which fruit tree to pick from while Vy runs and skips ahead. "There are so many guavas. Pick one for me, Sister Ha."

Two Sisters

Ha climbs up a guava tree and pulls down a branch full of fruit. She breaks off a stem to take with them as they walk on.

"Look at this guava tree," Vy cries loudly. "It has even bigger fruit than the last one. Let's pick some more."

Ha shakes her head because she has been eyeing a small star gooseberry tree that has just a few branches but bears big and juicy yellow fruit. She orders Vy to use her hat to catch the fruit as she climbs the tree and picks out the branch with the most fruit. Vy turns her hat up-side-down and holds it under the tree. Half of the gooseberries fall into the hat and Vy picks up the rest from the ground. Vy bites into one and scowls. "It is sour, Sister Ha."

Ha tastes one. "You're right. Too bad, they look so plump."

"That's because it's a sour star gooseberry tree. If you want sweet fruit, you need to go near the fish pond." Ha and Vy turn around to face the person who just spoke. She is short and skinny, wears a torn hat, and is chewing a concoction of areca-and-betel[11].

The woman looks at them not with unkind eyes. Even then, being embarrassed and scared because she is caught red-handed climbing a tree that does not belong to her, Ha feels weak in the knees. Her legs wobble under her. She turns pale and feels as if she is going to fall. Gathering all her strength and courage, she folds her arms, bows down in

---

[11] It is a mixture of betel leaves mixed with areca nuts. Chewing on it and spitting it out when it has become a red paste is a local custom for both men and women.

Two Sisters

deference to the figure before her, and timidly utters a greeting. "Hello...Auntie."

Vy follows suit. "Hello, Auntie."

The woman smiles gently. "Who are you? What are you doing here?"

Ha feels better at the gentle tone of the woman's voice. "We are children of Mrs. Fifth. Mom and her business partners said we could pick fruit."

"Your mother and her partners bought only oranges, pomelos, tangerines, sapoches, and soursops."

Ha's face turns red. Her lips quiver. "So...Mom did not buy this star gooseberry tree?"

The woman spits the areca-and-betel paste on the ground and wipes her mouth which has turned red from the mixture. "No, only oranges, pomelos, tangerines... But since you're here, go ahead and pick anything you like."

Ha calms down. "I just want to try it. I don't like the gooseberry."

The woman nods. "I know. It is sour, isn't it?"

"Yes, ma'am."

The woman continues to chew on the red concoction. "You need to know your fruit. If you eat sweet fruit first, the sour ones will taste even more sour. For example, if you eat the soursop or sapoche before the sour gooseberry, the gooseberry will taste more sour. If you come to my orchard, you should eat sour fruit such as star gooseberries, pomelos,

Two Sisters

carambolas first before eating sapoches, longans, soursops, and papayas."

"We picked only guavas and star gooseberries."

"I allow you to pick anything you want, but pick only what you can eat. Do not throw away any fruit because that's wasteful."

Ha and Vy feel guilty when they realize that the stem of guava Ha picked earlier is still full of fruit, uneaten. But the orchard owner makes an irresistible offer. "Do you want to eat sweet star gooseberries? I have a special tree near the pond."

"Is it far from here?" Ha asks.

"No, it's just past the soursop and sapoche trees."

Vy is excited. "I want to go. I never had sweet star gooseberries before."

Ha and Vy skip after the orchard owner. "You can pick all the fruit from my sweet tree," she says. "I make jam from the sour fruit, not the sweet one."

The fruit trees in the orchard were planted along straight columns in an orderly fashion. Ha and Vy walk past tall orange and tangerine trees that are heavy with fruit and short sapoche trees that are not taller than Ha. The golden sun shines and dances on the green sapoche leaves as though enticing the two sisters to look at the brown oval fruit underneath them. When they come to a vegetable field, there is a square fish pond that is fenced off by wires winding around surrounding trees. The wire fence is entwined with vines of purple wild flowers. Next to the pond, there are

Two Sisters

papaya trees with fruit of various sizes and at various stages of ripeness, sweet-smelling herbs, and a lone star gooseberry tree that provides shade to the duck house.

"This is the sweet gooseberry tree. You can stand on the wood stack next to the duck house to pick the fruit. Pick as much as you want. It's okay if you take all the fruit. I'll get a bag for you." Taking off her hat and giving it to Vy, the woman says, "Use this hat to catch the fruit. Your hat is too small. Be careful. The branches can break easily." She then walks to her house down the hill, a log cabin with a tiled roof.

Vy looks at the alluring branches hanging over the wood stack next to the duck house. "Let me climb and pick."

Ha gets up on the wood stack. "Come on up, I'll pull the branches down for you."

Vy climbs up after Ha and quickly starts picking and dropping juicy fruit into her own hat and shirt pockets. Ha takes a bite from one. "It is sweet but tart."

Vy puts a fruit in her mouth. "Sweet and tart is good. I'll share with my friends."

"Who?"

"The kids in my class - Be, Huong, Hoa, and Hong."

"So that you can fawn over them?"

."What does that mean?"

"So you can follow them and beg for food."

Two Sisters

"I don't fawn over them."

"I saw you do that."

Vy is stricken with shame, brimming with tears. "When?"

"Many times, during recess. I saw you ask friends for food. One time you and a friend licked the same ice cream cone over and over. Another time you followed a friend and I was sure you were begging her to share her food with you."

Vy jumps down from the wood stack and leans against the tree. She confesses in a resigned tone. "That girl is Hanh. She had a fried sesame mung-bean cake. I asked her to share it, but I did not fawn over her."

"That's fawning."

"Fawning is lying, but I did not lie. Mom will give me a beating if I ask for food, not for fawning over my friend."

"I knew but I did not tell Mom. I don't want Mom to give you a beating for asking for food." Ha continues when she sees no reaction. "But I don't like to see you follow your friends around." She tries to remember the words Mother teaches. "We should 'accept our lot' and not let others laugh at us or at Mom."

Vy transfers the gooseberries from her shirt pockets to the woman's hat, and then puts the best-looking gooseberries back in her shirt pockets. She asks, "What about you? Are you sharing with your friends?"

"No."

Vy looks at Ha in surprise. "So what do you do with them?"

"I'll save them for you. When you have nothing else to eat, you'll have these."

"You don't have friends?"

"Yes, I do, but I do not have very close friends."

Ha can still hear the taunts from her classmates ringing in her ears. *"Go away," "You're not in our group,"* or *"Do not let her in our group."* She says, "The girls in my class are rich and snobby. They don't care for gooseberries."

"I think my friends will like gooseberries."

Ha eats the gooseberries while watching the ducks. They are not timid, but waddle to the wire fence to watch for crumbs and quack loudly when their owner appears. Vy throws gooseberries over the fence and imitates the ducks' quacking sounds. From behind Vy, Ha laughs at Vy's short form and uncombed hair, and mutters a piece she just learned from school.

A flock of ducks, swimming in a pond,
Is threatened by a boy with a rod.
Quack quack they cry quack quack,
Rod comes down they run away.

The orchard owner comes back with two partially-filled bags. "You can add gooseberries in these bags. I put some soursops and pomegranates in the bags for you to try. Tell me if they are good. You can call me Seventh Aunt Luong-Son."

Two Sisters

Vy profusely thanks the owner for her generosity. Ha asks, "Are we at Luong-Son place, Auntie?"

"Yes. Now hurry up and put all the gooseberries in the bag. It's late. Your mother probably is ready to go."

On the way home, holding the two precious bags in their laps, Ha and Vy listen to the conversation around them.

"We earn much profit this time."

"Are you putting the cart before the horse? We have not sold anything yet."

"Just make a rough estimate and you'll see."

"I think so, too. When we first signed the contract for the trees, they didn't have many flowers yet. It is amazing they could bear so much fruit."

"We'll still have to come back twice to get them all."

"I don't think the owner even knew these trees would be so productive. After we sell, let's buy yellow rock sugar and rice crackers to offer thanks to the Kitchen God."

The Luong-Son orchard recedes in the horizon as the van pulls farther away. The pallid rays of the waning daylight still dance on the green leaves of the trees along the road. The van slowly turns its wheels under the heavy load of fruit baskets. It heads toward the city of Nha-Trang, where its passengers are eager to get back before dark.

CHAPTER TEN

•

Ha does not care for the yellow rock sugar and rice crackers that Mother and her friends offer to the Kitchen God, but she enjoys the Tet preparation otherwise. Each time she overhears the adults discuss their profits, she imagines that Mother's principal has multiplied many times. Knowing that Mother's business is going well, Ha has hoped to ask Mother for a gift of a doll, one that can open and close her eyes like the ones belonging to Elder Aunt's granddaughters. She will share it with Vy, so they need only one doll between the two of them. They will take turns and play house with cooking, shopping, teaching, sewing, and changing diapers. Ha plans to keep her wish a secret until after Mother has sold all the fruit from the contracted orchards.

The last trip before Tet involves two orchards that are farther away. The adults are tired on the day of the trip. They squeeze against each other in the van and doze off. As the peaceful country scenes roll by, Ha daydreams about a doll and a playhouse. She whispers in Vy's ears, "If we have a doll, what will you name it?"

Vy squeals loudly, "Doll? Where's the doll?"

Two Sisters

The adults wake up from their catnaps with a start. Without thinking, they respond to Vy by looking on and under their seats for a doll. "What doll? Whose doll are you talking about?"

Ha's face sags; she turns her head away and resumes looking at the scenery. The scenes keep changing from gardens to meadows, from meadows to dirt fields, from dirt fields to grass fields... just as those in films that Ha sometimes gets to watch on the television in Elder Uncle's living room as she sits with Vy and Mother on the front porch of the big house. Sensing Ha's silent disapproval, Vy stays quiet. The adults stay awake from that point on, but they are no longer interested in the doll. They get impatient and urge the driver to go faster. After a while, the van turns onto a narrow dirt road and passes large orchards as it bounces about on the uneven unpaved path full of loose rocks and pot holes. It finally stops at a gate adorned with pink and purple bougainvillea flowers on both sides. Before anyone gets off the van, the orchard owner is already at the gate to meet them. She is out of breath. "I have terrible news. All fruit including oranges, tangerines, and pomelos, have dropped from the trees."

Fourth Aunt, who is at the front seat next to the driver, jumps out. "What happened? We were here just a few days ago."

The other women immediately get off the van and form a circle around the owner.

"What happened to the oranges? The animals ate them?"

"What happened, Fifth Sister?"

Two Sisters

"Did you say all the oranges and tangerines have dropped from the trees?"

"How could that be? Are you teasing us, Fifth Sister?"

The owner scrunches her face into a painful expression. "Oh my God. How can I tease you when we do business together? I was so anxious for you to show up. Follow me to the orchard. You'll see I tell the truth."

The women run one after another in a hurry, without speaking to the driver or to Ha and Vy. The two sisters follow the adults without being told. The leaves underfoot have the autumn colors of yellow, orange, and red. They make a pleasant crunching sound as that of dry leaves being stepped on in a forest. The women do not stop to enjoy the scenery, but spread themselves about to examine the orchard in its entirety. They stare at each tree as though they wanted to either hypnotize it or be hypnotized by it. Ha and Vy are as stunned as the adults to see trees stripped of fruit and leaves, save some sick-looking yellow or brown ones still clinging on them.

The women of the Dam market gather en mass to cry out to their Gods. Ninth Aunt who is known for her calm seems to be the most agitated. "I've never seen such a sorry sight. The heat turned things brown and dropped them. We're ruined."

Third Aunt Ro jumps up and down on the leaves in a fury. "We're surely ruined."

Mother is no less upset. "Oh God, why does this happen to us at this time of the year?"

Two Sisters

Fourth Aunt chokes up. "Oh my God. We were just here last week when the leaves were green and the trees were full of fruit." She turns to the orchard owner. "Did you water the trees?"

This does not sit well with the owner. "What are you thinking, talking about watering a grown and mature orchard?" She pulls Fourth Aunt toward the red-roof house under a row of areca trees. "Come to my house and see. All of the fruit, large or small, dropped as if under a spell."

The women stop at the front door where a heap of oranges and tangerines lies on the cement floor. Ha and Vy insert themselves among the women to look at an assortment of lurid yellow and red fruit, appearing like dented plastic balls of different sizes. Third Aunt Ro squeezes one orange to test its quality. "We can't sell the rotten fruit without stems and leaves. People want nice, fat round ones for their altars."

Fourth Aunt does the same, picking up several oranges to examine them more closely. "Dear God. I don't understand how the fruit could be beautiful last week and rotten this week. We surely can't sell these."

Ninth Aunt sighs. "And this happened to the entire orchard!"

"I told you already. After just one night, half of the orchard was gone. My children and I worked like the dickens to gather and separate the fruit from the leaves."

Mother dejectedly sits down next to the fruit pile, squeezing a few as if she wanted to bring them back to freshness. "This will not be a happy New Year for us. No

Two Sisters

one will buy from us." She jumps up quickly. "We should go check Tenth Sister Dai-Dien's orchard."

Fourth Aunt calmly reasons. "I don't think the same thing happens over there. It can't. No place can be as pitiful as this."

The orchard owner lowers herself onto a chair, picks up a paper fan to give herself relief from the heat, and counters in an obviously irritated tone. "What are you trying to say? We've been doing business together for a long time."

Ninth Aunt tries to pacify the situation. "Let's all calm down. We should go to Tenth Sister Dai-Dien's place to check things out."

The orchard owner puts her fan down and stands up. "I'm going with you. She's Tenth Dai-Dien and I'm Fifth Dai-Dien. We're all Dai-Diens. I want to see with my own eyes how it is over there."

The agitated women all get into the van. As soon as they arrive at Mrs. Tenth Dai-Dien's orchard, they march straight to her house. They do not find her, but a pile of sick-looking fruit in a corner of the house. It appears to have been set up as a proxy to answer the questions the orchard owner knew would be asked of her. Mrs. Fifth Dai-Dien walks over to the table next to the window and pulls out a chair to sit down. She takes some areca-and-betel concoction from her shirt pocket and pops it in her mouth. "I told you the weather was not good this year. It was unpredictable. You didn't believe me."

Fourth Aunt rubs her forehead and shakes her head. She sits down next to Mrs. Fifth Dai-Dien and pours tea from a teapot on the table for herself. Ninth Aunt, Third Aunt Ro, and Mother walk outside in another attempt to look for the owner. Ha and Vy follow them. Third Aunt Ro calls out loudly. "Tenth Sister, where are you?" There is no answer but dogs' barking from the adjacent orchards and this causes a commotion of the birds overhead. The birds take flight in all directions from their resting place on the bare tree branches, void of fruit and leaves. Ninth Aunt joins in to call Mrs. Tenth Dai-Dien's name. Again they hear nothing but the dogs' barking and the birds' nervous tweeting in response. The party walks back into the house. Ha and Vy follow the women in silence. The two sisters have not uttered a word since they got off the van and witnessed the strange phenomenon. Vy refrains from asking Ha questions because she knows Ha is still upset with her about the doll. Ha has absorbed the worries of the women into herself. From their facial expressions, words, and actions, she can tell that there is a serious problem and it no doubt affects Mother's principal and in turn, her own dream for a doll. Mrs. Fifth Dai-Dien continues to chew on her areca-and-betel mixture. "I think you should gather all the fruit here and at my orchard."

Ninth Aunt sighs. "I want to wait until Tenth Sister comes back to talk to her first."

"What for? In the past, if she was not here, you would still pick the fruit and take them home, right?"

Fourth Aunt raises her voice. "How can you talk about the past? In the past, the fruit that I climbed up the trees to pick and put in baskets were fresh with stems and leaves still attached, not the same as this sorry lot."

Mrs. Fifth Dai-Dien's manner changes ever so slightly and her tone is a touch sharper. "You know the rules. You signed the contract. You either have profit or loss, and you just have to accept it. When you earned much last year, did anyone complain?"

"I know we already signed the contract, but just put yourself in our shoes. How can we accept the rotten fruit? We spent so much money and labor and who will buy these oranges? People will not want them even if they are free. How can we pay what we owe you?

"I don't know, but rules are rules."

Ninth Aunt entreats for mercy from Mrs. Fifth Dai-Dien. "Fourth Sister is speaking the truth. Think about it. Who will buy these fruit to set on their altars? How can we find the money to pay you back?"

"Don't you be many against one. When you made profit, did you share it with me? Why do you want me to share your losses? Did you sign contracts with dogs or with people?

Fourth Aunt gets angry. "Hey, I'll tell you. We're all adults. You should watch your language. There are two little girls here. Don't speak of dogs or cats. Aren't you ashamed of yourself?"

Mrs. Fifth Dai-Dien stands up and spits the dark red areca-and-betel paste into a basket. "Tell the girls to go outside. They do not need to hear the adults talk business. I cannot keep quiet if you speak nonsense."

Mother waves her hand to motion for Ha and Vy to leave. As the two sisters walk away, they can hear Mother plead with Mrs. Fifth Dai-Dien. "Please try to understand our situation. I don't have any profit yet. I just joined the group this year and already encounter this misfortune. We cannot sell..."

Two Sisters

Ha runs to the marigold and cosmos bushes under the window to listen to the adults' conversation. Vy, on the other hand, is happy to be outside. She does not care about business talk, but runs after the little chicks, spreading her arms wide and trying to catch them. The mother hen clucks and spreads her wings wide to gather her chicks under. She cocks her head and fixes her round black eyes at Vy, being ready to defend her charge. Ignoring the mother hen, Vy pursues the chicks that failed to run under their mother's protective wings. Ha cries out from under the window, "Vy, don't catch them. The mother hen will pluck your eyes out."

Happy that Ha is talking to her at last, Vy walks over to Ha and softly asks, "The little chicks are so cute! Can you catch one for me?"

"How can I?" Ha scrunches her face. "It will hurt when the mother hen pecks."

Vy tilts her head and pleads in a babyish voice. "I just want to cuddle a chick a little. I will let it go after a while."

"Which one do you want?"

"The yellow and brown one."

"There are four yellow and brown chicks."

"It does not matter. I just want one."

"I'll go to one side and you go to the other side. Then you catch one quickly and run away before the mother hen gets you."

Ha and Vy wave their arms, trying to lure the chicks into one spot. The mother hen frantically spreads her wings wider

Two Sisters

and calls to the chicks to hide under them. Cluck cluck cluck, she makes repeating sounds. In confusion, the chicks run around their mother's legs, chirp constantly, and are not entirely sure what to do. Ha reaches out for one. The mother hen pumps up her chest and pecks at her. A commotion of the little chicks ensues.

"Catch it, catch it," Vy cheers.

Ha bends down once more, but comes up empty-handed. "These chicks are too quick," she complains.

A black dog comes from nowhere and barks loudly. Ha and Vy, the mother hen, and the chicks all run off in different directions. A woman yells out while trying to quiet the dog at the same time. "Don't run. The dog will bite you if you run."

The van driver happens to materialize from behind the woman at that time and complains to her that his passengers did not give him instructions of what to do next and he still has to take them to another orchard in the mountains. She sweetly placates him. "Don't you hurry, Second Brother. Why don't you come in for a cup of tea? It's too hot out here."

• Ha and Vy follow them inside. Mrs. Fifth Dai-Dien is the happiest to see the orchard owner, as though she just won gold from a lottery. Acting as though she were the hostess, she pulls out a chair. "Are you Mrs. Tenth Dai-Dien? Sit down, Sister. I'm Fifth and also from Dai-Dien. People call me Fifth Dai-Dien."

Mrs. Tenth Dai-Dien invites the van driver to sit down and smacks her lips. "All the Dai-Dien orchards have bad luck this year."

Two Sisters

Mrs. Fifth Dai-Dien happily adds her opinion about the weather while fixing her eyes on the women. "The weather is unpredictable from year to year. The crop sometimes is good, sometimes is bad. If Heaven gives, we win. If Heaven takes, we lose. There's not much we can do about Mother Nature."

Mrs. Tenth Dai-Dien pours tea for everyone. "It's not Heaven's will that we lose the crop this year. They sprayed something to clear the land, I don't know what for, but they killed all the trees. From here to the highway, there are no more fruit on any tree and all the leaves have turned brown." She turns to the van driver. "Sit and drink some tea. Let's drink tea and we can discuss things."

Ninth Aunt says it is too depressing to eat or drink, while Mrs. Fifth Dai-Dien is anxious to get more information. "Who told you they sprayed the trees?"

"I've been talking to people around here. They all said the same thing."

"Do you see? It's not the weather." Fourth Aunt negotiates with the orchard owners. "It's the spray that caused this. Why should we bear the loss?"

Mrs. Fifth Dai-Dien ignores Fourth Aunt. "Who are they?" she asks Mrs. Tenth Dai-Dien.

"The people who cleared the fields. How do I know who they are?"

"When did they do it? How could they spray the entire area?"

136

Two Sisters

"They used helicopters, Sister. They had money to buy all the poison in the world to clear the fields."

The women argue that they should not bear the total loss if the disaster was not caused by weather and furthermore, they can ill afford it. Mrs. Fifth Dai-Dien again ignores the women, but directly addresses her concern to Mrs. Tenth Dai-Dien. "Who are these people? They should spray only in the mountains or forests, not on people's orchards."

"I already told you I don't know who they are exactly. I heard that they meant to spray only one area, but the poison spread. We are done for. This is not the only thing that will happen. People say that the trees will all die eventually. The spray is something very powerful."

Mrs. Fifth Dai-Dien continues chewing on her areca-and-betel mixture. "You keep saying *they*, and I am not happy because I do not know who *they* are. I did not hear or see any helicopters."

Mrs. Tenth Dai-Dien is as irritated as Mrs. Fifth Dai-Dien. "I just repeated what I heard. I don't know who they are either. I heard they cleared land to create a village."

The van driver interjects, "You need to make a decision of what to do soon. We need to get back before dark."

Ninth Aunt implores the orchard owners to figure out a fair way to handle the situation. Mrs. Tenth Dai-Dien calmly says, "I'll tell you what. Take the fruit and sell what you can. We'll share the losses equally."

Mrs. Fifth Dai-Dien smacks her lips. "I agree to one-third of the total loss."

Two Sisters

Fourth Aunt tries hard to negotiate to cut their losses further. But the two Mrs. Dai-Diens have made up their minds and won't budge. There is nothing the business partners can do but abide by the decisions of the orchard owners. They gather the sick-looking fruit into baskets to take with them.

On the way back to Mrs. Fifth Dai-Dien's orchard, Vy whispers to Ha, "Do you want me to name the doll?" Ha shakes her head. She has no time for dolls now, as her mind is occupied with what just happened. The words the women spoke are swirling in her head, droning on like the noise of the garden's insects.

"So why did you ask?"

Absentmindedly caressing the reddish oranges with her fingertips, Ha is uninterested. "I was just checking."

Vy casts her eyes downward in disappointment. It has been a bad day all around.

CHAPTER ELEVEN

•

The sorry-looking reddish oranges without stems and leaves bring curiosity and elicit bad manners from the customers of the Dam market. Etiquette dictates that customers do not question the quality of merchandise, especially when they do not intend to buy, but the shoppers cannot help themselves at the sight of the fruit. They also forget the custom against uttering negative things at Tet time.

"Oh my God, what kind of oranges are these?"

"What happened? I've never seen oranges like this."

"Why aren't the oranges fresh and why are there so many of them?"

At the beginning, the sellers are polite and try to appease the customers. They explain the situation, offer a substantial discount, and suggest the use of the fruit for juice. But when they realize they cannot convince the shoppers to buy, they stop responding to inquiries. They know full well that no one would be foolish enough to buy oranges from them when there is fruit galore in the supermarkets where people jostle

Two Sisters

to buy the best-looking and sweet-smelling fruit. Besides traditional fruits such as watermelons, pineapples, bananas, and papayas, people love to purchase anything called "American" such as American apples, American pears, or American oranges. Mother and her business partners have sold American fruits in the past, but they cannot afford to buy them wholesale at this time of the year. At the end of each day, the women gather at Mother's house to divide the small amount of profit, if there is any, among themselves. Pretty soon, words of the "poisoned oranges" spread and they no longer can sell but incur losses due to overhead. They decide to dump the unwanted fruit and with that, their business of selling fruit fails completely.

With the loss, the partnership breaks up and that allows Mother to stay home to take care of her daughters. Ha and Vy are happy about it even though that means they do not get to go to the orchards, meet with Mother's business partners, eat the face fruit, or have more meat and fish with their meals. The relatives in the big house are indifferent and do not ask why there are no longer carts to take merchandise to the market or why the women no longer gather at the little house. Young Aunt refrains from any tongue-lashing.

One week before Tet, on the 23rd of December, the day when the Kitchen God is believed to depart for Heaven, Sixth Aunt reaches out to members of the little house. She asks Mother to bring Ha and Vy to the market stand where she sells merchandise so she can treat her nieces to breakfast. Mother takes Ha and Vy and leaves them with Sixth Aunt at nine o'clock in the morning, then she goes to visit merchants whom she knows. Sixth Aunt gives Ha and Vy money and tells them they can buy anything they want for breakfast. While navigating their way around the market, Ha thinks of Mother who has never eaten breakfast at the market with the two of them. She thinks of all the hard work Mother has

Two Sisters

done and remembers the evenings after Mother had divided the profits among the business partners. Mother would give Ha and Vy money for breakfast, but she herself would eat the burned rice or other leftover food. Today Sixth Aunt gives them breakfast and Mother has nothing. Ha realizes that Mother walks around the market hungry, just to wait until they finish with their breakfast to take them home. She thinks of Sixth Aunt who is busy working and has to forgo breakfast. She appreciates the sacrifices of the adults in her life. She dreams that a fairy would come and grant her wishes so that she could repay her loved ones.

Vy asks Ha to take her around the food section once for her to look at everything before she decides what to eat. After breakfast, Vy wants to walk around the toy section where she can look at the plastic dolls and animals included in plastic candy bags. Before breakfast, Vy had expressed an interest in one of these cheap toys, but Ha insisted they use the breakfast money for breakfast, not for toys. When Ha and Vy return to Sixth Aunt's stand, Ha enjoys watching the hustle and bustle of people's coming and going and the busy exchange of money and merchandise. These real-world activities are similar to the games she plays house with Vy under the star apple tree. Sixth Aunt sells general merchandise such as hair clips, cologne, moth balls, eucalyptus oil, hair dyes, table cloths, clothes, and many other things. Since it is customary for people to buy new clothes for Tet, Sixth Aunt is constantly busy with customers. She gradually assigns work to Ha and Vy because she cannot handle everything by herself. Some of their duties are light such as bagging or re-organizing items that are misplaced by customers, but they are also given the task of tending the cash register.

When Mother comes back and sees that they are helpful to Sixth Aunt, she tells them she will return at the end of the day. Walking home by herself, Mother is pulled into the joyous Tet atmosphere. Fashionable dresses and beautiful shoes are hung high or neatly displayed in glass cabinets. Juicy kumquats proudly show off their green stems and leaves. Flower pots of ochnas, chrysanthemums, roses, marigolds, and dahlias in various sizes and colors have a beauty contest along the walkways. Deep-green watermelons brag of their sizes. There are plump rice cakes and colorful boxes of fruit candies galore. It brings Mother sadness and bitterness when she thinks of her daughters without new clothes and their little house void of festive items. With very little money, she does not dare stop at any market stand. Not until she passes the last stand where white mortar-shaped cakes wrapped in shiny colored cellophanes catch her eye and the seller gives her such a friendly greeting does she dare to ask their price. She is relieved to see that she can afford to purchase seven of these cakes for the altars, in lieu of fruit candy and flowers.

At the close of market, Sixth Aunt calls a cyclo to take the three of them home. Since there is not enough room for everyone to sit, Vy stands behind Sixth Aunt and Ha. There are so many food baskets that Sixth Aunt and Ha put some at their feet and hold some on their laps, while Vy carries flowers in her hands. Sixth Aunt says to the driver, "This is a heavy load. I'll pay you extra."

"Don't worry about it, Miss Sixth," the driver cheerfully says. "Two more little girls are no problem."

"I have a lot of stuff besides the two girls. I want to be fair to you and will pay extra. You see, I've been so busy that I almost forgot today is Kitchen God's Day. I quickly threw things together to make offerings to the Kitchen God tonight."

Two Sisters

The driver doesn't reply because he concentrates on balancing the heavy load and pedaling uphill on the crowded street. Vy is very excited to ride a cyclo for the first time and feels important. She leans out to wave to a friend.

"Hey, Hoa. Look! I get to ride a cyclo."

"Stand still," the cyclo driver admonishes her, "or you'll fall out."

When they get home, Ha and Vy help Sixth Aunt carry things into the big house before returning to their little house. Vy is full of stories to tell. "We're home, Mom. We took a cyclo home."

"Did you have dinner?" Mother asks.

"We did. Sixth Aunt gave us noodles and roast pork for dinner. We saved some for you."

"I already ate. Save it for tomorrow."

"What did you eat with rice, Mom?" Vy asks.

"Soy sauce."

"Why are you not eating meat? Is it the 1st or 15th of the month?"

"I don't need it to be the 1st or 15th to be a vegetarian."

"Eat what we saved for you, Mom," Vy insists. "Tomorrow we help Sixth Aunt and she'll give us food again." She pauses to think of something more convincing. "Sixth Aunt also says she'll give us more food tonight after she offers it to the Kitchen God."

Two Sisters

Ha asks if Mother also makes offerings to the Kitchen God. Mother says, "Of course. I also cleaned the little oil lamps on the altars." Ha walks to the kitchen where the Kitchen God is believed to reside. It is quiet there; the little oil lamp next to the stove casts a yellowish light on a ceramic plate holding three cellophane-wrapped cakes, two glasses of water, and three incense sticks. Ha walks out to the well and drops a bucket. The smell of ginger candy comes from the kitchen of the big house. The annual making of fruit candy and jams from ginger, taro, and squash in the big house must be going on. Ha can tell by the dim light casting on the patio and the shadows of people coming and going, laughing and talking. People in the big house must be busy preparing offerings to the Kitchen God. The joyous and festive atmosphere a garden away causes Ha to think that the Kitchen God would surely skip the little house and go to the big house, where *He* would surely find a bigger and nicer kitchen and better food. Ha absentmindedly pours water over her feet. The cool water makes her feel good. She swishes her feet together to clear dirt from her heels and between her toes. When she looks up at the electric wires that are tangled among the coconut leaves, she feels sad again. She wonders who planted these coconut trees that are indirectly responsible for their not having electricity and putting their house in perpetual darkness.

Ha offers to light the incense for Father when she gets back inside. Mother is surprised to see Ha being interested in doing the job Mother has been doing herself. "I just did, but you could do it again if you want." Ha quietly walks into the altar room. She lights an incense stick using the flame from the little oil lamp on Father's altar. This is the first time she lights an incense stick for Father. As in the kitchen, there are water glasses and cellophane-wrapped cakes on both Father's and Buddha's altars. No flowers. No fruit. No candles. In better times when business was good, there was

Two Sisters

always something on the altars. Ha wants to say a prayer and is not sure how to begin. She wonders how the adults do it. Thinking back to the orchard trips she and Vy took with Mother and her business partners and the evenings they gathered around each other, she manages to pray to Father to give Mother a chance to resume her business so that Mother will have fruit to put on the altars and the three of them will have enough to eat. She also prays that the coconut trees drop their leaves so that the electric wires come free and electricity can flow from the big house to the little house. As she continues, she feels more confident and bolder and begins to pray for more things. She prays that both Vy and she will do well in school, receive gifts, and have pretty dresses and expensive toys.

Ha lowers her voice when out of the corner of her eyes, she sees Vy listening in. When she is done praying, Vy follows her to the table at the window. "What did you pray to Dad for?" Vy asks.

"Why do you want to know?"

"Did you pray for me?"

"I prayed for good things for all of us," Ha says, then turns to Mother. "Why did you offer two cakes for Dad and three cakes for the Kitchen God, Mom?"

"Because there are three Kitchen Gods."

"Three? I thought there was only one Kitchen God."

"There are three. That's why the stove is made up of three pieces of bricks."

Two Sisters

"I don't think the Kitchen Gods will come to our house," Ha says sadly.

"Why not?"

"We do not have flowers or fruit."

"Don't say that and offend the Gods. Although we often say Kitchen God as singular, there are two male Gods and a Goddess. They are always present in everyone's kitchen in order to watch the household activities to report to Heaven for judgment. The Gods do not discriminate against the poor. Today the Kitchen Gods are going to Heaven. We will welcome them back after New Year's Day."

"I do not know anything about Kitchen Gods. Will you tell us the story before we go to sleep? Can we go to bed early tonight?"

When Ha and Vy do not have homework, they usually go to bed early and listen to Mother tell bedtime stories under the dim oil lamp. Ha eagerly tells Vy to go wash herself to prepare for an early bedtime, but Vy refuses. "I don't want to go to bed yet."

Ha is not used to an outright refusal from Vy. She narrows her eyes. "What do you want to stay up for? To be bitten by mosquitoes?"

"I'm waiting for our aunts to give us food after offering it to the Kitchen God. Look, they're coming."

Sure enough, Ha looks out and sees two shadows moving toward their little house. Sixth Aunt's voice pierces the air. "Fifth Sister, come out to get food for the girls."

Two Sisters

Mother comes to the door and is pleasantly surprised to see that the shadows are not of Sixth Aunt and Young Aunt, but of Sixth Aunt and Seventh Aunt. "Oh my God, you are here! But it's so late."

"I want to give you materials for new dresses for yourself and the girls," Seventh Aunt says. "Take them to a dress-maker. I'll reimburse you for the tailor's fee."

Mother bows her head. "Thank you. I failed in my business and cannot afford to buy things."

Seventh Aunt feels sorry for Mother when she looks at the empty house and bare altars. "What a pity! While you fail in business, we're doing so well." She holds Mother's hand. "I still have some old-fashioned flip-flops to get rid of. I want to sell them cheap, but I have no one to help me. How about if you help me out and we'll share the profit?"

Sixth Aunt tries to be helpful. "There is just a week before New Year's Day. When can she begin?"

"Tomorrow. Come to my stand tomorrow and take the flip-flops to Phan-Boi-Chau Street. I'll make a clearance sign so we can sell them quickly. We want to sell them regardless of price because we'll have new merchandise after New Year's Day and need to sell off all the old stuff before then."

After giving Mother instructions on selling flip-flops, the two women bid them goodbye. When the two shadows disappear beyond the well, there is much talking and laughing in the little house within its four walls. Each person is happy in her own way. Vy is delighted with the food given to them from the big kitchen after it was offered to the Kitchen God, Mother is elated with the promise of tomorrow, and Ha is happy with the pink silk cloth she's caressing in her hands.

Ha silently gives thanks to Father who has responded to at least one of her prayers.

CHAPTER TWELVE

•

The Dam market is the largest market in the city of Nha-Trang. The main street in front is always crowded with both foot and vehicle traffic. Therefore, Mother does not let Ha and Vy walk to the market by themselves. They are allowed to walk only on the familiar streets from home to school and back. The market is even more crowded when Tet approaches, not just with more buyers, but also with more sellers. A week before New Year's Day, a section of the main street is closed to vehicles and its sidewalks are used to extend the market where additional stands are set up. This is where Seventh Aunt sets up a stand for Mother to sell off the flip-flops. Ha and Vy are allowed to walk from this stand to Sixth Aunt's stand in the central market.

Ha and Vy are overwhelmed by the merchandise set up for sale on the sidewalks and at the stands. There are fruits and fruit candies, real and plastic flowers, statues and paintings of religious figures (such as Jesus, Mother Mary, Buddha, or Bodhisattva), incense sticks and burners, firecrackers, etc. Everything is pleasingly displayed in an inviting and seductive way. Sellers put on their best faces, smiling, greeting, and calling on the passersby to stop at their stands. The market is already full of people at ten o'clock in the morning. Buyers walk from stand to stand in search for the best products. Ha and Vy stop at a fabric stand to admire cloths of various colors and hues, from loud and bright to subdued and soft. Workers at the fabric stand are very busy, either serving customers or working the sewing machines, for the fabric stand also provides tailoring services. The steady humming of the sewing machines and the constant calling, talking, and bargaining create a lively atmosphere. Ha holds the two pieces of silk cloth from Seventh Aunt in her hands, but she does not know whom to talk to or what to do, so she takes the silk cloth with her to Sixth Aunt's stand. Sixth Aunt is very happy to see her two nieces, acting as if she has just found gold when they show up. She immediately orders them to work. "Go greet the customers. Ha, take the payment. Vy, bag the merchandise."

Ha and Vy stay busy helping Sixth Aunt from morning until evening. They hardly have a minute to rest. When the crowd finally thins out, Sixth Aunt orders take-out dinner for them. Ha pulls out the silk cloth. "Mother asked if you could take us to a dressmaker."

"Why doesn't she take you?"

"She's busy selling for Seventh Aunt. She's also afraid because she has no money to pay the dressmaker."

"Seventh Aunt says she'll pay. Why should your mom be afraid? Your mom can give the cloth to the dressmaker and she won't have to pay. At least not until the dresses are done."

"She doesn't have money and she doesn't want to go to any fabric place."

Two Sisters

Sixth Aunt smacks her lips. "It is a little late now. There are only six more days before Tet. I don't know if there are any dressmakers who can take on more jobs. Well, hurry up and finish your dinner. I'll figure out something."

Vy chews her food quickly and puts her chopsticks down. "I'm done."

"Eat more. You have not had anything to eat since morning," Sixth Aunt scolds Vy.

"Do you think you can find a dressmaker?" Ha asks.

"I'll take care of it. Don't worry. If I can't find one, I'll buy you two new Western dresses."

When Vy hears that she is going to have a new dress no matter what, she relaxes and eats more slowly. But this time Sixth Aunt pushes her to finish. "Vy, eat quickly and come with me to find a dressmaker. Ha, stay here to watch the stand. Vy will come back to fetch you when we're done."

Ha is nervous being at the stand all by herself. She protests that she does not know the prices, but Sixth Aunt says, "It's late, so there will not be many customers. If you can't sell something, wait until I come back. I'll still need to buy white cloth for pants to go with your Vietnamese dresses. Sit near the cash register in front."

Sixth Aunt takes the pink silk cloth, some cash, and Vy with her. Watching her harried aunt walk away in disheveled pants with one leg shorter than the one, Ha feels Sixth Aunt's love for them and feels love toward her in return. She thinks Sixth Aunt is trying to make up for the hardships she and Vy go through without a father. At the same time, Ha is preoccupied with the worry that no tailor would take on another job. The image of a pink silk Vietnamese dress coupled with the gold chain that Mother lets her wear during Tet is much more desirable to her than any plain Western dress that Sixth Aunt promised. Some customers come and browse, but no one buys anything. That is alright with Ha because she does not care to converse with customers while daydreaming about the beautiful Vietnamese dress that she will wear to the temple to receive blessings from Buddha on New Year's Day. While Ha cleans up and organizes the merchandise, she keeps her eyes toward the fabric area to watch for Sixth Aunt and Vy's return. She is anxious to see them but at the same time, if they come back too soon, they probably have not found a dressmaker.

While Ha is still daydreaming, Vy breathlessly runs back. "Sister Ha, we will not have new Vietnamese dresses."

"Why?... What happened?"

"No one wants to make them."

Sixth Aunt follows Vy and puts the dress materials on the counter. "They give us a hard time even though we just want two small dresses. They try to take advantage of us. We'll see what they can do after Tet."

When Mrs. Man, the seller at the adjacent stand, overhears Sixth Aunt, she asks what happened. Sixth Aunt is only happy to tell her. "You see, the dressmakers and I know each other well. When they come to buy thread, buttons, needles, zippers, I always give them a discount. Today they act high and mighty. I wasted my saliva begging them to make two dresses for my nieces."

Two Sisters

"That's because they don't think they can handle the extra load, not because they act high and mighty toward you."

Sixth Aunt tries to console Ha and Vy. "Don't worry. I'll buy you new Western dresses." When she sees that Ha still looks inconsolable, she adds, "I will go to the temple with your family and give you more li-xi[12] money than others."

Vy brightens with the promise of more li-xi money. "Can I use li-xi money for breakfast?"

"Yes. I'll keep the cloth and take you to a dressmaker after Tet and I will pay the dressmaker. We don't need to wait for Seventh Aunt to pay."

Ha is not totally happy. It won't do her any good to have the Vietnamese dress after Tet. What good will that do when she wants to wear it to the temple for Tet?

Mrs. Man tries to be helpful. "I know who will make the dresses. Take the girls to Mr. Hao. He's near the vegetable section. He doesn't have many customers. I think he'll do it."

Sixth Aunt takes Vy with her and leaves Ha behind as before. Ha wants to resume her daydreaming, but this time there are many customers. She seeks help from Mrs. Man when she does not know the price of something. After selling a few items, Ha feels more confident and becomes bolder in greeting and inviting buyers to come in and browse. More and more customers come. Ha is too busy to notice when

---

[12] Li-xi is a gift of money given mostly to children in red envelopes during Tet for luck.

Two Sisters

Sixth Aunt and Vy return. Sixth Aunt happily announces that Mr. Hao has agreed to make the dresses. Ha is surprised and happy. Leaving the stand to Sixth Aunt, she runs after Vy who has started ahead. Pulling Vy's arm when she catches up with Vy, Ha asks, "Did you get measured?"

"Yes."

"When will the dresses be done?"

"I don't know."

Seeing that Vy is not as talkative as usual, Ha asks, "What is wrong?"

"I don't want to wear a Vietnamese dress for Tet."

"Vietnamese dresses are prettier than Western dresses. They're special because we wear Western dresses to school."

"I don't like it that the tailor is a man."

"Well, no other dressmakers will do it. I think it will be fine."

Vy does not reply. Ha follows her cue and stays silent. They pass the nearly empty stands where vendors are clearing things out. The smell and water puddles at the fish stands are the only evidence that fish was sold there. Mr. Hao's stand is simple, having just one old manual sewing machine and a few wood planks on which fabric is stacked up, except for a small section of one plank where Mr. Hao sits and another slightly longer section used as a counter to cut fabric. The creaking sound the sewing machine makes when Mr. Hao presses his feet on the pedal makes Ha think that it is about to fall apart. Mr. Hao stops pedaling when Ha

Two Sisters

and Vy come in. The hand crank makes a shrill sound as it comes to a stop. Mr. Hao says to his daughter who's sitting on a wood stool, "Take measurements of the big girl for both dress and pants. She's Miss Sixth's niece. Make generous measurements just in case. As the saying goes: *'Relax the measurements for the young and tighten them for the old.'*"

The girl gets up and tells Ha to stand and look straight ahead while she gets out a measurement tape and a notebook. Ha is not used to being measured. She stands as stiff as a soldier at attention and stops her breathing. The tailor's daughter says, "Breathe normal. Your tummy is already so small, the dress won't fit if you shrink your tummy while I measure." Ha inhales and expands her tummy. The girl seems confused with two different measurements. She hesitates, makes some mental calculations, and writes something down in her notebook.

Just then an old hunchback woman walks in. She gives Mr. Hao a pair of pants and instructs him to replace the elastic waist band on them. She takes one look at Ha and Vy and shrieks, "Oh, poor girls. It is almost Tet and they have a death in the family. Who died?"

The already grumpy Vy looks even grumpier and appears ready to cry upon hearing this. Ha silently reproves Vy for looking so grumpy to cause the old woman to misread her and think there's a death in their family. She tries to stand still so Mr. Hao's daughter can finish quickly. However, she cannot help but stop breathing whenever she's touched by the girl.

Mr. Hao sounds irritated. "No one died. Don't speak nonsense. They're having new dresses made for Tet."

Two Sisters

"Oh my God. I've never known you to make dresses for anything besides funerals."

Ha is floored. She turns around to look at Mr. Hao's stand more closely. There is no colored but only white fabric. She jumps with alarm. "Are you using the funeral white cloth for pants?"

Mr. Hao's daughter shakes her head. "No, of course not. Be still. After I measure the inseam, we'll be done."

"So what will you use?"

Mr. Hao pulls some fabric out from behind him. "Here is the fabric your aunt gave me. I'm not as crazy as to use funeral materials for Tet clothes. Now are you finished? Take your little sister home and tell your aunt to pick up the dresses in four days."

Ha bows her head and crosses her arms to say goodbye to Mr. Hao, the woman, and the girl. As they walk away, she can hear Mr. Hao's irritated voice. "Do you think I don't know how to make anything but funeral outfits? I used to make traditional clothes and that is a lot harder than making new fashions nowadays. Of course I can make two little dresses for two little girls."

CHAPTER THIRTEEN

The joyful sounds of firecrackers celebrating New Year's Day entice Ha and Vy to the front door. They want to go out to join in the fun, but Mother stops them. "You two may not go."

"Why not, Mom?"

"Today is the first day of Tet. If you're the first one to walk into a house, then you'll be the one that '*set foot on the floor*.'"

• "I wear flip-flops, I won't set foot on the floor," Vy argues.

"Set foot on the floor does not mean stepping on the floor barefoot. It means you're the first one to walk into a house on New Year's Day."

"Why don't people want us to be the first ones to walk into their house?" Ha asks.

Two Sisters

"Because the first person who walks into a house determines the household's luck for the whole year. I already explained this to you two so many times and yet, you don't remember anything."

"I won't go into the big house," Vy whines. "I just want to go to the front porch to pick firecrackers."

Ha also wants to play with firecrackers, but she understands that they cannot go to the big house until a trusted relative like Seventh Aunt does. Mother has told them that people do not want poor folks to be the first ones to set foot in their houses because they believe that will bring them bad luck, sadness, and poverty. From what Mother says, Ha has a sense of where they stand in society in general and where they rank within their own extended family.

As they sit at their doorstep, Ha says to Vy, "We'll pick up the firecrackers later, Vy. When Mom takes us to the temple, we'll do it then."

"But by then they will all be gone!"

Mother says, "The two of you go wash yourselves, comb your hair, put on new clothes, and try to be more pleasant. Don't sit there being gloomy and bringing bad luck to our own house on NewYear's Day, not to mention other people's houses."

Ha jumps up. "Let's go, Vy. If Mom yells at us today, she will yell at us the whole year. Let's clean up and go places so we'll get li-xi money."

"No, you will not go anywhere until after we greet Grandma," Mother corrects her. "After you clean up and put

Two Sisters

on new clothes, write down a few paragraphs so that you'll be good students for the whole year."

Ha and Vy get their toothbrushes from an old tin can in the kitchen and walk to the water barrel to brush their teeth. On New Year's Day, they are not only forbidden to be the first ones to set foot in someone else's house, they are also forbidden to use the well until after Grandmother makes offerings to the Well God. Mother has filled the barrel with water the day before so they can use it this morning.

Vy wants to wear her new Western dress today. Ha knows that Mother would want them to wear matching outfits, so she will also have to wear her new Western dress. She had wanted to wear the Vietnamese dress on New Year's Day, but now it does not matter because neither the Vietnamese dress made by Mr. Hao nor the Western dress bought by Sixth Aunt fits her well. The Vietnamese dress is so big she can swim in it, even after she padded it with layers underneath. Her tall and lean body between its two flowing panels is like a stick leaning in an empty bottle. The Western dress is not much better. It is too long and runs all the way to her ankle. Sixth Aunt bought a larger dress to allow for growth, but it must be twice Ha's actual size. It feels like a borrowed dress belonging to someone with different height and shape. Ha does not want to wear either dress and suggests to Vy to wear their old outfits, especially since Vy's new dresses do not fit Vy properly either, but Mother scolds her. "Don't you wear old clothes on New Year's Day. You should be grateful that you have new clothes. What more do you want? You have to learn to accept gifts without complaining. If you don't wear the new dresses your aunts gave you, they'll be upset. It's not good to be so demanding. Hurry up. Put on new clothes and write down something."

Two Sisters

After Ha and Vy comb their hair and put on new dresses, they bring pens and papers to the table next to the window. They rack their brains for something meaningful to write. It is torture. Mother believes that if they write down something on New Year's Day, then they will be good students and do well in school the entire year. Mother used to wake them up at the first sound of firecrackers at midnight when New Year officially begins, but she overslept this year. Ha and Vy thought they could skip the writing because of that, but they were wrong.

After they dawdle by writing their names in big fancy letters and coloring them with ink, they still do not have a topic to write about. They look at each other in ill-fitting clothes and burst out laughing.

"You look funny in your new dress," Vy teases.

"Same with you," Ha scowls with mock disdain. "You look ugly."

Mother is not pleased. "Quit laughing and talking. Write!"

"I don't know what to write," Ha says. "I don't know how to write poems and I do not like to write anything."

"It doesn't have to be a poem or a piece of literature. It's for good luck."

"But I don't know what to write," Vy says. "We should not have to write on a holiday."

Mother clears her throat. "You're in second grade and don't know what to write? You should already know that I

Two Sisters

want you to write on New Year's Day. You'll be a good student for yourself, not for me."

"So can I write a poem I learned at school?" Ha asks.

"Yes."

"Can I copy what Sister Ha writes?" Vy asks.

"Yes. Anything you write down is good."

Ha dips her pen in the ink bottle and writes down what she has memorized.

Grandma, I love you so much,
You always buy me things.
Yesterday when we shared a cake you baked,
You gave me the biggest piece of all.
Each time I did something wrong,
You shielded me from punishment.
For you I want to be a good girl,
So you'd pat my head saying I'm the best.

Ha is pleased when she finishes. Vy copies the same poem word for word in her notebook. The shadows of the coconut leaves dance with the sunlight on the notebook's page as though wanting to imprint their images on it. Looking out the window, Ha suddenly notices something different about today. It is quiet except for the occasional melodious bird songs from the garden or loud firecrackers from the neighborhood. There is no noise indicating that children are playing outside the estate walls as usual. *Are these children also kept inside and forced to write by their parents?* Although the big house has a fresh coat of white paint and the flower bushes are newly groomed, there is no talking and laughing in the garden and no opening and closing of the gate. Everything is immersed in the silence of New Year's Day. Perhaps no one – rich or poor, educated or not – wants to chance setting foot on the floor of someone else's house. Grandmother, Elder Aunt and Uncle, Sixth Aunt, and Young Aunt must be sitting in the big house's living room at this moment, waiting for Grandmother's other children and grandchildren to come. Ha misses the days in the market with Sixth Aunt amid the hustle and bustle of holiday shopping, a contrast to today when everything suddenly falls into silence. Tet is supposed to be the time for families to gather to pay homage to their elders, to wish each other a happy year ahead, to feast, and to play games or cards together. But Tet in the little house is no different than any other days because Mother does not set up a table of fancy feasts, the three of them do not say magniloquent greetings to each other, and none of them plays games or cards. Tet at the big house must be as joyful and animated as theirs is boring and dull. It will remain a simple and subdued affair at the little house.

As if to remedy the forlorn feeling of the little house, music from an accordion breaks the silence. The sweet music spreads throughout the neighborhood as if wanting to fill its every nook and cranny with life and joy. The Chinese neighbor across the street has a habit of playing his accordion on New Year's Day. He often starts with a Chinese song praising the beauty of a Chinese young lady before playing traditional Vietnamese Tet music. This year he skips the Chinese song and begins with a Vietnamese song that Ha knows. She sings along with the music. *"New Spring comes amid happy days. I am drunk with the love of life. Beautiful flowers bloom everywhere. I want to pick a thousand roses—"*

Ha's singing is interrupted by Vy's loud declaration "I'm done." With a flourish, Vy throws her pen on the table.

Two Sisters

Ha is annoyed. "That's fine. Why do you have to yell so loudly?"

"My hands hurt from writing, but my writing is better than yours," Vy crows.

"So you're so good and you copied my poem." Ha's voice is tainted with sarcasm. She resumes singing while swaying with the music. Vy imitates, shaking her body about and singing loudly.

Mother admonishes them, "Stop singing and start cleaning up. Put away your paper and ink so that we have room to greet any guests who may be coming."

As they put away their papers, they hear the sound of the gate opening. Not wasting any time, they jump onto the table and throw their bodies forward, putting their faces against the window bars to look out.

"It's the family of Brother Ky and Sister Trinh," Vy yells.

"Yes, their three sons and three daughters are also here. Yay!"

Kiki and Yellow join in with joyful barking amid the laughing and talking at the gate. Ha and Vy do not want to miss out, but as they run to the front door, Mother says, "Don't stand at the door on New Year's Day. Finish cleaning up."

Vy lingers at the door. "Seventh Aunt is here! So many people! So much fun!"

Two Sisters

Mother says, "Now we can go over to greet Grandma, but only after you put away your writing materials."

Ha quickly puts things away and urges Vy to do the same. They excitedly put on their shoes. Mother reminds them of how to greet Grandmother and wish her a happy new year. Then the three of them take off for the big house.

CHAPTER FOURTEEN

Perhaps because Mother is afraid to set foot on the floor of the big house, even though she would not be the first one to enter it on New Year's Day, she walks her daughters to its back door.

Entering the big house from the back, they first pass by Grandmother's private parlor that also serves as the guest bedroom. Then they pass the dining room where Ha and Vy slow down to admire the holiday decorations and the spread of holiday food. Normally the dining table is covered by a simple plaid cotton tablecloth, but today it is covered by an elegant white lace cloth with white embroidery. On it a beautiful vase with fresh flowers is surrounded with an assortment of fancy food that dazzles Ha and Vy. There are an octagonal wood box of fruit candies, a big ceramic plate of fresh fruit, and a crystal bowl of roasted watermelon seeds. Two large green watermelons are placed next to two long stems of pink roses on top of the refrigerator. The china hutch shines brightly, showcasing beautiful things. Its top shelf holds bottles of liqueur and colorful candy dishes. Its lower shelf displays crystal glasses and fancy china. Ha and Vy feast on the aroma and richness of the food with their

Two Sisters

noses and eyes. Vy swallows hard at the displayed sweets, pointing and whispering in Ha's ears the different kinds of fruit candies: ginger, kumquat, sweet potato, pineapple, lotus seed, coconut, date, apple, and banana. Ha feels sorry for the two of them because this food is reserved for Grandmother's other grandchildren or rich guests and not for them. The most they can hope for is some leftovers after the holiday is over. Shaking her head sadly, she pulls Vy away from the dining room. The white walls smell of fresh paint as they pass the bedrooms whose doors are closed. They are tempted to take a peek inside each room through the thin lace curtain, but they do not dare dawdle. They follow Mother to the altar room which is brightly lit and at its entrance, Mother stops. In this room the living remember and pay respect to their ancestors. Glancing sideways, Ha and Vy hungrily take in the sight of bountiful food, not failing to notice the beautiful fresh flowers and the haze of smoke from the burning incense sticks. Standing close to Mother, they wait patiently for instructions from her of what to do next. They are between two rooms and can see that the living room is also brightly lit. No doubt it is also elegantly and beautifully decorated to create a dignified atmosphere, forcing people entering it to pay respect and show deference by softening their voices and becoming meek in manner. Mother stays still for what seems like an eternity with a look that does not betray her emotion. Ha and Vy vaguely sense Mother's hesitation and discomfort and her indecision of what to do. They surmise that Mother is not sure whether to enter the altar room to pay respect to the ancestors first or to the living room to greet the living and wish them a happy New Year first. Even though Mother has closely followed the decorum of her late husband's family since marriage, she is still unsure of her role and is not completely confident of the proper etiquette. Ha and Vy are aware that Mother often seeks permission and approval from her late husband's family before she does something, large or small, for she can

Two Sisters

be severely criticized and condemned if she is perceived to do something wrong. Mother pokes her head in the living room, perhaps hoping for a word from someone.

The noise level in the living room has lowered to a whisper as people close in a small circle to listen to a story, and then loud laughter erupts again. A lady in a purple dress turns her face from the group to wipe tears from her eyes while putting a hand on her stomach to control her laughter. That's when she sees Mother and her two daughters at the entrance and motions for them to come in. Not until then does Ha realize that the lady is Sixth Aunt. Standing shyly with Vy in the middle of the crowd, Ha feels out of place among her paternal relatives. In their fancy clothes, her relatives do not look familiar to her. She has a hard time distinguishing who is who. The children look more grown up and the adults look more beautiful. The perfumes disperse in the air, making Ha feel even more out of place. Ha and Vy stand close together and keep a safe distance from their relatives so as not to touch any of them inadvertently. Presently everyone is paying attention to a girl standing in front of Grandmother, who is wearing a light brown velvet Vietnamese dress and holding a stack of red envelopes in her hand. Grandmother is sitting straight and proper on the sofa, smiling encouragement at the girl in front of her. The girl is wearing white boots and a light yellow Western dress that falls to her knees, exposing the beautiful pink skin of her calves. The girl is reciting a greeting to Grandmother while pressing on the tiled floor with the tip of her shoes in nervousness.

- "Grandma, at the beginning of the year, I wish for you to live long, to be a hundred years old."

Grandmother nods. "Very good." She motions the girl to come close. "Come closer."

Two Sisters

The girl moves one step forward in hesitation and shyness. Grandmother pats her head. "I wish you a good academic year and for you to be a better student than last year. How old are you?"

"I am six."

"What year were you born?"

"The year of the pig."

"So you're seven years old according to our custom, even though you're only six on the Western calendar. Since you are seven, you will get seven dongs."

Everyone laughs at the reasoning and says that the adults should also receive the same amount of money as their ages, but Grandmother smiles gently. "This is for the younger children only."

Vy whispers to Ha that she should get eight dongs if Hanh gets seven. Ha is not sure about that as she sees that instead of giving Hanh a red envelope from the stack in her hand, Grandmother counts bills from her inner pocket to give to Hanh. Hanh happily takes the li-xi money to her mother, Seventh Aunt, who is standing near the door. Seventh Aunt wears a pink silk embroidered Vietnamese dress with red flowers and green leaves. Her hair is in a new wavy perm that cascades to her shoulder. She smiles sweetly at her child. Her pink cheeks glow with happiness. Standing next to her are Elder Aunt, Young Aunt, and Trinh. Trinh is the only daughter of Elder Uncle and Aunt. The women are pretty in colorful dresses and expensive jewelry that adorn their ears, necks, wrists, and fingers. Laughter arises from humorous greetings to Grandmother such as "I wish you success in your business," or "I wish you a son at the beginning of the year and a daughter at the end of the year;" the latter is a usual greeting given to newlyweds.

Ha glances at her own mother who possesses her own beauty despite wearing simple clothes. Mother looks especially beautiful today with her oval-shaped face, pointed chin, and well-shaped nose. She wears her hair high in a bun. A feeling of unbounded love and appreciation for Mother arises in Ha's heart. She wishes for a day when she will have money to buy Mother pretty clothes and exquisite jewelry just as those worn by her aunts. She will advise Mother to stand up straight, carry her head high, and shake off the feelings of inferiority, acceptance of fate, and complacency.

Ha's thoughts are interrupted by Vy's pat on her hand. "I already said a greeting to Grandma. Now it's your turn."

Startled, Ha removes herself from the crowd and wiggles her body through the throng of people and stands straight in front of Grandmother. "Grandma, at the beginning of the year, I wish you good health..." She can feel all eyes are on her and suddenly she is flustered and cannot remember the rest of the long greeting Mother has taught her. She looks down to her feet. Her dress is too long and too loose. It almost touches the floor at her ankle and the waist is at her knee. Her face feels flush as she tries to continue the greeting "...peace, prosperity, and much profit."

People burst out in laughter – laughter that is as crisp and clear as the sound of firecrackers. Ha joins in despite herself. She realizes that she has used Mother's prayer to Buddha as a New Year's greeting for Grandmother who smiles an understanding smile. In turn, Grandmother wishes Ha to be a good student and a good daughter and gives Ha a red envelope from the stack in her hand. Following the other children, Ha gives New Year greetings to Elder Aunt and

Two Sisters

Uncle, Seventh Aunt, Sixth Aunt, Young Aunt, and cousins Ky and Trinh. Each, in turns, rewards her with a red envelope for good luck.

After the greetings and disbursement of red envelopes, people disperse into small groups. The adults gather in clusters in the living room. Children either linger around their parents or play on the front porch. Ha and Vy would very much like to join their cousins, but Mother takes them into the altar room to pay respect to the ancestors. The fragrance from the incense sticks swirls and fills the air, forming a distinct scent when mixing with the smell of fresh new paint. Smoke fills the room. The copper bowls and candle holders shine brightly under the soft light formed by three different sources: the electric ceiling lamp, the oil lamp, and the candles. As in years past, Mother points out something about each ancestor to Ha and Vy. Although these are ancestors on Father's side, Mother knows their stories well. Through the stories, Ha and Vy become familiar with the ancestors they never met and, most importantly, know how to call to them in prayers. These include forefathers and foremothers of previous generations, and also relatives who had died young. More recent ancestors have pictures on the altar, whereas those from long ago are listed on a red plaque that is placed on the shiny brown shelf, behind the pictures of their great-grandfather and great-grandmother. Since the characters on the plaque look similar to Chinese characters, Ha thinks she must have a Chinese blood line.

After lighting the incense sticks and bowing in front of the altar to pay their respects to the ancestors and pray to them, Mother tells Ha and Vy additional facts about each ancestor and the relationship they have with that ancestor. Ha and Vy appear as if they were paying their utmost attention to Mother, but they are distracted by the fancy food. As they become older, they are more aware of the differences between their relatives and themselves. They feel insignificant when they think of the meager food on their own altars and the simple things they own in their little house. Looking at Father's portrait on the altar in the big house, they feel at least satisfied that Father gets to "enjoy" the fancy food that Mother cannot afford for him in the little house. They swallow hard as they bow before the altar, anticipating the fancy meal they are going to have with their rich relatives. Besides Christmas, they love Tet when they see cousins they don't often see and taste food they don't normally taste – food such as sweet rice cakes wrapped in banana leaves, head cheese, cured pork, abalone, fish fin, shrimp paste, egg rolls, meatballs, pandan cakes, bamboo-shoot cakes, and lotus cakes.

At meal time, the children have their own place set up in Sixth Aunt's house, separate from the adults' place. Their meal is not at a dining table with chairs but at a wood divan on which they sit around a large round metal tray of food. Ha and Vy put on their best behavior as instructed by Mother. They cannot help but look longingly at the food. Unlike their cousins who prefer playing over eating and whose parents have to nag them to eat, Ha and Vy are the first ones to come to the meal. Their cousins reluctantly eat only a little and hurry back outside to play, leaving Ha and Vy on the large divan by themselves. Although Ha and Vy would love to stay and eat more, they feel funny to be there without their cousins. They regretfully follow their cousins outside. After all, this is the one time of the year that all cousins gather together.

The ground has turned pink for it is covered with torn wrappings of fired and spent firecrackers. The children count the content of the red envelopes to see who gets the most li-xi money. The boys pick up firecrackers that have dropped on the ground but are still intact and set out to light them.

Two Sisters

They set one on a red brick and cover most of it with an old tin can, leaving the tip exposed. Trung, the third son of cousin Trinh and grandson of Elder Uncle and Aunt, lights it. When it catches and sparks, he waves his hand to disperse the crowd. Ha and Vy run together to one spot, keeping their eyes on the firecracker while cupping their hands over their ears, as the girls do but the boys do not.

Boom.

The firecracker explodes. The tin can flies into the air, making a spectacular sight and an ear-popping sound. The boys and girls cheer. Ky, Trung's father, and Seventh Uncle walk out from the big house, impressed. They ask if it was a "super-firecracker."

Trung shakes his head, flashing a big smile with a hint of mischief. "No. I fired a regular one under a tin can and it made that big a noise."

"Do it again. We want to see it."

The boys are delighted to oblige. They fire another firecracker, but nothing happens. The boys discuss among themselves, get another firecracker, set things up, and try again.

Boom.

The tin can is blown higher than the first time. The children cheer. Seventh Uncle flashes them a smile of approval before going back inside.

This is Tet all right. To Ha and Vy, it is real Tet when they hear the joyous sounds of firecrackers, see the tin can

Two Sisters

blown up and flying high in the air, and being a part of the laughing and talking among the young cousins.

CHAPTER FIFTEEN

A few days after Tet, Seventh Aunt makes a proposition for Mother to go to Cam-Ranh, a peninsula south of Saigon, to manage one of her stores selling lacquers and paintings. Ha and Vy would live with her family and would be well taken care of as her own children. With no other prospect of earning money, Mother agrees.

Seventh Aunt's house is located on Independence Avenue, a busy street in the business district of the city of Nha-Trang. The house is used both as a residence and a store selling general merchandise. The store is on the street level. The kitchen and dining room are behind the store. The bedrooms are on the two upper levels. On a roof, there is a flat terrace where Seventh Aunt keeps her potted plants. Seventh Uncle and Aunt have seven children whose names reflect the qualities that their parents wish for them to possess: Nhan (Kindness), Le (Decorum), Nghia (Loyalty), Tri (Knowledge), Tin (Trustworthiness), Duc (Virtue), and Hanh (Chastity).

The three youngest children, Tin, Duc, and Hanh, are excited about Ha and Vy's living with them and want to

Two Sisters

share their room. Seventh Aunt agrees because it is the largest room of the house, situated on the second floor, with enough bunk beds and dressers for five children. It is also adjacent to Nghia and Tri's room so that the two older girls can keep their eyes on the little ones. Seventh Aunt figures with five children under the age of ten living under one roof with their own inventions of games and mischief, the adults will need help in having the little ones closely watched.

After two months living with their uncle and aunt and cousins, Ha and Vy are used to the routine. The older children ride their bicycles or motorcycles to school while the five elementary-school-aged children go to school on a cyclo. The older children watch after their younger siblings (and cousins) and help them with homework. They also help out in the store at times. The little ones do not have chores to do. In the morning after washing up, they go down to the street level where an array of breakfast food awaits them. Seventh Uncle and Aunt have hired a cyclo driver to take their three little children to and from school for the entire year. He does not mind taking Ha and Vy in addition. He is always ready at the front door when the children finish their breakfast. The children know him well and call him Uncle Bay. School lasts until just past noon when Uncle Bay takes them home. They eat lunch and take an afternoon nap. Afterwards, they usually get to eat some kind of dessert from the street merchants who carry their wares in baskets hanging on the two ends of long poles resting on their shoulders. Then the children do homework and read until dinner time. School is held Monday through Saturday. On Sunday, the children usually go to a movie theater to watch a movie of their own choosing.

Since the time Ha saw the Indian movie *Two Orphans*, she has been partial to Indian films. She is obsessed with a scene in which a girl, sitting at a table of exquisite food,

Two Sisters

enjoys a cool drink while her older sister, sick and drained from a hard journey on an empty country road, must drink well water from a mud bowl given to her by a compassionate woman. The irony of the two scenes and the contrast of circumstances of the two main characters made Ha cry, but she was satisfied with the happy ending. The film not only had a happy ending, but it also transported Ha to a world of calm and peace as the beautiful actresses, with lovely red dots on their foreheads, sang and danced. Watching the movie, Ha felt as though she were at the same place with the women of beautiful voices and graceful bodies.

Only Ha wants to watch Indian movies. The other four children invariably pick a swashbuckling Chinese movie and being greater in number, they prevail. These Chinese movies are boring to Ha because they are predictable. There is always a beautiful girl in beautiful silk clothes falling for a handsome and courageous swashbuckler. The handsome and courageous swashbuckler sweeps his hair into a bun, wears a sword on his waist, and goes from place to place doing good deeds and saving honest people from treachery and tragedy. The story would not be complete without a love triangle made complicated by exciting sword or martial-art fighting. Sometime during the film, the hero would fall down a high mountain to be saved by a hermit and eventually come back to conquer the enemies and rescue the girl he loves.

After coming home from the movie theater, the four younger children would insist on play-acting. They hum and sing songs to the tune of *Luong-Son-Ba and Chuc-Anh-Dai*, a famous Chinese love story in which two young lovers end up dying for love. Ha does not enjoy play-acting because she always has to play the role of a swashbuckler who ties his hair with a rubber band and wears a bath towel as a cape, a ruler as a sword, and a piece of cloth around the waist as a belt. His heart would be torn for he has to choose between

Two Sisters

two beautiful girls. Vy would play the role of a mandarin's son who is rejected by both beautiful girls. To protect the girl her character really loves, Ha has to fight against the antagonist, the role that Duc plays. The antagonist is a bully who not only executes sneak attacks, but also collaborates with the mandarin's son to win the hearts of the two young ladies. The worst thing is that before the "costumes" and "props" are put away, Ha would be the one to be blamed because she is the oldest of the five children and therefore, the adults reason, must be the leader of the mischief.

One Sunday afternoon before they play-act, Uncle Bay comes to offer them a ride to the beach. Ha and Vy are ecstatic because they still remember their unfulfilled wish. The image of blocks of colorful clouds, painted with the pink hue of the early sun, resurfaces in its glorious beauty and gives Ha and Vy unfathomed joy. Uncle Bay tells Nghia and Tri, the two older cousins in charge of the little ones, that he already spoke to their parents about taking the five little children to the beach.

"But don't you have to work?" Nghia asks.

"I hardly have any customers in the afternoon nowadays. This morning, I kept riding around and no one called, so I stopped by to get my pay. I want to go to the beach anyway because it's too hot. I can take the children with me."

"But it's dangerous for them to be at the beach without adult supervision."

"I plan to sit at the beach to watch them. I will not let them out of sight."

"What will you do with your cyclo?"

Two Sisters

"I will park it at the coconut trees. I can keep an eye on it while I sit below. I want to relax and feel a nice breeze while the children go in the water. We'll be there for one to two hours to cool down."

"You just want to spoil them," Nghia laughs. "I think it will be hotter at the beach than at home."

Uncle Bay waves his hat and smiles. "I have this fan to help me."

Tri asks sweetly, "Can I go too?"

"There are already five children," Nghia says. "There won't be enough room."

"That's okay. Tri and Tin can sit on the cushion, Hanh and Duc can stand behind them, and Ha and Vy can sit at their feet. They're all little and don't weigh much, I'll be able to handle the load."

Vy is relieved, not noticing she has been holding her breath. Exhaling, she pulls Ha's hand and whispers in Ha's ear, "We're going to the beach, Sister Ha." Ha nods and tries to listen to Nghia's instructions. They are to hurry and pack swimsuits and towels and not make Uncle Bay wait. Uncle Bay says he'll be waiting for them and they do not have to hurry.

Ha is not sure what to pack but does not want to ask questions. She watches her cousins pull out their swimsuits and after a moment of hesitation, she says to Vy, "We do not need swimsuits. Bring me your regular clothes and I'll pack."

Two Sisters

Vy reports, "Tin and Hanh already put on their swimsuits."

"They are not doing things right. We are supposed to pack clothes, not change clothes."

Vy is not sure. "But Sister Tri[13] also put on her swimsuit."

"We do not need to change because we do not have swimsuits. Let's hurry because they are waiting for us."

Ha is right. Their cousins are already on the cyclo. "Hurry up," Tri says. "What took you so long?" Ha and Vy quietly get on and sit at the feet of the other children. They only have room to squat next to each other.

"Sit closer to me or else you'll fall out and bump your head," Ha says to Vy.

Uncle Bay visually checks that the children are secure before pedaling away. He struggles to keep the cyclo in balance. "If you fall, you'll break your head, not just bump it. Sit still. I'll be in trouble if anything happens."

The cyclo rolls away slowly on Independence Avenue, passing through the business district where there are various shops on both sides of the street. An office complex is being

---

[13] By custom, younger siblings pay respect to older siblings by addressing them with the title "Brother" or "Sister." They do the same to cousins who are children of aunts and uncles who are older siblings to their parents, regardless of age. Since Ha and Vy's father was Seventh Aunt's older brother, their cousins are supposed to call them "Sister." Ha and Vy break traditions when they address their four older cousins as "Brother Nhan," "Brother Le," "Sister Nghia," and "Sister Tri."

Two Sisters

built and the rumor is that the new building will be seven stories. A whiff of cakes and pastries from a bakery makes the children hungry. There are street merchants on the sidewalks. In front of a bar, a few American soldiers mingle with beautiful young women wearing fancy clothes. Showy colorful store signs are everywhere. Shops display merchandise in shiny glass cabinets. The tailor's shop has a mannequin draped in a Vietnamese dress – flowing on her arm is a piece of beautiful fabric that falls gracefully to her ankle. An Indian fabric store is on the opposite side of the street from the tailor's shop, creating a near one-stop shopping experience for the customers' convenience.

As they go along, Tri points out things to her siblings. "Here is the Nha-Trang City News Network. If we go straight ahead and turn right, that's where Grandma, Ha, and Vy live." The younger cousins say they already know that because their mother has taken them there before.

The cyclo takes a sharp turn; Ha and Vy scramble to hold on to each other and to any part of the cyclo they can get their hands on to keep from being thrown out. When they come to a six-way intersection, traffic is bad. Even the sidewalks are crowded. Some cyclists are on foot, pushing their motorcycles or bicycles, looking for a place to park. Buyers haggle on the black market. Ha is surprised to see a theater. She wonders aloud why they have not gone here. Her cousins say that this theater shows only *Cai-Luong*, a type of Vietnamese musical, that they don't care for. Besides, the cousins say, it costs more and is farther away from their house. They want to know why Ha and Vy who lived nearby did not know about this theater. Vy says that is because they do not watch *Cai-Luong* movies and Ha adds that no one ever took them to a theater before.

Uncle Bay has a hard time maneuvering the cyclo at this intersection. He begs the other drivers to give him room, "Please move your vehicle to the right," but to no avail. Traffic is so bad that he finally asks Ha and Vy to get off to lighten the load. Ha and Vy follow the cyclo on foot until traffic thins out.

Ha reads the street sign aloud. "Yersin Street."

"This is the correct way to go to the beach," Tin says. As if to prove that Tin is correct, a cool breeze blows from the opposite direction. Yersin Street is a pretty street with royal poinciana trees lining it. Their deep red blossoms add beauty to the square brick buildings and the iron gates carved in beautiful and exotic designs.

"Are we almost there?" Ha asks.

"Almost," Hanh says.

"Give me the float, Sister Tri," Duc says.

"Stand still or else you'll fall," Tri admonishes him. "I'll give it to you when we get there."

Ha feels deprived because Mother has never taken her and Vy to the beach before. Although she understands that rich people have the time and financial means to go places, whereas Mother has to work all year long and has no time to think of pleasure, she still wishes that Mother would have taken them to the beach, even just once, so that she does not have to be so ignorant. Sadly, Mother never had time to learn about her children's simple wishes. Ha is sure that Vy and she would be so happy if Mother had taken just a few minutes to walk them to the beach. She wishes Father were still alive. He would surely take them places just as Seventh Uncle takes his children places.

Ha gets off the cyclo when it stops at the beach where a stunning view is before her. Sunbathers are lying on the smooth sand behind the coconut trees. Beyond the white sand, the blue water glistens under the sunlight all the way to the mountains in the distance at the horizon. White clouds are suspended in the light blue sky. The sunlight is reflected off the blue sea and white wave crests. The ocean is gorgeous, much more beautiful than the image Ha had formed in her mind. It is both alluring and poetic. Ha and Vy silently admire the ocean's enigmatic beauty. They have imagined the blue water and the sandy beach, but they did not know about the harmonious blending of the colors of the sea and sky, the glistening of the dancing waves, the softness of the white sand underfoot, and the graceful swaying of coconut trees in the breeze. They follow Uncle Bay and their cousins past the coconut trees down to the sandy beach. They walk slowly and stay behind the group, partly to enjoy the beautiful scenery and partly because they are unsure of where to go.

"Let's go into the water, Sister Ha," Vy says when she sees their cousins do so.

"Okay, let's run."

Vy breathes heavily as she is not used to running on the sand. "I love this, don't you?"

Ha runs after Vy. She has to yell her reply over the sound of the waves and the laughing and talking of people. "Of course I do. I want to come here again and again. What about you?"

Two Sisters

Vy trips, falls down, and laughs hysterically. "The sand is so smooth. It didn't hurt a bit."

Ha removes her plastic flip-flops. "Everyone is walking barefoot. Take off your flip-flops."

"The sand is hot. I'll leave mine on."

They leave things with Uncle Bay and run to the water with their cousins. The waves pound on the wet sand. Water splashes amid white foam. They watch the dark tanned children ride the waves in and then swim out again. Tin and Hanh call to them. "Come out here with us. You can't swim there where the waves hit."

Ha and Vy get in the water and go farther out to where their cousins are. Ha shivers in the cold water, stops, and refuses to put her face under. Vy slips and falls. "Ah, I fell." She coughs out water as Ha pulls her up and smoothes her hair.

"Are you okay?" Ha asks.

Vy spits into the ocean. "The sea is too salty."

The other children laugh. Ha is not sure if they laugh at Vy's falling or at her and Vy's wearing regular clothes instead of swimsuits. She walks Vy back to the sand. "The rocks at the bottom are very slippery. Be careful."

"I am not scared. I want to go back into the water. But...my pants are down."

Ha shows Vy how to roll up the pant legs and tie her shirt around the waist to keep the pants up. Then they stay in the shallow part, ignoring their cousins' calls to go to deeper

Two Sisters

water. Vy imitates Ha who acts as if she knew how to swim, stretching herself into a horizontal position and kicking her feet and waving her arms.

Suddenly Duc screams, "Ouch, my foot hurt."

"You got hit by a jellyfish," Tri says, pushing Duc's float toward shore. "Let's get out."

Ha suspects that a jellyfish must be some kind of sea monster that she has read about in fairytales. "What is a jellyfish? Is it big and mean?" she asks.

A little boy near them laughs out loud. "Where are you from? Don't you know what a jellyfish is? Look. Here's one."

Ha and Vy look at a soft round form that is as transparent as the sea water, bobbing gently in the little boy's hand. Ha asks, "Where did you catch it?"

"We don't need to catch them. The waves bring them in. Look carefully in the water, you'll see them and can pick one out if you want."

"Why does it look just like water?" Vy asks. "Where is the mouth? How does it bite?"

"They don't bite. They 'hit' you and put a sore on your skin. You get hit if you're near shore. If you want to avoid them, go farther out."

Ha and Vy shake their heads and return to their cousins. Uncle Bay is putting wet sand on the red welt on Duc's leg. He says soothingly, "It will stop hurting in a moment. Don't cry."

Two Sisters

"I'll stay and build a sand castle with you," Hanh offers.

Tri helps Hanh dig a hole in the sand. Vy joins in. Together, they build a mound around the hole. Tin runs after the little crabs on the sand. Duc stops crying and runs after the little crabs with his big sister. The older children build a castle around the water hole, while the younger ones throw the little crabs they catch into the hole.

Ha dreamingly looks at the blue calm water where sailboats are gliding and a few heads are bobbing up and down. She does not pay attention to people around her or to their laughing and talking. She wishes she could be in the midst of the immense sea and sky. The thought of lazing in the middle of the cool blue sea while looking up at the blue sky above gives Ha pleasure. The hot sun dries out the beads of water on her skin. She stands up and asks to borrow the float from her cousins.

Tri wipes the sand off her hands. "I'll go with you. I want to swim again."

"I want to go too," Tin says.

Uncle Bay says, "The three of you go ahead. I'll watch the younger ones."

When they reach the water, Tri and Tin swim to the deep part. Ha follows while hanging onto the float. "If you want to learn how to swim, you'll have to let go of the float," Tin says.

"Is it deep?"

Two Sisters

"It's not very deep, but you won't be able to touch the bottom. However, you can't swim in shallow water. If you want to learn how to swim, you'll have to do it here."

"You think so?"

"You won't be able to swim if you're too scared."

Ha lets go of the float and starts kicking her feet and waving her arms. The more she tries to get above water, the more she is pulled under. She tries to raise her head above water to cough and screams out, "I can't swim. I'm sinking. I'm sinking."

Tri quickly pulls Ha up and pushes her toward the float. She scolds Tin, "Ha doesn't know how to swim, why did you tell her to? She could drown."

"I didn't know she cannot float," Tin nervously says.

Ha shivers. "I don't know how to float."

"Let's go to the shallow part," Tri says.

"Can we go home?" Ha asks while resting her face on the float. "I swallowed too much water. I'm tired. I don't want to swim anymore."

CHAPTER SIXTEEN

Seventh Uncle and Aunt decide to take their young children to visit Uncle's parents and leave Ha and Vy behind. With no one to play with, Ha and Vy venture to the study room where Nhan is painting on a large piece of paper spread out across two tables. He looks up. "Do you two want to study here?"

"No," Ha says.

"Then go play."

"Everyone is gone," Vy says. "No one is here to play with us."

Nhan waves his hand to stop Ha and Vy from getting closer to the painting. "Ah yes, they go visit Grandma and Grandpa. Be careful! If you dump water on my paper, my effort will be wasted."

Ha sits down next to Vy. "Why didn't you go visit your grandparents?"

Two Sisters

"I have this painting to do. Besides, I visit them often. I don't wait until Sunday to visit."

"What are you painting?"

"A landscape. I have to turn this painting in tomorrow. You can sit and watch if you want. But don't dump the water. I can't turn in any messed-up work to my teacher."

Ha is surprised that Nhan who is a big boy still has painting homework. She thought only little children draw and paint. Ha thinks of the pictures she drew and colored with the colored pencils Mother bought with money she made from her own business. Ha used the pencils until they were too short to be sharpened, but she still keeps them in their box. She also keeps the picture of Snow White and the seven dwarfs that she drew. She likes to draw and watch people draw to learn from them. She learns that Nhan does not use colored pencils, but what he calls watercolors. He asks casually, "So you two cannot play with each other?" and laughs as they shake their heads.

Ha likes the way Nhan draws and paints with little effort. First he sketches a house at the right bottom corner of the paper, and from there, he adds two lines going up to the top of the paper. The lines go toward each other so that they are closer to each other at the top. He intersects the two long vertical lines with short horizontal lines and fills the rectangular areas with brown color. He makes graceful curves from the top of the vertical brown lines with green color. The green curves look like fish bones or leaves that either stretch high up, spread out, or hang down. Ha asks, "Is it a coconut tree next to a thatch house?"

"Yes, I'm making a country scene."

Two Sisters

Nhan continues to work on his coconut tree, drawing a clump of big round fruit from the brown tip of the trunk, at the same place where the leaves begin. He works steadfastly, but stops to check his progress now and then. The thatch house and the coconut tree look so real, making Ha homesick for her own little house. This feeling turns into a melancholy that she feels she cannot share with anyone. She decides to leave the room and takes Vy with her to the street level.

At the store front on the street level, the children's nanny and two female helpers look bored as they sit behind the glass cabinets until some American soldiers enter. They stand up to greet the white-skinned, blue-eyed, blond-hair customers. The soldiers point to the lacquered paintings while speaking in a strange language. The helpers answer them in the same strange language. No one bothers to tell Ha and Vy to get lost as usual. This is a business place and children are not encouraged to linger here. The only time Ha and Vy walk through the store is when they are on the way out of the house. It seems the sellers and buyers finally agree on a price because the helpers start to wrap up a painting and put it in a box. With nothing else to do, Ha pulls Vy outside.

"Where are we going, Sister Ha?"

"We're going home."

"I miss Mom, too."

"Yes, but Mom is not home. She's away selling merchandise for Seventh Aunt."

"So why are we going home?"

"To visit Dad. He's home alone."

Two Sisters

Vy chokes up. "Why are we not home with our parents as other kids?"

"Because God let Dad die."

"Can we ask God to bring him back?"

"I pray all the time, but God does not do that."

"But dead people come back to life after drinking a potion in Chinese movies."

"Chinese movies are fake."

"Then why do people watch them?"

"Maybe because the stories are interesting."

Vy does not completely understand the logic, but she is distracted when she suddenly spots a bill on the ground. "Look, I found five dongs."

Ha examines the bill carefully. "You're right. It's five dongs."

"Did someone drop this or did God give us this money?" Vy asks.

Ha and Vy look up at the construction workers who are busy painting the exterior wall of a multi-story building. "Do you think they dropped this?" Vy asks.

"I don't think so."

"Can we take it?"

"Perhaps someone dropped it. But since no one is here and you found it, it's yours."

"Does that mean I'm a thief?"

"No, you're not a thief or a beggar. I will not tell Mom."

"Keep the money and buy me anything you want. It's ours."

Being wise, Ha puts the bill in her pocket. "We'll save this money and use it only when we really need it. Now we'll live independently."

"Does that mean we are not going back to Seventh Uncle and Aunt's house?"

Ha shakes her head. "No, we're not."

"I like to live with just the two of us."

"You're right. Our house is small but it's ours."

When they get to the big intersection near the news network, Ha makes sure the traffic is clear before taking Vy's hand to cross the street. They approach the Hoa-Hoa bakery and stare at the bakery goods in the glass cabinets, but everything is expensive. A street merchant greets them warmly. "Do you want to buy?"

"Can we buy something, Sister Ha?"

"We can't. We don't have enough money."

"Can we buy something for five dongs?"

Two Sisters

"I don't know how to ask."

The street merchant offers again. "Buy something, my dear children."

The street merchant offers them a variety of food: green guavas, green mangos, cut-up pieces of jackfruit and pineapple, sweet potatoes, boiled jackfruit seeds, and some kind of black seeds.

"How much is the jackfruit seed?"

"Half a dong for ten."

"Let's buy jackfruit seeds," Ha says. "Then we still have four and a half dongs."

They eat the jackfruit seeds on the way home. When they get to their little house, the gate makes a loud noise as Ha unlatches and relatches it, but no one from the big house comes out. The sun is bright and casts the girls' shadows at an angle. Kiki and Yellow, recognizing the familiar scents, do not bark, but jump at them and follow them to the little house. They find the door unlocked. Ha gently opens it and lets the sunlight in. The two of them stand there looking at the familiar sight. Everything is in its place just as before, except there are a few bottles of water at the bottom of Father's altar. Being thirsty, they each grab a bottle and drink it. After taking a gulp, Ha runs outside and spits it out. "It's oil, not water. Don't drink."

"I already drank some," Vy says in disbelief.

"A lot?"

"No."

Two Sisters

"How could you not tell it's not water? You swallowed too fast."

Vy's voice shakes. "Will I be okay?"

"Oil is used to light oil lamps," Ha reasons. "It will burn your stomach. Spit it out."

Vy tries her best but cannot spit out what was already swallowed. Her mouth foams up with saliva. She whimpers, "Will I die? I can't spit it out."

"I don't know if you will die," Ha says. She's hoping that by chance someone from the big house will come and tell them what to do. Seeing the water barrel next to the well, she says, "Go rinse out your mouth. Drink a lot of water so that the oil will not burn you."

After Vy rinses out and drinks water, they go lie down on their bed.

"How do you feel?" Ha asks.

"I'm sleepy."

"Go to sleep then."

Ha waits until after Vy falls asleep before getting up to sit at the front door. But when she sees movements in the garden, she figures people from the big house are preparing lunch and not wanting to be seen, she goes back inside and sleeps next to Vy.

They wake up when Sixth Aunt comes in. From the time Mother started working in Cam-Ranh and Ha and Vy lived with Seventh Uncle and Aunt, Sixth Aunt has been visiting the little house each evening to light incense for her late brother. Sixth Aunt almost screams when she sees her nieces. "When did the two of you come home? Who told you to?"

"No one," Ha stammers. "We just wanted to be home."

"Why?"

"I'm homesick."

"How long have you been home?"

"Since this morning."

"Your cousins won't play with you?"

"They went to visit their grandparents."

Sixth Aunt gets worked up over the thought that Seventh Aunt is not treating Ha and Vy well. "Why didn't they take you with them? For Heaven's sake, we're all relatives..." Ha tries to explain at first, but Sixth Aunt does not stop talking. Ha figures the best way to avoid being questioned is to be quiet and since she does not want to be punished for leaving Seventh Aunt's house without permission, she stops explaining. After a long monologue about the blameworthy Seventh Aunt, Sixth Aunt asks, "Have you eaten?"

"No, I'm very hungry," Vy quickly says.

"We ate some jackfruit seeds, that's all," Ha adds.

Sixth Aunt is incredulous. "Let's eat in my house and then we'll go to Seventh Aunt's to have a talk."

Two Sisters

After lighting incense for her late brother and feeding Ha and Vy, Sixth Aunt takes them back to town. Ha gets butterflies in her stomach and prays that they will not be punished. They get to Seventh Aunt's house during dinner. Nghia invites them to eat, but Sixth Aunt's voice drips with vinegar. "That's alright. Thank you. We already ate."

"Vy and Ha, did you eat with Grandma?" Hanh asks innocently.

"Where else would they eat?" Sixth Aunt says to Seventh Aunt. "Why did you go away without taking the girls and leave them hungry since morning?"

"This morning I had to take the children to my in-law's. I already asked the helpers to feed the girls, but they left without telling anyone. We spent so much time looking all over for them."

Sixth Aunt's voice softens. "I came to check out the situation because they said you left them home. They had no food from morning until just now."

Seventh Aunt is not pleased with the implied accusation. "How could I not feed them? How could you think of me as being so mean? I just had errands to run. They did not tell anyone when they left and we were so exhausted from looking all over for them. I was going to go to Mom's after dinner to find out if they were there. I figured that's where they went."

Sixth Aunt tries to placate her sister. "I misunderstood. Now you don't need to look for them anymore." Sixth Aunt turns to Ha and Vy. "You two may not leave without permission any more, you hear? Wait until your mother comes back, then you'll get to go home. Now apologize to

Two Sisters

Uncle and Aunt and go wash up and get ready for bed. You have school tomorrow."

Ha and Vy timidly mutter apologies before going up to their room. As they leave, they hear Sixth Aunt say to their cousins, "They have no father and their mother has to work far away. Make sure you include them in your activities so they don't feel sorry for themselves."

"We include them in all activities. It's their fault if they feel bad."

When the cousins join them in the room, Tin asks, "Why did you tell Sixth Aunt that we didn't feed you?"

"I didn't say so."

"So why did she think that?"

"I just said I was hungry. I didn't say no one fed me."

"Why did you leave the house and be hungry?"

Tri says, "It's already bad that the two of you left without saying anything. It's worse when you cause the adults to fight about it."

Ha cries silently inside. She puts two sets of clothes into her knapsack and walks to the bathroom. Vy follows, whispering, "Why did you put clothes into the knapsack?"

"I will go home tomorrow and not come back here."

"I want to go home with you. So I should put my clothes in my knapsack, too."

Two Sisters

"Okay, when school is over, we will not get into Uncle Bay's cyclo."

The cool bath water calms them down and takes away their worries. They go to bed early. Lying next to Ha, Vy says, "I already put my clothes in the knapsack. Tomorrow we'll go home."

"Do you have a tummy ache?"

"No. I guess oil does not kill you."

"Of course it can kill you. You didn't die because you drank just a little bit. Next time we'll have to be more careful."

They stop talking when they hear Tin, Duc, and Hanh come in. Their cousins stay quiet and do not ask them to play the *Man-eating Crocodiles* game as usual. There is tension in the air. The cousins turn the light off early. Vy falls asleep easily, but Ha stays up, reliving the day in her mind. When she remembers about the money Vy found, she realizes it is not with her. Figuring that the money must be in the dirty clothes in the kitchen, she waits until she hears snoring before getting up to go get it. After finding the money, she does not return to the bedroom right away, but climbs the stairs all the way to the flat terrace. Passing the dark rooms, she figures that her aunt and uncle have closed the shop and everyone is asleep. She whispers in the dark, "Mom, why are you gone for so long? Why don't you come home to be with us and with Dad?" and bursts into tears. In loneliness, she takes comfort from the quietness and darkness of the night. A strong wind shakes the house roofs below, startling her and making her feel cold. There is a faint light from the seventh floor of a building that is being renovated. White clouds in funny shapes move in tandem with the flickering yellow light as if teasing her. Ha suddenly recalls the ghost stories told by her cousins about the seventh floor and an eerie sensation runs down her spine. Her limbs freeze and she thinks she sees various ghostly apparitions that come and go. Although scared, she feels comforted when she thinks of Father. She figures the ghost of Father would be a kind one, just as the ghost of the Lady Cuc-Hoa who comes at night in a fairytale to comb lice off the hair of the two boys Nghi-Xuan and Tan-Luc who, on their way looking for their father, have fallen asleep on her tomb. Thinking of Father, Ha asks him for his blessings and prays to him for good things to come.

CHAPTER SEVENTEEN

After school, Ha and Vy meet at their agreed-upon place and begin their journey home. When they come to Uncle Bay's cyclo, Ha says, "Today we'll go back to our own house."

"No one told me about this. Do you know the way? Do you want me to take you?"

Ha speaks fast as she sees Tin and Hanh approaching. "We know the way." Then she takes Vy's hand and walks away quickly.

When they get home, Ha is gentle with the gate latch so it doesn't make as much noise this time. They walk through the quiet garden to their little house. As soon as they put their school knapsacks on the table, Ha runs to the kitchen to check the rice container. Seeing that there is rice in it, she says, "I'll cook the rice. But you have to go gather wood."

"Where is the wood?"

"Pick the dry branches on the ground."

Two Sisters

"Can you help me gather the wood?"

"Okay."

While they gather dry branches, they are startled by Cuu, Elder Uncle and Aunt's new helper. "What are you two doing here?"

"We're gathering wood to cook rice," Ha stammers a reply.

"What rice?"

"Rice to eat."

"Why are you not at your aunt's house?"

"We like our house better."

"So you're brave, huh? Wanna be independent? You're just a kid!"

Ha doesn't appreciate Cuu's sarcasm. She looks straight in Cuu's eyes. "We can live by ourselves. I can take care of my little sister."

Cuu narrows her eyes and raises her eyebrows. Her lips tremble as though she wants to say something, but then she sulkily turns and goes to the well where she picks up a tray of dishes and walks back to the big house. Cuu's disappearance makes Ha feel lonely and abandoned and she starts to cry.

Vy shakes Ha's hand. "Is this enough wood? Can we cook yet?"

Two Sisters

Ha wipes away her tears. "Yes, that's enough. I'll cook now."

Vy scratches her head. "Why are you crying? Did... Sister Cuu make you sad?"

"No, I just miss Mom."

"I want Mom home too, but I won't cry any more. I cried and Mom didn't come home," Vy says while squatting down next to Ha. Although she says that she doesn't cry, tears fall on her face and the two of them cry together.

Trying to remember and mimic how Mother used to cook rice, Ha puts rice in the pot and rinses it a few times before adding water and putting the pot on the stove. She lights some old school paper with the flame from the little oil lamp on Father's altar, and uses it to start the fire. The dry leaves and branches catch and burn brightly. She puffs her cheeks with air and blows at the flame. Vy watches and cheers when the flames spread and make cackling sounds. They happily feed the fire with more and more dry branches until there is black smoke and a burning smell.

Ha feels important because this is the first time in her life that she has cooked a pot of rice. She sets things up as though they were going to have a feast. Vy gets the chopsticks. Ha pours fish sauce into a little bowl. "Today we'll have rice with fish sauce. We'll get meat another day."

Vy does not mind rice with fish sauce. She swallows hard. "I like rice with fish sauce, especially rice we cook ourselves."

"Oh, the rice is not done and it's also burned," Ha says disappointedly when she opens the lid.

Two Sisters

"That's okay," Vy says.

Ha digs deep into the pot with chopsticks and tastes a few pieces of rice that stick on them. She is happy to find that the middle layer is cooked, albeit a little soggy. The soggy and burned rice is not entirely bad; in fact, it tastes quite good with fish sauce. As usual, Vy eats more than Ha. They finish up the cooked part, so there is none left to save for another meal. Ha takes the dirty dishes to the well and soaks them in a big pot of water. She is afraid to throw the under-cooked rice in the kitchen scrap pot because Mother has said that people who waste as much as a grain of rice will have to eat maggots in their afterlife. Ha hopes that the birds flying above in the coconut trees will come down to consume the rice she spreads on the ground. Vy thinks that the birds may not want to eat the rice that has touched dirt, but Ha assures her that is okay.

"Then why aren't they coming?" Vy asks.

"They are busy singing songs... No one gave them rice before so they do not know."

"Why do you want the birds to eat rice?"

"If the birds eat the rice, we won't have to eat maggots in our afterlife."

"I don't think the birds will come. What do birds eat when they don't have rice?"

"Worms or fruit."

"I think they prefer worms and fruit."

Two Sisters

Ha is anxious and abrupt. "I know. Let's not talk about it anymore."

Ha hopes people from the big house are taking a nap after a busy morning. She hopes no one will come out to the garden at this hour and if they do come out, they won't pay attention to the little house. To be sure, she closes their front door.

Vy says, "I do my homework first and I'll check the birds later for you."

"Okay. When you check, don't open the door wide. I don't want *people there* to know we're home."

"But Sister Cuu knows."

"She doesn't know we're staying. I don't think she will tell anyway because it will just be more work for her."

"How?"

"She may have to take us back to Seventh Aunt's house."

Ha gets out her homework assignment. She doesn't understand the notes she took in class this morning. They look so random now as she tries to read them. She was so preoccupied with making plans to come home and live independently that she was absentminded. She wrote things down without understanding them. She reads and rereads the assigned math problem, wrestling with all combinations and permutations of numbers and operations, without coming up with a solution. After writing, erasing, rewriting, and erasing again, she gives up, heaves a deep sigh, and puts away her notebook.

Two Sisters

"You can't do your homework?" Vy asks.

Ha admits her defeat, shaking her head and feeling miserable. "No."

"If we are at Seventh Aunt's house, Brother Nhan can help you, right?"

"Yeah."

"Do you want to go back?"

Ha shakes her head.

"It would be great if we have an older brother or sister," Vy says.

"I have an older sister," Ha says dreamily.

Vy opens her eyes wide. "Why don't I know?"

"Because she's my big sister. I'm the only one who knows."

"Where does she live? What's her name?"

"Her name is Snow White. She lives near the ocean."

"Did you meet her?"

"Of course. She's my big sister."

"Does she look like Snow White in *Snow White and the Seven Dwarfs*?"

Two Sisters

"Yes, she's as pretty as Snow White in *Snow White and the Seven Dwarfs*, although the other Snow White lives in the forest and my sister lives near the ocean."

"Is her house pretty?"

Ha's imagination comes alive as she looks out at the garden. "It is very pretty. She plants lots and lots of flowers in front of her house. Butterflies and bees come to drink the nectar and spread the pollen. She has a swing next to a big tree with beautiful green leaves where the birds come and sing."

"What does she do for you?"

"She lets me sit next to her on the swing and put my head on her shoulder. She reads me stories. It is so nice when she talks, the birds sing, and the waves clap."

Vy exclaims, "I have an older brother."

"Does he love you?"

"Yes. He gives me cookies and candies, even French cakes and chocolates."

"What's his name?"

"His name is Hoa-Hoa"

"Why does he have a girl's name?"

"That's because he works in the Hoa-Hoa bakery."

Ha remembers the other day when they stood in front of the Hoa-Hoa bakery, looking longingly at the cakes and

Two Sisters

pastries. There was a Chinese young man working in the shop. "So we are alike. Our big sister and big brother are only in our imaginations."

Vy lowers her head. "You're right. My big brother is just in my imagination. He does not give me sweets in real life."

In Ha's mind, Snow White has turned into her cousin Lily in the elegant long white dress. "And my big sister Snow White does not really want me to sit next to her on the swing because that will make her dress dirty."

"My brother Hoa-Hoa never knows what kind of cakes I like."

Ha puts her arms around Vy. "I will be your good sister. Tomorrow I'll get you a real good sandwich on the way to school. It will cost us two dongs."

Vy raises her head. "Really?"

"Yes. We still have four and a half dongs."

"Don't forget your promise."

"Okay. I'm going to take a nap. I will do homework when I wake up."

"Me too. I'm going to nap with you."

The little house stays quiet during their sleep. In the garden, the under-cooked grains of rice silently wait for the birds that have not come.

CHAPTER EIGHTEEN

When Ha wakes, it is dark. She is not sure if it is morning or evening until she hears the street merchants chanting. *"Who wants to buy mung-bean, peanut, or red-bean sweet rice."* She jumps up and shakes Vy. "Vy, wake up. Hurry up or we'll be late for school."

Ha and Vy wash themselves as fast as they can. Theirs are the only souls awake in the dimness of the foggy air. The gate is closed and the garden is quiet. Everything is still immersed in sleepiness.

"Can you still get me a sandwich? Are we late?" Vy asks.

"The street lamps are still on, so we're not late. I can get you a sandwich."

They remember falling asleep late yesterday afternoon and did not eat dinner. Sixth Aunt must not have lit incense for Father yesterday evening and did not notice that they were home, so they went hungry. Vy feels like ants are marching on her empty stomach. She swallows hard in

Two Sisters

anticipation of the delicious sandwich she is about to have. Ha makes a calculation in her head to see if she should also get a sandwich for herself. If she buys two sandwiches, they will have only half a dong left.

The sandwich stand is already crowded with customers. Ha is happy to know that she can buy half of a sandwich without meat for half of a dong, so that is what she orders for herself. Vy offers to share the meat from her sandwich but Ha declines. Although Ha is hungry, she does not feel much like eating. She is preoccupied with the undone math homework. She has memorized the math problem, but still does not know how to solve it. She shakes away the idea of asking classmates for help. To her, they are a bunch of selfish little snobs. She remembers the time she helped a student by giving away two words of an essay they were supposed to memorize, the class leader tattled to the teacher to have her punished. She knows she cannot ask the class leader for help, nor can she ask other students. The students who do well academically usually get help from their parents or older siblings or are from rich families who can afford tutors. These kids would not understand her situation nor would they want to help her. She resigns herself to the consequences of not having done her homework. She tells herself whatever will happen to her is what often happens to students with unlucky circumstances.

As Ha fears, she is scolded by the teacher in front of the entire class for not having the math homework solved. She is also scolded for wearing untidy and dirty clothes. When the teacher checks the students' hygiene, Ha is always singled out as the one with dirty fingernails. She can feel her classmates' disdain by their looks, facial expressions, and manners. She can hear her teacher's familiar words: *"Students who wear dirty clothes to school are bad students. Students who have learned about hygiene and still stay dirty do not know how to take care of themselves."* Ha sometimes cries when she's alone, but now as she stands in front of the class and listens to the teacher's lecturing, she is free of tears. After denouncing Ha, the teacher has her stay up front to listen to the math solution. But Ha's thoughts are not with the math lesson. Being called "dirty" by her teacher is similar to being called "uncivilized" or "barbarian" by Elder Aunt. The words swirl in her head, telling her that being dirty is a terrible and serious crime that makes people cringe and look down on the culprit. Not only that, her father's name is dragged out when Elder Aunt says things like *"The Giu children..."* Ha blames herself for not bathing and not wearing clean clothes. Her eyes follow the white chalk on the blackboard, but her mind is elsewhere. She says "Yes" as a robot without comprehending when her teacher asks, "Do you understand now?" She heaves a sigh of relief when she is finally sent back to her seat and instructed to copy the math solution from the blackboard. She does so while avoiding looking at her classmates.

Seeing that Ha is quiet on the way home, Vy figures Ha is worried about not having food to eat. Vy suggests that they go to sleep when they get home to forget about their hunger, but Ha says, "We will eat rice with fish sauce again. When Mom comes back, we'll get meat. I'll buy you candy tonight."

"I will eat rice with fish sauce. I don't need candy. I'll pick up wood for you to make a fire."

When they get home, Cuu greets them at the well. "You slept at home last night?"

Ha nods.

"And yesterday you burned your rice, right?"

Two Sisters

Ha nods again.

"Oh my God, I have no idea how you can be so bold. What happened? Why didn't you stay with your aunt?"

"We are homesick."

"Why, girls? You come home and eat burned rice instead of having maids do things for you!"

Cuu goes back to the big house after washing dishes, but returns to the little house with a tray of rice and fish for them. "When you have time, will you teach me how to cook?" Ha asks.

"So you really want to stay home?"

"Yes, until Mom comes back. Don't tell anyone because they'll make us go back to Seventh Aunt's house."

"Okay. I'll teach you. You're at the right age. But what will you eat with rice?"

"We'll eat rice with fish sauce or salt."

"No, I'll make extra food until your mom comes home. Now eat!"

Seeing there is not much rice, Ha says she's not hungry and will give rice to the dogs if Vy doesn't want it all. Watching Kiki and Yellow stick out their tongues in anticipation, Vy says, "I'll eat it all."

Cuu admits that the rice she gave them is supposed to be for the dogs when Ha asked her about it. "How else would I have extra rice for you? But no worry, the dogs have other food."

"I'm not worried, but will you also show me how to wash clothes?"

"There's nothing to it. You soak clothes in water, throw dirty water away, brush clothes with soap, rinse them, and hang them up."

"Oh yes, I remember. I used to carry rinsing water for Mom."

"It's not hard. Just watch and you'll learn."

"What about lighting an oil lamp?"

Cuu goes to the altar room to retrieve the little oil lamp that is always lit and the large oil lamp for daily activities. Putting them on the floor, she explains while giving a demonstration. "You take the lamp cover off and put it on the floor like so. You turn this knob until the wick shows like so. You light an incense stick with the flame from the little oil lamp like so. You use the incense stick to light the wick like so. When you have the flame, you put the lamp cover back on like so."

Ha is eager to try. She follows the directions and lights the lamp to Cuu's satisfaction. "See, it's not hard. Make sure you push the lamp cover all the way down like so or the cover can fall and break," Cuu says.

"I will remember. And how will I turn it off?"

"You turn this knob like so. When the wick disappears, the light goes out."

Two Sisters

Cuu looks around the house. "Aren't you scared in the dark?"

"Scared of what?"

"Of ghosts."

"I have not met any ghosts to be scared of. But I think some ghosts are nice and also, Dad will protect us."

"Okay, I have to go. I already fed you, so now you're free to do whatever you want."

"Thank you. Please do not tell anyone we're home."

Cuu shakes her head and rolls her eyes. After Cuu is gone, Ha puts things back to where they were. She dusts the altars and the table, sweeps the floor, and makes the bed. She tells Vy to take the dirty dishes to the well so she can wash them along with those left there from the previous day. Then she tells Vy to take a bath while she washes clothes.

"Why do I have to take a bath in the afternoon?"

"Because we did not bathe yesterday."

"Why do you wash clothes?"

"How else will we have clean clothes for school?"

"Why do you clean everything?"

"So our house will be clean and no one can tell us we're dirty anymore."

"But everyone says that we're dirty."

Two Sisters

"I don't want to hear that again."

Looking straight at Vy, Ha speaks loudly and clearly as if issuing a command. "I will not let anyone say we are dirty. And Vy, don't you let anyone call out Father's name when they yell at us."

CHAPTER NINETEEN

Under the star apple tree, Ha and Vy sit next to each other on the uneven exposed roots. Ha has a hard time with peeling a sapoche with a knife. She tries to peel off only a thin layer of skin so she does not waste the edible part, but the more she tries, the clumsier she feels as the blade keeps sliding off. The sapoche is not ripe, but a section of it has been bitten off. Vy is impatient with the progress though she remains silent. She closely watches Ha's hand, not wanting to miss any action.

"Ah," Ha makes a loud cry.

"You cut yourself?"

Ha throws the knife on the ground, transfers the sapoche from her left hand to her right hand, and puts the injured left finger into her mouth to suck it.

"You got cut?" Vy asks again.

Ha nods. The blood tastes salty in her mouth. She is not sure if she should swallow it or spit it out. She sucks a little harder and decides to spit it out. Vy is alarmed to see red blood. She darts her big eyes back and forth from Ha's face to the bloody spit, and eventually her sight lands on the sapoche. Ha hands the sapoche to Vy and says, "Eat it. I will not try to peel it anymore."

Vy is disgusted. "I can't eat it. It has blood on it."

"So what? See how I suck my own blood? You can bite off the bloody part first if you want."

"I'm going to wash it."

"You can't go to the well by yourself. Use the water barrel."

Vy hesitates. "I am afraid Young Aunt will ask where we get the sapoche. I'll wait for you."

"Okay. Wait for me."

Ha wipes the knife's blade against the rough roots of the star apple tree, attempting to get the blood off, but the red stain stubbornly remains.

A voice comes from behind. "What you two doing? Oh my God, you play with a knife and cut yourself?"

Ha and Vy turn around and are relieved to see Cuu instead of Young Aunt or Elder Aunt. Nevertheless, they freeze.

"Who let you play with knives? That will hurt you, don't you see?" Cuu gets more agitated when they stay silent. "Who did this?"

"Me," Ha says very softly.

"Where did you get the knife? You're only nine years old and are so bold!"

Remembering the custom of adding another year to a person's age on New Year's Day rather than waiting until the actual birthday, Ha contradicts, "I'm already ten."

"You still do not play with knives. I'll put this knife away and give it to your mom when she's back."

Ha stays silent. She is not pleased with the way she is treated and how Cuu speaks so loudly. Watching Cuu disappear behind the trees in the garden, Ha wonders if Cuu realizes that her words can carry. If Young Aunt and Elder Aunt overhear, the information can be used as a weapon against Ha and Vy and they will be severely scolded and punished. Vy figures they are in trouble, so she does not care to go to the well anymore. She tries to take a bite of the fruit but it is too hard. When Ha bites it, she immediately spits it out. "It's too bitter. It's not ripe at all. No wonder I could not peel it."

Vy is surprised that Ha throws the sapoche away. They stay silent for a long time before Ha speaks again. "Do you know what animal in the world is the most stupid?"

"The cow. I hear people say 'as stupid as a cow,'" Vy eagerly says.

"No. Cows are not the most stupid animals."

"So it's the pig. I also hear people say 'as stupid as a pig.'"

Two Sisters

"No. Pigs are not stupid. They are just greedy."

Vy scratches her head and scrunches her face and cannot come up with another guess.

"You give up?"

"Yes. So what is the most stupid animal?"

"The bat."

"How do you know?"

Ha speaks in a serious tone, wanting to sound wiser than her years. "Because a bat does not know what is what. That's why." She laughs at Vy's puzzled look. "The sapoche was still green, totally, and a bat tried to eat it. So that's why it's stupid. It's stupider than the cow for sure. I thought that bats would know which fruit is ripe and that's why I picked up something that was already bitten by a bat."

"How do you know a bat had it?"

"What else? If a bird had it, it would be pecked and not bitten off like that."

It does not matter to Vy if Ha is correct. She does not feel good losing the sapoche. "I'm hungry," she says.

"Me too, but we don't have anything else to eat. Let's go inside."

Ha's finger is still bleeding. She gives it a hard bite. When she remembers that Mother used to put spider web on a cut, she goes into the kitchen. Under the kitchen's low ceiling, all sorts of webs string from one corner to another and from one column to another. She picks up a handful and squeezes it into the cut.

Ha and Vy have been home for five days, and Mother has not returned. Perhaps Seventh Aunt assumes that they are taken care of by the adults in the big house and did not feel the need to inform Mother of the situation. Ha and Vy have been depending on Cuu's generosity for secretly bringing them food. Grandmother, Sixth Aunt, and Young Aunt see Ha and Vy in the garden now and then, but no one asked them any questions. They probably think Ha and Vy are visiting and do not imagine that two little girls can take care of themselves. The oil lamp Ha and Vy light each night is drowned out by the bright electrical light from the big house, the street, and the nearby houses. Unknown to the paternal relatives, their indifference and ignorance abet the two sisters' living in hunger.

In the last five days, either Sixth Aunt has not come to light the incense for her late brother or else she did it after Ha and Vy had gone to school. Ha has mixed feelings about letting Sixth Aunt know of their living situation. She is afraid of being scolded, but also craves Sixth Aunt's approval and wants to be taken care of. Cuu feels sorry for them, but she has limitations. She cannot keep cooking extra food under the watchful eyes of Elder Aunt. Ha also has mixed feelings about Cuu. She appreciates that Cuu can keep a secret, but Cuu can be sarcastic and loud. Thinking of how angry Cuu was at her using a knife, Ha does not expect dinner from Cuu later that day. So Ha spends the rest of their money, which is half a dong, to buy candy in lieu of food.

That evening Ha and Vy lie on their bed in the dark, suck on candy, and retell each other fairytales that Mother used to tell at bedtime. They are startled when Sixth Aunt walks in on them. Sixth Aunt is beside herself. "Oh my God, you two are sleeping here?"

Ha and Vy jump out of the mosquito net. "Yes, we are home."

"When did you come home? Who let you sleep by yourselves?"

"We've been home for a few days."

Sixth Aunt screams while walking in the altar room to light the large oil lamp to see them more clearly. "How many days? The two of you came home to visit and then decided to sleep over?"

"No, we've been home since Monday."

"Since Monday? Why didn't I know about this?"

"I don't know."

"Five days! And I didn't even know? I did not have time to light incense for a few days. You two are just too much!" She looks at their skinny forms. "What did you have to eat?"

"We cooked by ourselves and..." Ha does not want to mention Cuu's name.

"And what?"

"... Uh...uh... We stayed hungry."

Sixth Aunt's anger subsides at hearing that the girls are hungry. She ponders for a while and gives in. Her voice is mixed with bitterness and resignation. "Did your mother give

Two Sisters

birth to you on a rock for you to be so stubborn and so hard to deal with? Why couldn't you stay with Seventh Aunt? Why do you make it so hard on me?"

Ha bends her head low but stays resolute. "I just want to stay at my own house where Dad's altar is."

"And you are not afraid?"

"Of ghosts? Dad will protect us, I'm not afraid."

Sixth Aunt sighs. "Okay. You can stay. I'll ask Young Aunt to bring you food and talk to your mother when she comes home." Sixth Aunt lights the incense and tells them they will have to go to sleep after dinner.

Ha and Vy are happy for not being sent back to Seventh Aunt's house. They figure from this moment on, they will live freely in their little house without having to hide from anyone.

•

CHAPTER TWENTY

•

It is the most unlucky day for Ha and Vy – all because of the stupid bees. Upon seeing them on the Western hibiscus bush, Ha is inspired to play a game. Knowing that people in the big house are taking solace from the heat, Ha calls Vy out to the garden.

"What game are we going to play, Sister Ha?"

"We'll be the bees and drink nectar."

"Yay, nectar is sweet. I want to play!"

"Ok, you can be a bee, but don't talk too loud."

Ha picks a hibiscus flower and gives a demonstration. "Pick a flower and tear this part out, then suck from this hole."

Vy leans forward, putting her mouth around the stem, and sucks in the flavorful juice – slowly and deliberately – taking time to enjoy its sweetness. She darts her eyes back and forth as she puckers her lips rhythmically and stops only

Two Sisters

after draining all of the nectar from the flower. "It is so sweet! That's why there are so many bees around the flowers. Let's drink it before the bees get it."

Ha feels proud that she can provide fun activities for Vy who is under her charge since Mother is not around. "Good. Be a bee and find nectar yourself. Drink as much as you want."

Taking a clump of flowers from the bush, Vy separates the sepals from a stem. "So I pick the flower and tear the leaves like this and suck the sweet water, right?"

"Yes, but it is nectar, not sweet water."

"Ok, it's nectar because the bees drink nectar. I am a bee drinking nectar—"

Ha chides Vy, shaking her head. "I told you to speak quietly!" Vy is often oblivious, especially when food is involved, and needs to be reminded to be discreet. Vy is momentarily taken aback by Ha's scolding, but she understands, so she lowers her voice and walks softly.

Mesmerized with the game, they keep playing until Ha starts with a realization that all the red flowers, which she sometimes imagines to be little red lights, are gone from the bush! Not only that, there are dead flowers all over the ground. "Vy, that's enough. Let's go home."

But Vy is too much into the game to pay attention to Ha. She lingers to search for more flowers until Elder Aunt appears and she runs away as fast as she can into the little house's kitchen. Vy does not stop to think that something is wrong with flowers being splayed on the ground until it is too late. Vy is caught, frozen and terrified, at the crime scene. In the meantime, lying low and curling up to make herself as small as possible in the little kitchen, Ha wishes that Vy had been smart and quick. Ha can hear her own heart thumping loudly as though wanting to jump out of her chest. She scrunches up her face and tries to peer through the cracks in the wall to monitor the situation outside, but her vision is blocked. She tries to listen and hears the thumping of her heart match the intensity and volume of Elder Aunt's voice. That makes her more determined to stay put rather than risk revealing herself in Vy's defense.

Ha waits for a long time on the kitchen floor. When Elder Aunt's scolding subsides, Ha still does not know where Vy is. She half wants to walk out to check and half is terrified to. When she hears a whimper that is louder with each footstep on the leaf-covered path, she stands up, intending to walk out to greet Vy. But she sits back down when Elder Aunt's and Young Aunt's voices sound near. Through a crack in the wall, she sees Vy fumbling with the front door's knob. "Why did you leave me?" Vy cries.

Ha quickly calls out in a soft voice, "Vy, come here. Don't cry anymore."

Vy turns and her whimper becomes a loud anguished cry. Ha jumps, waving her hands frantically. "No... No... Do not cry! Elder Aunt may hear us. Come here."

Vy walks into the kitchen and sits down next to Ha who is about to issue a harsh command for Vy to stop crying, but stops when she sees snot and tears on Vy's face. Ha swallows the sound of each sob to the pit of her stomach as guilt engulfs her. She pulls Vy close and they stay together in their hiding place until the garden is totally quiet.

Two Sisters

In the evening, after checking that no one is in the garden, Ha and Vy go to the well to wash themselves. After laying down their clean clothes, Ha lowers the plastic bucket into the clear water. She works in a hurry and pulls it up when it is only one-third full. She pours water from the bucket into a faded green bowl and tells Vy to hurry. Without being told, Vy understands they should not dawdle and be in the garden longer than necessary. Not until Ha empties the bucket the second time does she notice something unusual. Ha points to Vy's legs. "What happened?"

At first, Vy is not sure what Ha refers to, but when she looks down at the bruises on her thighs, she bursts out crying. "Elder Aunt pinched me!"

Ha is speechless. When she recovers from shock, she reaches out to hold Vy. "Stop crying. If Elder Aunt hears us, she may come out and pinch you some more."

Vy chokes at her suppressed crying. Ha feels as if a part of her died with each sob. She blames herself for not pulling Vy away with her when she ran to the kitchen. She feels an intense hatred toward Elder Aunt as the image of Elder Aunt's fingers twisting into Vy's flesh plays out in her mind. She splashes water on the bruises in hopes that they will somehow fade away or the water will take them with it as it flows down the young flesh.

After drying out and putting on clean clothes, Ha and Vy return to their little house to wait, hoping to receive a call from Cuu or Young Aunt, but suspecting they will not get leftover food for dinner. Then they will stay hungry and their hunger will only be relieved by falling asleep. They do not think today is a good day to walk to the big house to declare that they have not eaten. When it is dark and they still have not heard from anyone, Ha says, "I don't think we'll get food tonight. Let's read on our bed."

Amid the mosquitoes' buzz, Vy asks, "How do we read in the dark? Can we use the oil lamp on our bed?"

"No, we'll use candles."

Fumbling her way to the altar room, Ha goes to the corner where Mother keeps the end pieces of used candles and takes a few with her. She lights a piece using the flame from the little oil lamp on Father's altar. Holding the lit candle at an angle, she lets the wax drip on the mat on their bed and anchors the candle on the melted wax. With the burning candle between them, Ha and Vy read books that Mother recently bought with the money earned from her business. When the flame of the first candle sputters, Vy goes to sleep, but Ha lights another candle and continues to read. Ha feels more comfortable now that Vy has turned her body and leaves more space on the bed. Ha lies on her side with the arm holding the book behind the candle so it does not block the light. She has finished a comic book and chosen a fairytale as the next one to read. She does not mind that the fairytale book has only words and no pictures, and it is perfectly alright with her if she reads the same story over and over. She loves fairytales because they always have happy endings and they reward honest characters with living happily ever after. She wants to believe that if she behaves as decently as the good characters in the fairytales, she will have the same good fortune that they do.

When the words on the page begin to dance to the flickering flame as Vy's snores drone on, Ha's eyes get heavy. The book falls out of her hand as she drifts off to sleep. The candle continues to burn until there is no wax left.

Two Sisters

The flame spreads. Not until Ha's arm is hot and Vy feels the heat on her back do they wake up and scream, "Fire! Fire!"

"Oh my God, the mat is on fire, and my arms are, too," Ha cries.

Vy jumps up and hits the fire with her pillow. The flame spreads farther as a book catches fire. Ha and Vy take turns pounding the flame with their pillows until it is finally extinguished. Ha runs to the altar room to examine her right arm next to the little oil lamp. It is burned to a bright red color between the elbow and the palm. Her skin looks translucent and she can see veins and muscles beneath. Vy is appalled. "Oh my God. Your arm has holes!"

While Ha is still dazed, Vy runs out of the house wailing. "Sixth Aunt, come. Grandma, come. Come quick. Sister Ha is dying."

Vy disturbs the nocturnal birds who make loud cries and flap their wings. Kiki jumps up and barks as if wanting to help wake up all of the adults in the big house. Sixth Aunt and Cuu run out and speak in unison. "What happened?"

Vy sobs. "Ha is burned."

Sixth Aunt relates the news to Grandmother and Young Aunt who also run to the little house. Young Aunt is not too happy to be awakened. "What the dickens! These two are full of trouble during the day, and now at night, too?!"

Grandmother tells Young Aunt to be quiet so Ha and Vy can tell them what happened.

"We lit candles to read books," Vy explains.

Two Sisters

Grandmother asks her daughters to go check on Ha and kindly grasps Vy's hands. "Your aunts will take care of Ha. Don't cry anymore."

Ha is nervous when she hears voices and sees people come in. She has fortunately escaped punishment for destroying a flower bush, but surely she cannot be so lucky as to also escape punishment for burning the mat *and* her own arm! She tries to find a place to hide, but there is nowhere to go. Her arm throbs as she stands glued to the floor when her aunts walk in. Young Aunt picks up the little oil lamp from Father's altar and holds it so that Sixth Aunt can look at Ha's arm. How Ha could stay asleep while being burned to this degree, Sixth Aunt wonders. Grandmother instructs her daughters to use fish sauce to treat the burn. Sixth Aunt promptly agrees. She tells Ha to stand at the front door and stretch out her burned arm, then she pours half of a bottle of fish sauce over the burned area. Ha screams as her pain intensifies, "It hurts!"

Sixth Aunt says Ha needs to suffer through it because fish sauce is the only treatment for burns known to men. Ha cannot help but scream. Cuu tries to console her. "The more it hurts, the faster it heals."

Young Aunt is not as kind. "Scream some more and Elder Aunt will hear you. Don't you complain when she comes and chews you out."

Ha stops crying as loudly but continues to whine, "Fish sauce stinks."

Sixth Aunt asks Cuu to clean Ha's arm while she inspects the bed. Vy is quick to give Cuu a wet cloth and offers her opinion. "I think fish sauce makes it worse."

Two Sisters

Sixth Aunt yells from the bedroom. "Nothing will heal burns as much as fish sauce, but it will take time. It's not a magic potion that can make everything normal right away."

Grandmother says to Sixth Aunt, "The girls cannot sleep by themselves anymore. From now on, they should sleep with you."

Ha immediately utters what she has rehearsed many times in her head, "I only want to stay in my little house where Dad's altar is."

Young Aunt snaps, "What for? So that you can burn the whole house down?"

Sixth Aunt says she works all day and suggests the girls stay with Young Aunt instead. Grandmother makes a compromise. She says that Ha and Vy can stay in their little house after school and go to Sixth Aunt's house for the night. She tries to placate Sixth Aunt. "It will be just a few more days until their mother is home. It won't be long."

Everyone remains quiet and that is the way they accept Grandmother's proposal, which pleases her. Grandmother asks for the leftover yarn from Sixth Aunt's knitting and asks Cuu to fashion two pairs of knitting needles from bamboo sticks. She declares she'll teach her granddaughters how to knit so that they will have something to do and not get into more trouble.

Cuu offers to have the girls stay with her that night. Young Aunt wonders out loud if Ha can go to school with her burned arm. Ha says she does not want to miss school and that she will hide her arm under her shirt sleeve.

Two Sisters

Ha and Vy are saddened that they will no longer be free to do what they wish. From this moment on, they will be closely supervised by the adults of the big house.

CHAPTER TWENTY-ONE

Evidence of the many times Ha and Vy suck candy during the night to alleviate their hunger is the cavities of Ha's teeth. The pain keeps Ha from falling asleep. "Uh...uh...my teeth hurt."

Sixth Aunt, asleep on her soft bed, wakes up. "Stop crying. What's up with you?"

"My teeth hurt so much. I can't sleep."

"Didn't I tell you to brush your teeth before bed?"

"I did. Uh...uh... I'm hurting."

Sixth Aunt falls back to sleep while Vy tries to be helpful. "Bite down very hard to kill the tooth bug, Sister Ha.'

Ha shakes her head. "I'm hurting so much, Vy."

Sixth Aunt wakes up again. "My goodness, are you still crying? Can't you shut up so I can sleep? How will I get up

Two Sisters

to go to work if you don't let me sleep after a hard day? How can you be so heartless, Ha?"

Ha tries her best to suppress her sobs. She cries out for Mother. "Mom, where are you? My teeth hurt so much. Come home to me."

Sixth Aunt jumps up. "Are you not listening to me, Ha?"

"My teeth hurt," Ha wails more loudly.

Sixth Aunt runs to the door and opens it wide. "If you want to sleep here, then stop crying. Otherwise, get out!"

Vy pleads, "Stop crying so you can sleep here."

Still crying, Ha gets up and walks out the front door, which is held wide open by Sixth Aunt who is shaking with anger. The door shuts close behind Ha, making her feel rejected, abandoned, and lost. There is nothing else for Ha to do but continue walking into the garden. She walks all the way to the wax jambu tree under the yellow street light and no longer hears Vy's whimpers.

Ha feels sorry for herself. Her short-sleeved top does not protect her from the cold wind. She shudders and scrunches down next to the tree, hugging herself with her arms around her legs and putting her chin on her knees. The night brings strange sounds and sights to her ears and eyes. Things are very much alive and active. She hears noises and sees the moving shadows of dancing leaves, falling fruit, flying birds, and scurrying nocturnal creatures. She yearns to be in her cozy little house, but it is now locked each evening after Sixth Aunt lights the incense for Father. Ha stares at the tree shadows but cannot make out the shapes of the familiar fruit trees. She imagines the trees play a trick on her by switching

Two Sisters

places with each other in the dark. They remind her of ghost stories told by classmates during recess. Scared, tired, numb, and cold, Ha shuts her eyes and tries to reassure herself that what she sees and cannot make sense of are optical illusions, not ghostly figures. She regrets leaving Sixth Aunt's house and starts with the realization that her toothache, the reason for her boldness in walking out, is gone. So even her toothache has been eradicated by the ghostly magic of the night! Ha inches herself backward to lean against the tree.

Ha opens her eyes in fright at a rumbling and is relieved to have Kiki next to her and feel his wet nose against her body. Kiki sniffles for a familiar odor and licks the tears falling down her face. The dog makes a whinnying sound and wags his tail. Ha reaches out and pulls his furry head into her bosom and breaks out in sobs. "Kiki dear, I'm so scared. I'm so scared."

Kiki replies with meaningless grunts. Ha holds Kiki for dear life and refuses to relax her grip for a long time. Precious Kiki is her lifesaver in the ghostly garden of darkness and eeriness. Feeling a cold wind at the nape of her neck, she wraps her arms around Kiki and whispers in his ears. "I am very scared. Please stay with me, Kiki."

Kiki settles down. His regular breathing lulls the lonely Ha to sleep. She sleeps soundly until Kiki jerks away from her embrace, barks loudly at something, and chases the shadow of that something all the way to the well. Ha wakes up, feeling empty without Kiki next to her, and is confused by the barking. She tsks softly. "Kiki, come back."

Kiki's object is a shadow of a wild cat at the barbed wire on the top of the garden wall. Kiki tries to appear most ferocious by baring his teeth at the cat. After some time barking and growling with no effect, Kiki lies down at the

Two Sisters

carambola tree, while continuing to keep watch with his ears erect. Ha walks over to sit next to Kiki, leaning her back against both the tree and the dog. She feels as though she is lost in the middle of a large forest of dark shadows. The toothache returns. A sharp pain from her upper right molar shoots up the nerve path to the very depth of her brain. Ha puts two fingers into her mouth to grasp the hurting molar. She squeezes her fingers to tighten the hold and tries to dislodge the affected tooth by shaking it back and forth, as she used to do with loose baby teeth. But the molar stubbornly stays put, safely tucked under the swollen gum of tender pus. The pus breaks and she can taste the saltiness of the thick mixture of blood and pus. She spits out continually in throbbing pain, puts her head down on her knees, and cries out for Mother in despair. Kiki turns his head toward the source of the noise and, after determining that nothing is out of the ordinary, resumes watch over the stray cat. Ha's loyal friend stays quiet and does not mind the crying and the mosquito slapping that Ha executes on her arms and legs. As the night gets colder, Ha nudges closer to Kiki. She silently hopes that nothing will disturb them and Kiki does not run away from her again. Receiving the warmth from Kiki's body and feeling safe with him next to her, Ha eventually falls back to sleep.

Ha survives the night in the garden and does not hear Vy's calls in the morning. Looking at Ha's skinny body in dirty and disheveled clothes lying on the ground, Vy feels bad that she has to rouse Ha from her peaceful sleep after what must have been a tough night. It is a pitiful sight to see. Ha's forehead is lower than her chin, her nose sticks straight up in the air, and her mouth hangs open as she breathes through both nose and mouth.

"Get up, Sister Ha. We're late for school!"

Two Sisters

Ha wakes with a start. "We're late?"

"Almost."

"Did Sixth Aunt unlock our door?"

"Yes. She gives you this."

"What is it?"

"Milk with honey and orange juice."

"Did you have some?"

"She did not give me anything to drink. She feels sorry that you slept 'on the street.' Also, I'm not as skinny as you."

Ha examines her bare arms that are now swollen with mosquito bites. She cries when she remembers the previous night's events. Getting up, she wipes her tears, straightens out her clothes, and walks to the little house.

Vy runs after her. "Drink this. It's too full for me to carry."

"Do you want it?" Ha asks, scratching her arms and legs.

"Yes, but it's not for me."

"Drink it. I give it to you."

"Really?"

"Yup."

"What will I tell Sixth Aunt?"

"Tell her I drank it."

"But that's not true."

Ha gets annoyed at the technicality. In a not so gentle tone, she says, "I told you that I gave it to you, so it's the same as if I drank it."

Vy takes a sip. "It's very good. Drink some with me."

Ha shakes her head, getting her knapsack ready. "No."

"Are you mad at Sixth Aunt? Is that why you don't want the milk?"

Ha shakes her head again, but falling tears betray her emotions. She playfully picks up a pen and draws circles on her arms. "One, two, three, four, five, six…"

"What are you doing?"

"I'm counting the mosquito bites."

"…fifty, fifty-one, fifty-two, fifty-three…"

"You're bad."

Ha ignores Vy. She pulls up her pant legs and draws circles on her legs as well. "…sixty-nine, seventy, seventy-one, seventy-two…"

"You're dirty."

Two Sisters

Ha is amused. This is the first time Vy has called her dirty. She finishes drawing the last circle. "One hundred and twelve! I believe no one else in the world has one hundred and twelve mosquito bites."

"You won't be able to wash it out."

"Drink up your milk and hurry. We need to wash ourselves before going to school."

At the well, Ha scrubs her arms until they are red, but the ink stays on as tattoos. The burned area near her elbow has been covered with a new layer of pinkish skin that feels itchy all over.

"Your teacher will see your arms. What are you going to do?"

"Today my teacher will not check hygiene. I will wear a long-sleeved shirt and no one will see my arms."

"Your cheeks look swollen. Do you still have a toothache?"

Ha shakes her head. "Don't remind me because the pain may come back."

"So when you cried 'It hurts' yesterday, did that make it hurt more?"

Ha changes the subject as she changes clothes. "Hurry up. I'm almost done."

Vy does not give up. "You cried too much and Sixth Aunt was right when she did not let you sleep inside."

"I did not say she was wrong."

"So why didn't you drink the milk she gave you?"

"I gave it to you because you didn't have breakfast."

"I already had sweet rice this morning."

"I don't like to eat breakfast and you like milk. I'm not mad at Sixth Aunt."

"But Sixth Aunt is mad at you because you did not come back."

"I thought she closed the door when I walked out."

"Maybe she tried to scare you so you'd come back. She waited for you."

"Then why didn't you come out to get me?"

"I was afraid...of being scolded. Also I was afraid of the dark."

"I am not afraid of the dark," Ha lies. Vy looks at her big sister with awe and admiration. Ha continues, "But I'm afraid of mosquitoes. There are only mosquitoes, not ghosts."

"How did the toothache go away?"

"Maybe because I forgot about it."

Vy whispers softly, "I hope you will not have a toothache so that you can sleep in bed with me tonight."

CHAPTER TWENTY-TWO

"Give me more."

"They already have many. Give *me* some more."

"You should share. I want more."

The commotion near the Hoang estate arouses curiosity in Ha and Vy as they walk home from school. Clutching the knapsacks to their chests, they inch their way inside the circle of the neighbor children. Vy spots Hoa, a classmate of hers, among the crowd.

"Hey Hoa, what are you doing?" Vy asks.

A boy answers for Hoa. "We are sharing Jamaica cherries."

"Where did you get them?"

"Over there," the boy answers, "where the barber shop is."

Two Sisters

"Are they good?"

"Of course."

"Can I have one?" Vy asks expectantly.

"Sure. You and your sister each can have one."

Ha smiles knowingly. Food is often a connection between Vy and others. It is through giving and sharing food that Vy makes new friends. The boy hands Vy two shiny red cherries and Vy passes one to Ha. "This one's for you. Try it."

"It looks too pretty to eat. I'll save it."

"Eat it. I'll ask for another."

But the other kids are not happy that the boy shares the fruit with Ha and Vy.

"Why share with them? They did not pick cherries."

"They have their own fruit trees. We do not need to share with them."

The boy scratches his head and makes an offer to the other kids. "Okay. I'll give each of you one more."

"Will Ha and Vy get one also?" Hoa asks.

"I don't know, we'll see."

Hoa turns to Ha and Vy expectantly. "Maybe you can share your fruit with us?"

Two Sisters

Vy hesitates. "I don't know."

Hong, Hoa's sister, chimes in, "Your family throws away fruit and that's wasteful."

"But we are not allowed to pick."

"So who does the picking?"

"Nobody, unless there is time."

"So when you have time, pick carambolas to share with us."

"We need permission," Vy says.

"So go ask for permission."

"But I know we will not get permission."

"Why not?"

• Ha intervenes, "What fruit do you like?"

"Carambola, jambu, guava, whatever. They're all good."

"When are you free?"

"We gather outside your wall every day. You can come play with us."

"Okay we will. Now we have to go home."

As Ha and Vy walk away, Vy asks Ha, "What is your plan?"

Two Sisters

"No one will be in the garden when we get home—"

"But Sister Cuu doesn't take afternoon naps and she may be at the well."

"Sister Cuu will not tell."

Vy is not sure of Ha's plan. "I don't want you to get in trouble. I want you to sleep with me tonight."

"I will sleep with you. I will not cry about my toothache."

"So will you go to Grandma's house to eat lunch with me?"

"No, you go ahead, but come back right after lunch."

Setting her knapsack on the table, Vy asks sadly, "Why don't you want lunch?"

"I'm not hungry."

"I'm scared to go by myself."

"You'll get hungry if you don't eat. Hurry up or there will be nothing left."

Ha hands Vy the empty milk glass that Sixth Aunt gave them in the morning. "Return this to the big kitchen. It is your excuse to go there. Grandma will invite you to eat and Young Aunt will have no reason to scold you. Everything will be fine."

"Are you going to sleep?"

Two Sisters

"No, I'll pick carambolas for Hong and Hoa."

"So...I have to beg for food myself?"

"Yes. Go and hurry back."

Ha waits to go to the carambola tree after Vy is gone. After checking that no one else is in the garden, she plucks two carambolas from the branch close to the ground, then runs home to put them under the table. Running back and forth several times, Ha is able to amass a number of carambolas. Feeling satisfied with herself, Ha brags when Vy returns, "Look. I picked carambolas and no one saw me."

Vy puts a bowl of rice and pork on the table. "Grandma saved this for you. Young Aunt thinks you're still upset."

Ha ignores the food. "I had to run back and forth several times to get this many."

"So you're giving them to the kids?"

"Yes. When we hear them play outside, we'll join them."

"Eat your lunch," Vy reminds her.

"I don't want it. You can have it for dinner. Then you don't have to go to Grandma's tonight."

"If I return the empty bowl, I'll have an excuse to be there for dinner. You should eat."

Ha bites a carambola. "I can eat a carambola. It's very good. Do you want some?"

Two Sisters

"Wow, this is a big fruit. Did you climb up the tree to pick?"

"No. I just picked those near the ground. The ones high up are very ripe. They'll be falling down any time."

"The jambu tree also has ripe fruit up high."

"We can get the picking stick after the adults go to sleep," Ha suggests. Vy scrunches her shoulders and shakes her head no.

"That's okay," Ha says. "We can wait until the fruit fall down."

Although Ha says to wait for the wax jambus to fall down, she is deep in thought, trying to figure out a way to get them before they are too ripe. She is confident in her plans. "If you want jambus, I'll get you jambus."

Vy does not protest this time, but sits down next to Ha to wait for Young Aunt and Cuu to finish washing dishes at the well. When the garden is quiet, Ha tells Vy to get a hat and follow her out.

"You want a hat for shade?"

"No, for catching jambus. I'll pick and throw them down to you."

"I don't think I can catch them."

"You can't do anything, can you?" Ha scoffs. Seeing that Vy is upset at the remark, Ha changes her tact. "You do not need to catch. I'll throw jambus on the ground. You'll pick them up and put them in the hat."

Two Sisters

At the wax jambu tree, Ha puts her right foot on the split between two branches, wraps both arms around the widest part of the trunk, and pulls herself up. Working her way to the branch with the most fruit, she picks and throws them on the ground. Vy is not comfortable. "That's enough. Get down now."

Ha drops herself down. They gather the fruit and take them inside. They divide the fruit into two piles and play *Rock, Paper, Scissors* to determine who gets to choose which pile to have. Vy wins. After choosing, Vy wipes the dirt off each wax jambu with her shirt. "Should we put some jambus on the altar for Dad?"

Ha is surprised that Vy is the one to think of Father. Ha does not recall that garden fruit was ever used for the altars. The altars in the big house always have fruit, whereas their own two altars are empty at times. Ha knows that the fruit on the altars in the big house are from the market, and Mother could not have picked fruit from the garden for their altars. Now that Ha thinks about it, she does not understand why her paternal relatives own so many fruit trees and yet they are not put to use.

"The jambus are all bruised, we can't put them on Dad's altar," Ha says. "Also, if Young Aunt sees them, she'll know we picked fruit without permission. If Dad wants to eat, he can go to the garden. He doesn't need us to put fruit on his altar. The fresh ones on the tree are much better anyway."

"But how could Dad eat?" Vy asks, putting her hands under her chin.

"Dad is invisible. No one can stop him from doing what he wants. He can even eat the fruit at the market if he wants to. We cannot see what he does, but he knows what we do."

Two Sisters

Vy knits her brows in worry. "So does he know we steal jambus?"

"Yes."

"Then why did you do it?"

"Because you want them... If we let the jambus rot, the kids laugh at us and say that we are wasteful."

"But Mom says those who steal get their arms cut off after they die."

"I know."

"So if I eat these jambus, my arms will get cut off."

"I climbed the tree and picked the jambus, not you. My arms will be cut off, not yours. You can eat." Biting a jambu, Ha complains. "I don't understand the adults. Why are we not allowed to do what we want?"

"I can hear the kids playing now," Vy says. "Let's go play with them."

Ha listens to the laughter outside the wall. "Yes, but let me check that no one is in the garden first, then we'll climb the wall."

"I can't," Vy gets nervous. "I will fall."

"I will help you. If we go through the gate, someone may see us." Ha is encouraging. "You can do it, I'm sure. If you want to go play with the kids, you'll have to climb the wall."

250

Two Sisters

Vy looks at the gate and back to the little house, still unsure. "Why don't we have a gate in front of our house?"

"I don't know. I want a gate too, so no one sees us coming or going. But you can climb the wall. The jambu tree is even higher than the wall and I climbed it. I'll help you."

Ha pushes Vy up the wall from under and calls on the neighbor kids to help lower Vy down on the other side. After putting a bag of carambolas through a wall opening, Ha climbs to the other side as easily as a squirrel. While Ha distributes the carambolas to the neighbors, Vy gives Hoa a wax jambu from her pocket and says, "This one is just for you."

"Why don't I get any?" the boy who gave Ha and Vy cherries earlier protests. "I gave you Jamaica cherries, remember?"

Hoa says to Vy, "This is Man. He lives next-door to me. Do you have more jambus to share?"

Vy hesitates. "I have only one for you. Jambus are harder to pick."

Ha says, "I have two jambus in my pocket. We can share."

Everyone is satisfied. The children sit down and lean against the Hoang estate wall, eating, talking, and watching traffic go by. Hoa gushes, "Your jambu looks green and yet it is so sweet."

"The carambola is also very sweet," another says.

"We want you to share fruit with us again!"

Two Sisters

"Come play with us!"

"Can we be friends?"

"I want to be your friend, too."

"Me too."

"Me too."

"Make sure to give me more fruit next time."

Ha stands up and smiles. "Okay. We'll bring fruit again next time. Now let's play a game."

Man suggests *Hit-the-Can* game and everyone agrees that it is a fun game to play.

"Okay, there are ten of us," Man says. "Each team will have five players, but brothers and sisters cannot be on the same team."

A girl pulls on Ha's hand. "Can I be with you?"

Ha nods her head repeatedly as more kids want to be on her team.

"I want to be with you too."

"Me too."

A warm feeling spreads over Ha. It feels so good to be accepted and liked. She thinks to herself. *I will pick more fruit for my new friends.*

CHAPTER TWENTY-THREE

"Nguyet, Vinh, come home for dinner!"

Vinh was trying to rescue his teammates who were "captured" by their opponents. When he hears the call, he announces, "I have to go home."

"No, let's finish our game first," Nguyet, his sister, says.

"I have to go too," Hong says and calls to her sister. "Let's go home, Hoa."

But Hoa shakes her head. "I'm having fun."

"It's late," Hong insists. "We'll play again tomorrow. We'll get in trouble if we're not home when Mom gets home."

As the children scatter, Ha asks Man to help get Vy across the wall. Man suggests that Ha climb it and get in the garden first so that she can help Vy down more easily. When Ha gets to the top of the wall, she feels dizzy and has to stop to catch her breath and rest.

Two Sisters

"What happened to you?" Man asks.

"I feel like the ground is going round and round."

"That's just because you played too hard," Vinh says.

"Hurry down, but don't fall," Hong urges.

Ha puts one foot in a wall opening for support and lowers herself down. When she looks up for Vy, all of a sudden, she sees stars dancing and clouds and sky merging into one huge mass. The mass swirls and twirls around Vy who, with the help of Man and others, is already perched on the top of the wall. Ha feels the need to bend down and close her eyes. She leans her head against the wall to rest and recover from the dizzy spell. After she manages to get Vy down, she says to the friends waiting outside, "You can go home now." Then, drained of energy, she sits with her back against the wall until the swirling of clouds and sky fades away.

Looking at Ha's pale face, Vy is concerned. "Are you okay?"

"I'm okay. Just let me lean on you." Ha gets up and puts an arm on Vy's shoulder for support. Vy helps Ha walk slowly back to the little house.

Being concerned does not stop Vy from chiding her big sister, "Why did you have to play so hard? You already saved two teammates, you didn't have to try to save more."

Ha does not have the energy to contradict Vy. She concentrates on making out the familiar surroundings that do not at all look familiar. She struggles to get past the door. As soon as she is inside the house, she runs straight to her bed and collapses on it. She thinks she hears Vy say something. She mumbles a message for Vy to eat and not wait for her before totally passing out.

When Ha wakes the next day, she hears voices. She tries to open her eyes, but the bright daylight shoots a sharp pain up through her eye sockets. Her head feels hard like a rock and her limbs feel limp like noodles. She wants to call out to Vy; but her mouth is dry and her throat is constricted. She closes her eyes, lies still, swallows to ease the pain and dryness, and listens to discern what is going on around her. She momentarily feels arms under her and has a sensation of being lifted. She reopens her eyes. As her eyelids flutter, she can see wax jambu branches passing by the blue sky. She makes an effort to raise her head and what she sees makes her cry out in happiness.

"Mom, Mom. You're home!"

Mother squeezes her tight while running. "Yes, it's me. I'm taking you to the clinic."

Ha bursts out in sobs. "Mom, don't leave me ever again."

Mother shakes her head and chokes up. "No, I will not leave you two alone again."

They are greeted warmly at the clinic by a doctor in a white lab coat who looks to be in his fifties. "The nurse already briefed me about your girl's conditions and I am ready to see her." Mother appreciates the fact that they get to be seen ahead of other patients in the waiting room. The doctor extends his arm and guides them into a small room with a white bed on which he directs Mother to lay Ha down. Mother looks haggard and worried. Ha feels for her. The

Two Sisters

blameful words she's been harboring within, ready to be unleashed when she sees Mother next, vanish into thin air. At this moment, she feels only love and tenderness toward Mother whose presence brings a sense of peace and calm that has eluded her during the past few trying days.

The doctor listens to Ha's heart and knits his brow when he sees an unusual amount of mosquito bites on her body. He is taken aback with Mother's claim of ignorance of the bites. He opens his mouth as though wanting to say something, but holds back. Instead, he grunts some unintelligible sounds as he continues to examine Ha. He raises Ha's right arm to look at the burned skin. His brows come together again. "What about this burn? It's recent, isn't it?"

Mother puts her face right at Ha's arm to look at the burn, being surprised herself. She stammers a reply, "Well...I do not know about that cither." She feels the need to explain. "I...I was not home the last two months. I had to go far away to earn money to raise my two children. My husband is gone, I am the only one—"

But the doctor does not have time for the long explanation; he pulls Ha's lower eye lid down and gravely says, "Your daughter is very anemic. She's in critical condition." Not waiting for Mother to answer, he hurries out of the room, leaving Ha and Mother behind.

Sitting on a chair, Mother curls her back, appearing even smaller than her small frame, and cries like a baby. "Please cure my daughter. Please save her."

Ha cries along. "Please don't cry, Mom. I will not die."

"It's all my fault," Mother wipes Ha's tears and massages the inked circles around the mosquito bites on Ha's arms. "I will do everything to save you. I will not leave you again."

"Mom, where's Vy?"

"She went to school."

Ha tries to get up. "What about me?" But she feels dizzy. She is blinded as though thousands of moths had descended on her eyes to block her vision, and her head hurts as though thousands of needles were penetrating it. She feels powerless, and yet she cannot fathom the severity of her illness. "I don't want to miss school," she moans. "I will get behind. I am already behind."

A nurse walks in and stops Ha with her hand. "Lie down and do not talk. You're very weak." Sitting down on the bed at Ha's feet, the nurse informs Mother that the doctor wants a private conversation with her.

Ha keeps an eye on Mother as she walks out of the room. Ha, feeling uncomfortable with a stranger, wishes Mother to be with her. No matter how gentle the nurse appears, Ha sees this person as an adult, a figure of stern authority like a teacher who lives in a world of rules and regulations. Ha sighs when she cannot think of anything to say to the nurse. She knows she does not relate well to adults. She admires those cousins of hers who can start conversations with adults and even make them laugh. She attributes their ease and openness with adults to their upbringing, their parents' education level, and their being influenced by Western culture. Mother is the only adult in her life Ha feels comfortable being with. Besides, Mother always says: "Speak only if you know something. You should listen more and speak less, especially as a child." Ha is used to being quiet around adults, a habit she finds hard to break.

The nurse breaks the silence. "Would you like some milk?"

"No, thank you—" Ha is about to add a reason for her refusal when a frightening thing occurs. She stops mid-sentence to stare at a big long needle attached to a bloody red tube in the hand of the doctor who has reappeared. Mother comes in from behind the doctor and turns Ha's body to the facedown position. As Ha's pants are pulled down, she feels something cold and wet on her exposed bottom. She jumps when a searing pain shoots from the wet and cold spot. She grits her teeth and thinks of the immunizations she has had in school. She was always the first to line up for shots to show her classmates how brave she was. The immunization shots were quick and did not hurt for the needles were small. But this shot gives her a sharp pain and a numbness that spreads as the large needle settles deep inside her muscle and the bloody liquid begins to flow into her. "It hurts so much, Mommy," Ha cries out. "It hurts!"

"It's almost over," Mother says. "You need to get better."

The doctor pushes and grinds a cotton ball at the site of needle penetration while saying to Mother, "Your daughter needs this shot every day while she's still in critical condition. She will have to stay home from school until she's better."

"Yes," Mother replies.

"I'll give you a prescription and a list of food she needs to regain her strength."

Two Sisters

"Doctor..." Mother hesitates. "Can she be home alone while I work? I can't afford not to go to work—"

"Are you saying you'll go far away again?"

"No...I mean I'll go to the market each morning."

"I think you should be at home with your daughter for two weeks," the doctor says. "I understand your financial situation. You can pay me later."

Mother says, "No, I can pay you today."

The doctor speaks slowly to emphasize his point. "The most important thing is that you take care of your daughter and bring her here every day for shots."

Ha does not feel better even after the needle is removed from her body. She has never experienced this kind of pain before. Not only that the pain is still so strong, she is also terrified of what the doctor said. Thinking about having to stay home from school and come here every day for more shots, Ha buries her face in the pillow and weeps.

CHAPTER TWENTY-FOUR

Everything looks too bright to Ha. After being cloistered in darkness for several weeks, Ha knows she needs time to adjust to sunlight again. She is excited to go back to school and ecstatic to be outside. She skips on the street while Vy follows behind on their way home from school. As they approach home, they spot new flower pots in front of the big house.

"Where are these flowers from, Vy?"

"I don't know."

"Oh look at the lilies! I've never seen a lily plant before. And there are so many pretty roses! I love the yellow ones, and also the pink baby ones."

Vy points to the far end. "Look, there are also orchids and chrysanthemums."

"Let's go look at them."

Two Sisters

They continue to the far end of the big house where the carport is. As they pass the house, they throw a surreptitious glance sideways. They seldom venture over to this side of the estate because they do not like to walk this part of the street in front of the big house. There is a shiny black car parked under the carport. "Elder Uncle has such a pretty car," Ha gushes.

"Yes, it is pretty, but we are never allowed in it, so what do you want to look at it for?" Vy jeers.

Ha dispenses her wisdom. "We're not allowed in it because we are dirty."

Vy disagrees. "Even if we're clean, we do not have pretty clothes. But..."

"But what?"

"If you tell Elder Uncle you want a ride, he'll give you a ride."

"Why?"

"Everyone is nice to you since you were sick."

"What do you know? Elder Uncle did not know I was sick. He never visited me and he never came to our house."

"Grandma, Sixth Aunt, and Young Aunt were nice to you. They gave you milk, oranges, and candy every day and they even begged you to eat. I want to be sick!"

Knowing that the longan tree at the corner of the house is off-limits, Ha teases, "So if I want to pick longans, will Elder Uncle let me?"

Two Sisters

Vy grins. "Elder Aunt won't let you, you know that." She pulls Ha back. "Let's go pick jambus in the garden. Grandma and Sixth Aunt will not scold you."

"So you think I'm allowed to?"

"No, don't ask. Just pick. If you ask, they may not let you"

"But...I don't want to climb the jambu tree. I'm afraid I'll fall and get hurt and then I can't go to school tomorrow."

"What if we use the picking stick?"

"Ok, you get the stick and I'll get the jambus."

"I'm scared."

"If anyone asks, say that I told you to."

"I don't dare get it myself. Can you go with me?"

"Okay, then we can be scolded together."

Ha and Vy walk back to the gate. They go through the gate and the garden and tiptoe to the big house's kitchen. When they see no one around, they quickly run to the corner of the kitchen to grab the picking stick, which is a long wood stick with a metal hook at the end to grasp fruit. They carry the stick to the green wax jambu tree where the sight of juicy fruit on high branches makes their mouths water. Working deftly, Ha wields the stick to pull down jambu after jambu. Sometimes she even pulls down a whole branch with fruit and leaves still attached. There are so many ripe jambus. Vy gets busy telling Ha which branch to go after and neglects to pick up the fruit from the ground. When Vy spots a branch that holds the most beautiful jambus, Ha does not mind that it extends beyond the estate wall. The neighbor kids stop playing and gather to watch. They, as a group, remind Ha and Vy of the promise of friendship and the virtue of sharing. Vy delivers jambus through the wall openings and lets the kids fight over them.

Man is not happy with the distribution of the jambus. He climbs to the top of the wall and shows his face. "Ha, Vy, why do I get only one jambu? Remember the time—" Man has not finished his sentence when Kiki jumps almost to his face, baring teeth, while barking and growling at the perceived intruder.

All the children scream and run away. Some run across the street before daring to look back. Some stop at the curb to pick up rocks and throw them at the wall. Ha yells at them, "Why are you throwing rocks at my place?"

Man says, "Because you sent your dog after us."

"I didn't. You just made too much noise."

"But you did not divide the jambus equally," Vinh says.

"That's not true. It's you—"

Ha is interrupted by a booming command from the big house. "Both of you come back here right now." Ha starts and turns around. Standing at the patio is Elder Uncle in white pajamas, with a baton in his hand. Ha lays the picking stick down and walks with Vy to the hibiscus bushes to face Elder Uncle, head bent and arms crossed in deference.

"So you and those kids have to make noise and disturb the adults' afternoon naps," he says while pointing his baton

Two Sisters

at the wax jambu tree. "Who allows you to play with those kids?"

Ha looks up at Elder Uncle's angry and distorted face. It is a rare occasion that she sees him face to face. She has always imagined him to be kind and loving because of the adage: *"Without a father, you are cared for by uncles. Without a mother, you are nursed by aunts."* She had hoped for a different kind of meeting between the two of them. The warmth and affection she imagined would exist when they had a chance to meet are erased from her mind. As bitterness and anger grow within her, she loses fear of her uncle. Looking straight at him, she says, "I want to play with them because no one in our family plays with us. We are the dirty and barbaric people. We are poor and we play with the poor. The Hoang relatives are high class people and are not our friends."

When she stops to get a breath, she half expects the baton to land on her back, but strangely, the anger in Elder Uncle's eyes seems to dissipate and the baton is slowly lowered until its tip gently touches a tile on the patio. Elder Uncle stares at her without a word.

Ha continues through tears. "I don't want to carry the name Hoang. We do not deserve the family name. Since Dad died, the name died with him. We are not happy with the famous name. I will change my name one day. I'd rather change my name than have people with the same name look down on us."

Elder Uncle looks shocked. He silently walks back into the big house while Ha goes back to the wax jambu tree to have a good cry there. When she and Vy return the picking stick to the big kitchen, they hear Grandmother's call. "Ha, Vy, come here."

Two Sisters

Grandmother and Young Aunt are at the patio waiting for them. Ha and Vy automatically cross their arms in deference to the two adults. Ha is surprised to hear Young Aunt plead with Grandmother. "Don't be harsh on her. She just recovered from illness."

Grandmother dismisses Young Aunt, "What do you know?" and directs a question at Ha. "So is that true that you want to change your name, Ha? Why?"

Despite the usual ability to control herself, Ha cannot help but let the bitterness that has been held inside come alive and overwhelm her. A stream of fresh new tears flows from her already-red-and-swollen eyes. Sources of her unhappiness appear rapidly one after another in her mind: her orphanhood, the unjust treatment from her paternal relatives, Mother's place, and the disparity of education and social standings within the extended family. Ha swallows hard and is unable to speak for she is overwhelmed with emotions. She cannot understand how her paternal relatives fail to see her family suffer when they all live on the same estate together. Could the paternal relatives not see the contrast between the little house dimly lit by an oil lamp and the surrounding bright houses that enjoy the benefit of electricity all these years? Could the paternal relatives not see their yearning for tutelage that cannot be fulfilled by their under-educated mother? Could the paternal relatives not see that they go hungry at times depending on their mother's earnings? Could the paternal relatives enjoy wealth while ignoring their hardship and poverty when they carry the same bloodline and family name? Does the "extended family" concept refer only to families living in the same physical address and not to the need to take care of one another? Do the paternal relatives enjoy the power that comes with the high social standing that stokes their egos and makes them feel important?

Two Sisters

Ha does not completely understand why she said she wanted to change her name and she does not even know what name she would want. She has said something that is totally contradictory to a secret wish she has been harboring – the wish to become successful as a Hoang so that Father would look down from heaven with pride. Now perhaps her dream cannot be fulfilled because she has been imprudent and made a stupid statement. She feels bad that she did not listen to Mother's teachings of crossing arms, bending head, listening, and complying so that she would not find herself in this sticky situation. As she feels helpless and confused and does not know what to say, she remains silent.

Young Aunt feels sorry for Ha. "Mom, let her go. She's still as weak as a noodle."

"Do I interrogate and punish her? I just want to know why she doesn't want to carry her father's name. What makes her feel that way?"

Vy looks back and forth from Ha to Grandmother and is not sure what to do. She tries to be helpful. "Don't cry anymore, Sister Ha. Grandma is not punishing you."

They are distracted by Kiki and Yellow who jump and bark at the rattling gate. Hearing Mother's voice shooing the dogs away, Vy has a sense of urgency. "Mom's home. Tell Grandma why you want to change your name so that she lets us go. Otherwise, we'll get in trouble with Mom."

But Ha stays still as a statue while tears continue to run down her cheeks. Mother comes as Grandmother calls her over and asks, "What did the girls do wrong, Mother?"

Two Sisters

"They were scolded by their uncle for playing with the neighbor kids and Ha wanted to change her name, I was told."

"Your daughter has a mind of her own," Young Aunt chirps.

Mother grasps Ha's hands. "Why were you so brazen, Ha? Why do you want to change your name?" But Ha's cold hands startle Mother. She turns to Grandmother. "Mother, I need to take the girls home. Ha's hands are frozen."

"Let her change her name if she wants," Young Aunt mumbles to Grandmother. "Will you be happy if she gets sick again and can't go to school?"

Before leaving, Mother manages to say, "I will tell her to apologize to Elder Brother."

Grandmother's wrinkles deepen a bit more. "I just want to know why she wants to change her name. That's all."

When they get back to their little house, Mother leaves Ha alone. She does not tell Ha to go lie down, nor does she ask for the reason Ha wants to change her name. Perhaps she knows the deep wounds that are buried within Ha and does not wish to stir them up. Without speaking directly to either Ha or Vy, Mother says, "We are suffering, but we have to endure for the sake of your father's name. We cannot escape our fate."

CHAPTER TWENTY-FIVE

•

The end of the school year marks a happy time for Ha and Vy because Vy is ranked second in her class. On the day of the award ceremony, a crowd of happy parents, teachers, and students gather on the school ground. Ha, being the only family member in attendance besides Vy, represents the Hoang family to witness a momentous event, an event that had been a dream of hers for so long. Ha solemnly listens to the announcement of awardees, paying special attention to the list of second grade students. Her chest is about to explode with pride.

"Hoang Thi Thao Vy[14] receives the award for second place in her class. Please come up."

When Vy's name is announced by the teacher of class 2A, who is decked out in a beautiful green dress, Ha cannot contain herself. "That's my sister's name," Ha gushes to a classmate standing next to her. The girl looks at Ha, shrugs her shoulders, and turns away with her eyes back on the

---

[14] Vy's full name with the last name listed first.

Two Sisters

stage straight ahead. Other classmates also remain silent and do not share Ha's enthusiasm. Ha feels embarrassed. She stops talking, but stands on tiptoe to look for Vy in the seating area of second graders. Vy, in a bouffant white dress puffed up with a stiff layer underneath, makes her way to the front. Since Mother can afford only one stiff layer to wear under a dress, Ha and Vy resort to playing *Rock, Paper, Scissors* to decide who gets to wear the layer under her dress each day. If Vy had not won the right to wear it today, Ha would gladly have let Vy wear it anyway. She is so proud of Vy who will accept her award in front of the whole school. Ha watches Vy step up to the wood stage, receive a big package wrapped in shiny red cellophane, and carry it back to her seat. Ha wants very badly to run over to congratulate Vy and see what the package contains, but restrains herself through the ceremony.

On the way home, Ha feels important walking next to Vy. She is amazed at Vy. She was not sure if Vy would even pass, much less receive an award. She remembers the many evenings they studied together under the oil lamp and how they challenged each other to recite lessons in their loudest voice in order to fight boredom and sleepiness – that is, until the relatives in the big house and the neighbors complained. After that, Mother required them to recite lessons softly and Vy lost interest in studying. Ha tried to incite Vy by citing the consequences of not doing well in school, but she was not sure how effective that was.

Ha is proud of Vy because the award package is something Vy earned by hard work, not a charity given by people who feel sorry for them. Looking at the shiny red package, Ha implores, "Is it heavy? Do you want me to carry it for you?"

"No, I want to carry it. You have your knapsack to carry."

"Can I look to see what's inside?"

Vy searches the contents by feeling with her hand inside the package. "There are notebooks and pencils." She raises the bag above her head to look through the cellophane wrapping. "There's a knapsack with Snow White on it. Can you see?"

"Is there a doll?"

"No."

"How do you know?"

"I didn't feel a doll when I put my hand inside."

"Maybe there is a doll in the knapsack. Let's hurry home to see."

Half way home, Vy relents and lets Ha hold the package. Ha puts it on top of her knapsack and holds both out in front of her, walking slowly, not wanting to hurry home. She feels good when she sees heads turn with looks of envy. She does not mind if others think she is the recipient of the award.

"Let's hurry home," Vy says, "Mom will be so proud."

Vy's mentioning of Mother reminds Ha of her own dismal school record. She did not graduate to the next level because she had missed too many school days due to illness. When Ha's teacher handed Ha her school record, she said, "You'll have to stay back one year because you were sick, not because you were lazy. It will be good for you to prepare for the next level. I hope you'll be able to come to school more regularly next year." At that time, Ha did not feel bad because the teacher was kind and she knew the reason she stayed behind was not her own doing. But now comparing her record with Vy's, Ha feels like her heart is being squeezed. She returns the award package to Vy. "You hold it."

"Why don't you want to hold it anymore?"

"I am sad."

"What happened?"

"I'll have to stay behind one year."

Vy almost drops the package to the ground. "Why?"

"I missed too many school days and do not have enough credits to pass the grade."

"Really?"

"Really!"

"But it's not your fault, it's because you were sick. The teacher should let you pass."

Ha shakes her head. "But I know I'm weak in math."

"That's because you don't have a tutor to help you, right?"

Ha feels like crying. "Mom will give me a beating."

Two Sisters

"I don't think so. Mom knows that you were sick."

"Mom says she'll give us a whipping if we do not pass. You get an award and I stay behind a grade. I'm sure to get it."

"I will plead with Mom not to whip you," Vy says. "I wish that Elder Uncle helps us with homework."

"I do not need his help."

"Is it because you're afraid of walking into the big house?"

Ha nods. "Elder Uncle never asks us about our homework or walks into our little house. He has rich friends and does not care about us. I don't think he wants to help." As they enter their little house, Ha adds, "I wish Mom could help us."

"Mom should not punish you because she cannot help you with homework."

Putting the award package on the table, Vy does not feel so excited anymore. "You dared to talk back to Elder Uncle and even slept in the garden, so why are you so scared of being punished by Mom?"

"I deserve a punishment for not passing my grade. Mom works hard so we can go to school. We need to do well." Ha sighs. "Not passing the grade is a sin. I'm sad that I am not good enough to pass."

"Why are there so many sins?"

"Like what?"

"Like stealing, lying, being dirty,...and not passing a grade."

"But they are different."

"How?"

"We will be punished for stealing and lying after we die. The devils will cut off the arms of thieves and the tongues of liars. But we are punished by living people for being dirty and doing badly in school. Living people do not know about all our sins, but devils do."

"Do you think Mom got a beating for not doing well in school?"

"Sure, she got a beating from Grandma. But we can't ask her that."

"But...I don't think you're right."

Ha puffs her cheeks in self-defense. "What is not right?"

"You said we cannot see dead people. So how can devils cut off their tongues?"

"I just repeat what Mom says. I think devils can do it because they are also invisible."

"Only if Dad could help us with homework even when he's invisible..." Vy dreams.

"It's better if he's alive," Ha wishes aloud. "He was Mom's teacher, so I'm sure he could help us with homework. He could even teach us music and how to play instruments."

Two Sisters

"How do you know?"

"Don't you remember when we opened the box under Dad's altar? There were books and a mandolin and even a radio that he made himself. He was good at many things."

"Yeah, because he was a teacher."

"You did well in school and got an award. You'll be as good as Dad when you grow up. You'll be rich like Elder Uncle and Aunt, but I will be poor like Mom."

Vy is happy to hear she will be rich. "I'll share my money with you. I'll buy you clothes and take care of you and Mom."

Vy starts to open the package and that makes Ha forget about her problem. "Is there a doll?"

"No, but there are four notebooks, you can have two. I'll use the knapsack and we'll share the colored pencils," Vy says. "When I'm rich, I'll share many other things with you."

"And if your children are clean and mine are dirty, you still let them play together, right?"

"They'll play with dolls together inside and they won't get dirty."

"Don't call poor people 'dirty' or 'barbaric' when you're rich, okay?"

"No, I'll teach them to stay clean so they can be healthy. I'll help them and give them money."

Two Sisters

"I wish to be good in school so I will be rich, too, but that won't happen." Feeling miserable, Ha bursts out crying.

Vy consoles Ha, "I will share my money with you."

Ha is still crying when Mother gets home. Mother wants to know why. Vy says, "Because...she has to stay behind in school."

Ha cries harder. "Please don't hit me. I was not lazy."

Mother is relieved to know it was not anything more serious. She calmly says, "I knew you didn't pass the grade because you missed too many school days. Don't worry. I will not punish you for this. Next year you will study hard and pass."

Snuggled in Mother's embrace, Ha is surprised to hear that Mother is not going to follow through with the punishment she has threatened. Mother's words have been repeated so many times that they are clear in her mind: *"You will get a whipping if you fail your grade."* Instead Mother calmly confides in them, "I do not know enough to help you with homework. So you need to pay utmost attention to your teachers. If you do not understand something, ask your teachers and classmates for help. My life is hard without an education and I want you to have a better life. If I scold you, it's only because I love you and want you to advance."

Ha wants to tell Mother that one cannot do well just by listening to the teachers. She wants Mother to know that teachers usually pay more attention to the strong students and call on these students to read or solve problems, and do not spend much time on the weak students. She wants to say that with the way teachers teach, she will hopelessly fall behind unless she has a personal tutor or someone from the family to help her. She wants to tell Mother that asking classmates for help is not an option for her. She finds that the strong students are selfish. Since they want to maintain their class rank and receive an award at the end of the year, they do not want to help anyone. Furthermore, the discord between Mother and Young Aunt, the disparity of wealth between the big house and little house, the lack of electricity in the little house when the whole neighborhood has it, the unjust treatment, and the scolding and disparagement from the paternal relatives distract her while she is in class. She often daydreams and dwells on the family situation rather than listen to the teacher.

Ha is moved by Mother's sincere confession about being illiterate. She spares Mother the bitter feelings she harbors, but she asks Mother for the reason Mother did not complete school. Mother explains that her parents did not allow her to attain a higher education because they did not think girls needed an education, and because they thought educated girls would write letters to boys. Like many other girls of her time, Mother had to stay home and help on the farm.

"I have not met my grandfather, but..." Ha cannot finish what she intended to say when she sees worry and pain on Mother's face. She thinks of her grandfather as being as strict and harsh as the relatives in the big house.

•

CHAPTER TWENTY-SIX

As the bus zigzags its way up the mountain pass, Ha feels dizzy. She rests her forehead against the seat in front of her and throws up into a plastic bag that Mother gave her for exactly that purpose. Her excitement at visiting Mother's village and riding a bus for the first time decreases with each wave of nausea. The unpleasant mixture of odors from human flesh, gasoline, and fume makes her sick. Her head hurts, her throat throbs, and her stomach lurches each time the bus brake is roughly applied. She is exhausted. She tries to control her nausea by closing her eyes and reclining to a horizontal position as much as possible within the limits of a bus seat.

Vy complains, "You throw up too much and it smells bad. Are you really sick?"

Mother searches in her travel bag for more plastic bags and hands one to Vy. "Hold this for your sister. It is the last bag I have. If she needs more, she'll just have to lean out the window. She's not ill. It is motion sickness."

"But we're not on a ship."

Two Sisters

"You can get motion sickness on a bus."

"Then why am I not sick?"

"You are stronger than your sister."

Vy pinches her nose in disgust. "But it smells so bad that I want to throw up too."

"I told the two of you to go to bed early last night and you didn't listen," Mother chides them. "If you don't have enough sleep, it's easy to get motion sickness."

Before Ha has a chance to wipe her mouth after the last vomit, she throws up again. Her body shakes uncontrollably. Mother changes places with Vy to sit next to Ha. Mother wipes Ha's face with a wash cloth and puts eucalyptus oil on Ha's neck and forehead. "Close your eyes and rest."

Putting her head on Mother's lap, Ha lies down and closes her eyes. She stays put even though she dearly wants a drink of water to clear out the sour taste in her mouth. She does not want to get up lest she get nauseated again. Despite being bounced with each bump on the road, she feels good being stroked by Mother and soon falls asleep. She wakes up only when the bus stops at the station.

Ha opens her eyes. "Are we there yet?"

Mother says, "Stay put. We can wait until after everyone else gets off."

Ha sits up to look out through the window. The bus station is full of people walking about, around and between parked buses.

Two Sisters

Vy asks, "Are we at your village, Mom?"

"No. We'll have to take a van, and then walk."

"Oh no, do we have to walk far?"

"About three kilometers. We could take a horse carriage if we got here earlier."

It is late afternoon when they get off the van to find that they are the middle of nowhere. As Mother predicted, they do not see any horse carriages about. Ha and Vy follow Mother on the lone dirt road that begins on top of the hill where the van drops them off. As they walk on, houses appear on both sides of the road. The afternoon breeze makes Ha feel better and she does not mind walking. It is better walking than being sick on the bus. Now that she has experienced motion sickness, she does not wish to be invited to ride in Elder Uncle's car anymore.

"Look at them strange clothes."

A group of tanned-skin children are playing with a shuttlecock, bouncing it on their foot, on the side of the road. They stop to stare curiously at the three strangers who wear clothes that are not the usual attire of people in their village. Ha figures they are about her age. The girls wear tops and pants whereas the boys wear shorts and are shirtless. Most of the children wear no shoes and their clothes are either brown or black. Ha and Vy have a hard time making out many things they say. Ha feels paranoid and embarrassed because she thinks they talk about her. She pulls down her hat a touch to cover her eyes. Vy has no such reservation. She turns around to look at the children. "Look, Sister Ha. They are barefoot. They are even dirtier than us."

Two Sisters

Ha whispers, "Don't look at them."

A few kids throw dirt at Ha's and Vy's backs. Ha and Vy turn around and give them a stern look and are somewhat gratified to hear their tormentors being scolded by their parents. "What's ya doing that for? Scoot!"

A man on a bicycle rides past Mother before turning his head. "Going to village? Wanna ride?"

"No, thank you," Mother says. "There are three of us, plus bags."

The man stops. "Where's ya going to? Wanna ride for one?"

Ha and Vy shake their heads. Mother puts her bags down and wipes her forehead. "We do not go with strangers. If you can, please stop at Mrs. Fifth Dien to tell her that her daughter is visiting from Nha-Trang. Thank you very much."

"I'll tell her."

The man takes off down the hill. Mother and her daughters resume walking. At the bottom of the hill, the scenery opens up to a large rice field with no end in sight. There are tall bamboo trees all around. Mother quickens her steps. Vy admires the scenery. She says to Mother, "Your village is so pretty. It is the prettiest place in the world."

It is indeed very pretty here. Ha has never seen or imagined anything greener and prettier than the different shades of green around her. The fresh green of grass, the yellow green of ripened rice stalks, the bright green of banana plants, the light blue green of bamboo trees, and the dark green of leaves have a calming effect on Ha. Her eyes

Two Sisters

follow the undulating waves of the rice stalks to the horizon. She imagines herself to be a lone traveler on an empty road. The trees dance and sing in the breeze while the white clouds from the blue sky above descend to flirt with the flying birds. Mother's village is so beautiful and inviting, not a run-down place that her paternal aunts wanted her to believe when they disparaged Mother. Ha breathes in the earthy smell of leaves and grain and feels content and happy walking behind Mother and Vy, the two most important people in the world to her.

After they walk the length of the rice field, the landscape changes to thatched houses and banana trees. Villagers stare and talk aloud among themselves with no discretion about the three city people. Besides not being used to the incomplete sentences uttered by the villagers, it disturbs Ha that these people talk about the three of them as though they were not there. When they reach the market, they are suddenly surrounded by three women.

"O my God. It's Hao. Got married and left for City long ago."

"Ya daughters' this big? Why not come home sooner, Hao?"

"It's bad ya not come home when ya Pa died. He waited a long time, Hao."

Mother makes grunting sounds and Ha cannot make out if they were answers to the blunt and indiscreet questions or if they were meaningless syllables to avoid talking to the nosy women. Ha throws a less-than-friendly glance at the three barefoot women in tattered hats and disheveled clothes. She startles with the realization that "boorish hicks" and "country bumpkins" have not just popped into her inner mind, but were actually uttered aloud. These are the same contemptuous words Elder Aunt and Young Aunt have used against Mother – words that Ha hates with all her being – and she immediately regrets saying them. She tries to justify her action by telling herself that she did not judge the women by their appearance, but by their impolite behavior. She feels bad all the same.

The women must not have heard Ha. They do not appear to understand that their behavior is not in accordance with city etiquette and they seem totally oblivious to the discomfort they cause Mother. They do not talk directly to Mother, but loudly discuss her among themselves.

"Not come back since she got married?"

"Nah, not even when her Pa was sick and dying."

"Oh my!"

Mother walks as fast as she can, but she cannot escape the words of the three women who decide to follow them. To Ha's astonishment, as the three of them continue on their journey, other women join in to form a line as if they were members of a marching band. When Mother comes to a fork, she turns and takes the straighter and narrower road which is lined with bamboo trees and houses in a similar layout. Each house has a gate that is constructed by two large pieces of rocks and a yard with banana trees and flower beds. The children come out of their houses to watch the lively march. It must be the most exciting thing of the day for them. They join in the fun and form a longer and noisier line. Their clothes are drab compared to Ha's and Vy's city clothes, a fact that does not escape the villagers. It is a topic to be added to whatever else they find to talk about city people and their peculiarities.

Two Sisters

Mother stops at a gate anchored by two large shiny flat rocks that do not look too different from others. She puts the two bags she has been carrying on top of one. Ha and Vy figure that Mother wants to take a rest and are about to do the same when a swarm of people – men, women, young adolescents, and little children – run out from the two houses behind the gate, squealing and talking all at once.

"Third Sister's home."

"Ma's inside. Come in, Third Sister."

"Them are ya girls? Come say hi to Nana."

Ha and Vy are confused with the commotion and the way strange people freely take their bags away without asking. They quietly follow Mother and these people through a yard of orange flowers and banana trees. Once they pass the front yard, they enter a large cement square, covered with rice grain spread out to dry under the sun. At a corner, a red flower bush is planted next to an old water barrel. Behind the square is a large thatched house which they pass by. They walk toward a smaller thatched house where ducks and chickens roam freely and where the collective noise of fowls and pigs is louder than the talking of people.

A pale old lady in a long black dress, whose face is dry and wrinkled and whose white hair is high in a bun, comes out from the small house. She looks at the three city people with bewilderment. She appears confused until a woman pulls Mother's hand and pushes Mother toward her. "Ma, this is Third Sister. She's home."

As the old lady's eyes search Mother's face to register reality, Mother walks closer to the lady and her voice breaks. "Ma, I bring the girls home to meet you."

Two Sisters

Mother instructs the girls to cross their arms and bend their heads to greet Nana, their maternal grandmother. "Nana, we're visiting."

As if she just got blasted by cold air, the old lady's face suddenly becomes icy. She swiftly turns around, walks back into the small thatched house, and sits down on a chair next to the altar decorated with polished inlaid concha. She speaks slowly and enunciates each word as though that would do a better job to convey what she wants to say to her estranged daughter. "Go away. What ya come home for? Ya city girl forgot ya roots!"

Mother stands at the door and cries. "Why do you want me to leave? It is not because I forgot you, but since my husband died, I had to work day and night to raise my little girls. I could not afford a bus ticket to visit you before. I married a city man, but it did me no good. Don't you know that I am only a maid for my husband's family? I thought you'd be happy to see me. I did not have enough money to come home when Pa was sick or when he died. I am not an animal—"

Mother's voice became louder and louder throughout the speech as if she was fed with strength and assertiveness, but her body finally betrays her. It falters and sways and it looks as if she may collapse at any minute. Her siblings quickly hold her up and guide her to the bamboo bed next to the altar.

A middle-aged man in brown clothes walks toward the white-haired lady. "I told ya, Ma, she had no money to bring her children home. It's her fate not to see Pa when he died. We just have to accept it."

Two Sisters

A young woman takes Ha's and Vy's hands and places them on the white-haired lady's shoulder. "I'm your Seventh Aunt. Say sorry to Nana for ya Ma."

Vy pulls her hand back in fear and uncertainty. Ha throws burning rays of hatred at the white-haired lady, but suddenly the old lady clasps Ha's hand in hers. "My granddaughter lives in City and she's so skinny. Ya ma has no plenty to feed ya!"

Ha is taken aback and does not know what to think. The old lady tightens her squeeze while sobbing on Ha's chest. Ha thinks of an adage that Mother sometimes recites in a sad voice: *"Poverty robs the filial piety from people and makes them forget their parents' love and labor."* Mother must have recited this adage so many times because Ha has it memorized word for word. She feels she understands better the hardship that poverty can bring. Although she is still upset with her grandmother for making Mother sad and therefore giving her a bad first impression, she stands still and lets her grandmother cry on her.

A man hands Ha and Vy a box of incense sticks. "Go bow at ya Pa's altar." They each take three sticks from the box and bow three times in front of a picture of Father. Mother has the presence of mind to extract fruit, incense sticks, and pastries from one of her bags to add to the altar's offerings.

A few curious neighbors have gathered at the front door. When it is clear that the old lady has relented and forgiven her estranged daughter, family members ask the neighbors to disperse so that the family can reunite in private. There is so much catching up to do. Everyone stays at the small thatched house and they talk and talk until late. Through the conversations, Ha and Vy know that the tall middle-aged

Two Sisters

man is Second Uncle[15] who is the oldest of Nana's children. His wife, Second Aunt, is as short as he is tall. Second Uncle inherited most of his father's properties. He and his family own the large thatched house, the cement square, and three rice fields. They have six children, having the largest family among the siblings. Vinh, their oldest daughter, is two years older than Ha. Vuong, their second daughter, is the same age as Ha. The next four children – Dan, Tin, Tien, and Teo – are younger than both Ha and Vy.

Mother is the second child of her parents and is called Third Aunt by nieces and nephews on her family's side[16]. Fourth Aunt looks very much like Mother and is the plumpest of all the sisters. Ha understands she was the one who pretended to be Mother and went to the hospital to accept Father's proposal of marriage after he tried to kill himself. Fourth Aunt, Sixth Aunt, and Seventh Aunt have two daughters each. Eighth Uncle attained the highest level of education in the family. He lives with Nana and so does Thu, the only son of Fifth Aunt who has died. Thu helps Nana in the farm. Eighth Uncle is soon to be married.

After the relatives depart to their respective homes, Thu helps Nana cook dinner. It is a simple meal of rice, boiled spinach, and grilled fish. The food is fresh and the city guests have a good appetite. Eighth Uncle and Thu give up their beds for the three female visitors and sleep over at Second Uncle's large thatched house.

---

[15] Local custom dictates how the oldest son is called. In other places, he may be called First Uncle or Elder Uncle.
[16] Mother is called Fifth Aunt by nieces and nephews on her husband's side because her husband was the fifth child in his family.

CHAPTER TWENTY-SEVEN

The pigs' oinking disturbs the morning's quietness and wakes Ha and Vy. Following their noise and scent, Ha and Vy come to a wood pigpen with a half-thatched and half-tiled roof.

Thu is washing the pigpen with water while Nana and Mother are adding bran and banana trunks to the trough. Mother tells Ha and Vy to wash themselves at the well. Although Ha and Vy are not used to the strong farm smell, they find the sight of four pink piglets pushing and shoving their snouts into their food intriguing. Ha and Vy linger a while at the pigpen before joining their cousins at the well. When they see their cousins scrub their teeth with bare fingers and wipe their faces with shirts' sleeves, they follow suit and do not bother to go inside to get toiletries from their travel bags. Vy is interested in the way water is brought up from the well because of its novelty. A heavy piece of rock is tied at the far end of the handle. To lower the water bucket which is tied to the other end of the handle into the well, she raises the end with the heavy rock. When she lets it go, the rock's weight pulls it down and allows the bucket of water to rise up. At home in the city, Vy is not allowed to pull up

Two Sisters

water from the well because she has to stand at the well opening to pull up the rope, a task deemed too dangerous for her. Here, Vy is allowed to work the handle because she can do it from afar and does not have to stand right at the well opening. She happily agrees to the task of bringing water up for the banana trees.

When Mother calls Ha and Vy to breakfast, their cousins join them even though breakfast is not their usual meal. After breakfast, Nana takes the basket of bananas and banana leaves that she and Mother have gathered earlier to the market. Nana takes her grandchildren, including Ha and Vy, with her. After selling both fruit and leaves, Nana gives her grandchildren the money she got from the transactions. She tells them to buy whatever they want and while they are off by themselves, she spends time bragging to other villagers about her city daughter's visit. As if to clear her daughter's reputation of being a heartless daughter, Nana makes sure people understand why Mother could not come home when her own father fell ill and when he died.

Ha is moved by her newfound cousins' generosity and friendliness. The cousins help her and Vy buy what they want and let them keep the rest of the money from Nana.

In the afternoon, Nana and Mother go to the marshy field to harvest water spinach, or ong-choy as it is called in the village. Watching Mother work alongside Nana, Ha concludes that mothers are a comforting figure even for grown-ups and adults also like to spend time next to their mothers, as much as she does her own.

Vuong, the second daughter of Second Uncle, invites Ha to attend summer school with her since they are of the same age and both are in fifth grade. Vuong changes clothes for school. She puts on a light green shirt and nice black pants that do not have holes in them like the ones she wore to the market. She combs her hair and puts a hair pin through it. She wears flip-flops whose strap is held together by a safety pin. Ha thinks Vuong looks lovely and unpretentious and feels a bit self-conscious in her city clothes.

Vuong and Ha walk to school along the same dirt road that they took to the market in the morning. The school is a one-room building with a thatched roof and mud walls. There are eight sets of wood desks and chairs to be shared among twelve students. The teacher is not surprised to see a new face. He just asks Ha a few questions to determine her level and later calls her up to solve some arithmetic problems. Ha solves them with ease since they involve multiplication and addition that were taught at lower levels in city schools. Ha enjoys being praised by the teacher and admired by other students and wishes she could attend school here so she would not have to solve harder math problems. Vuong whispers in Ha's ears that she will want help in math.

When Vuong and Ha get home, all of her aunts and cousins are already at the large thatched house. The extended family gathers in front of Second Uncle's house to chat and enjoy the afternoon snacks of sweet rice with peanuts, boiled bananas, and rice cakes with ginger sugar syrup. Ha joins in, but is taken aback when asked by her aunts if she loves Nana. Vy is asked the same question. Ha thinks that it is an unfair question that presses for a positive answer. She feels that Vy and she are not taken seriously by their aunts. After all, it is only the second day since they met their maternal relatives for the first time, and did Seventh Aunt forget about Mother's crying the first day? When Vy says yes, that she loves Nana, Seventh Aunt wants to know why they did not ask Mother to take them to the village sooner. As though that was not enough, Fourth Aunt has the audacity to ask which grandmother they love more.

Vy is diplomatic and unperturbed. "I love them both the same."

Ha, on the other hand, is more blunt and straightforward with her feelings. "I like to keep my feeling inside and do not want to discuss it." Ha senses embarrassment and even anger from her three aunts. She feels bad because Mother had told her that these three aunts came to the city to help Mother out both times she gave birth. These aunts took care of Mother and brought gifts from Nana. Although Ha does feel a loving connection with her aunts, she does not like to have to analyze and bare her feelings to them.

After some time with their aunts, Ha and Vy learn to make bracelets and necklaces from their cousins by weaving bamboo leaves and tying weaved strands into circles. Then they go with Vuong who decides to lead her younger siblings and cousins to the highest hill that she calls the mountain of the village. Ha observes that houses on the hill are not thatched houses made from dirt as houses on the field below, but have cement walls and red tiled roofs. Colorful flowers grace the landscape where butterflies and dragonflies flutter by. The hill grows steeper once they pass horse stables and mangers. Horses neigh as if giving warning to their owners of the intruders. The odor from the horse manure makes Ha sick in her stomach and causes Vy to pinch her nose. "This smells so bad," Vy complains.

Their cousins walk on. They do not pinch their noses or spit or complain. They walk on pebbles and rocks with no difficulty even though some of them are barefoot. The path opens up and widens after they pass thick bushes. Vuong

Two Sisters

points to a thicket. "Let's pick chim-chim[17] before going up the mountain."

Ha is excited to follow Vuong, although she does not understand why Vuong thinks they are not already on the mountain. As they approach the thicket, a flurry of flapping wings of frantic brown birds ensues. The birds have covered the green tops and made the thicket look dark, but after they fly away, an array of bright colors opens up, from green to yellow to red. There are many different kinds of fruit, each a different color. Ha, influenced by Mother's teaching, is cautious. "Are you sure this is not poisonous? Do birds die after eating them?"

"Oh my, we eat them fruit all the time," Dan says. "We not die. Ya should try."

Vy immediately pops a chim-chim in her mouth. She gushes, "Chim-chim is so delicious."

Ha relents and tries one. She likes the taste and begins to explore other fruits. Dan recites the name of each fruit and tells Ha and Vy which ones are edible. Ha and Vy abandon all caution and stuff their stomach with all kinds of fruit until Vy exclaims, "I have a tummy ache. I need to go to the bathroom."

"There's no toilet. Go in the bush," Vuong says. She picks up Teo, her littlest brother, and heads to a bush. Ha is surprised to see that each cousin immediately takes off in a different direction in search of his or her own bush. Ha thought Vy was the only one in need of a toilet until she starts to feel a funny sensation in her stomach. After doing

---

[17] A type of fruit.

Two Sisters

her "business" at a bush, Ha wonders how to clean herself. She looks around to see what others do and to her astonishment, she sees her cousins leave their pants down while scooting from rock to rock until they find a rock to their liking. Then they gently lower their behinds onto their chosen rock and begin to move back and forth, to and fro, in a rocking motion. Not only that, Ha's own sister Vy is doing exactly the same thing. Each round bottom swishes in a well-choreographed cleaning session.

Ha is appalled. "What? How barbaric!" Immediately she is horrified and covers her mouth with her hands. Vy, as horrified, looks at Ha as if wanting to ask what the devil has gotten into her. Ha and Vy have promised each other never to utter the "b-word" against anyone, even if and when they become rich and successful in life. Now the word "barbaric" is being echoed back to Ha. Feeling eyes on her, Ha lowers her head on bended knees in shame.

"Who ya call barbaric?" Vuong asks.

"Uh...No..." Ha stammers. "Nothing. I just...just want to ask why you wipe your bottom on the rock where maybe someone else did the same thing."

"No need to worry," Vuong says. "It rains at night and washes it out and the sun dries it out just like washing clothes. We pick clean rocks and never get sick. There are many rocks to pick."

As if Vuong understands that Ha needs privacy, she calls on her siblings and the local cousins to go off a distance to wait before they resume their walk.

When they get home, the children of Fourth Aunt, Sixth Aunt, and Seventh Aunt go back to their houses with their mothers. Ha and Vy follow Second Uncle's children to wash themselves at the well. They leave their clothes on and splash each other until it is dark, before changing to dry clothes.

Dinner at Nana's place consists of leftovers from the previous day's dinner plus crab caught at the field by Thu and sweet and sour soup made with fish that Mother brought from the city. After dinner, Thu works under an oil lamp, shaping clay into the shapes of a pot, a kettle, two bowls, and two cups to give to Ha and Vy as gifts. While he works, Ha goes over to Second Uncle's place to help Vuong with math.

A few neighbor children linger around the perimeter of the house, still curious about the strangers from the city.

CHAPTER TWENTY-EIGHT

The full moon, appearing as a giant round lamp suspended in the clear sky, shines gently at the foot of the mountain in Mother's village. The peaceful moonlight blends with the quietness of the night as it spreads over thatched roofs and high guava branches and threads its way through the banana leaves to the bamboo shoots on the ground. When the sky is clear and the moonlight reaches the ground, the villagers can navigate their ways on the main dirt road. The day's noisiness is taken over by the night's calmness at the first sight of the moon which slowly brightens the darkened sky.

Relatives and neighbors have gathered at Second Uncle's cement square to say goodbye to Mother and Ha and Vy. They come bearing gifts of rice, flour, rice paper, and sugar cane. Ha is surprised that no one, including the little children, bothers to drink the tea or eat the cakes, baked by Eighth Uncle's fiancée, set out on a little table. People seem to be more interested in Ha, staring at her as if expecting something from her and making her the center of attention. Ha is glad she is not sick, for she would be even more uncomfortable than she is now with all eyes on her. For two weeks, Ha has been drinking water straight from the well

Two Sisters

that is full of visible squiggling little things instead of boiling it first as Mother told her to do and as they do in the city.

An old woman clears her throat while plopping down between Mother and Ha. "I hear ya tell good stories. Do tell one before ya go back to City."

Ha feels embarrassed and shakes her head no, but Vuong pleads, "Please do. You'll be gone tomorrow. Auntie comes to hear you."

Ha looks up at expectant faces around her and remembers the first time the neighbor kids got over their shyness and entered Nana's house. She had recited some well-known stories to them, making things up and adding things as she went along to make the stories more interesting and elicit some laughter. The kids loved her stories and challenged each other for the privilege to stay overnight at Nana's house, for Nana had her limit of how many kids she could take. Ha loved it when the kids listened attentively and laughed on cue. That bolstered her confidence and encouraged her to be more imaginative and lively in her story telling. The more they laughed, the more elaborate the stories became. So now she has earned the reputation of being a great story teller. But telling stories to peers under the covers in the dark is not the same as telling stories to adults under the full moon. The adults will not be easily amused by slapstick humor and crazy embellishments of familiar fairytales.

Mother pours some tea for Nana while urging Ha on. "Tell a story. Don't make people wait."

Vy chimes in, "Any story will do." Vy's innocent face reminds Ha of the younger sister in the Indian movie *Two Orphans*, but the Indian story is too long to tell. Ha thinks

Two Sisters

hard for a suitable story. Her senses are heightened as the moon shines a bit more brightly, the fireflies dart a bit more quickly, and the insects chirp a bit more loudly. Second Uncle and Eighth Uncle roll their cigarettes while stealing a glance her way now and then. What story, Ha wonders, would be more interesting than the story *The Girl Hidden In The Melons* in which Ha has the prince urinate on the melon field and kill off all the melons because he cannot see the tiny girl hidden among them, or the story *Thach-Sanh Ly-Thong* in which Ha curses Ly-Thong with ugliness so that the princess declares she'd rather die in the cave than be rescued by him, or the story *Sea God and Sky God* in which Ha gives an alternative reason why the two gods continue to fight bitterly for eternity and wreak havoc on the weather every year. The story *Eat Starfruit to Return Gold* may hit too close to home. In this story, the older brother arranges to inherit everything from the parents and leaves his younger brother destitute. Since Second Uncle inherited three large rice fields while Eighth Uncle got only a small field, the former may think that she is imprudent and rude and that Mother did not do a good job raising her. It is probably best not to mention wealth and poverty. Ha tentatively begins a story after Vy impatiently pulls on her sleeve.

Once upon a time, there was a woman who did not want to get married or have children. She went up to the mountain to live as a nun by herself. She walked and walked and walked until she came to a cave next to a stream of clear water in the green forest. There were red chim-chims, yellow apricots, wild maracujas, and black berries to eat. She decided to stay, using the cave for shelter.

Ha pauses. She waits for people to tell her to stop. She names local fruit from the village in this well-known story. Part of her hopes that the adults will dismiss her story because it is not told in the traditional way. But as all eyes

Two Sisters

are on her, riveting and waiting, she gains some confidence and continues.

One day, while she was bathing in the stream, she saw two pieces of grapefruit in the water, even though there were no grapefruit trees in the area. After she ate the delicious grapefruit, she became pregnant. After nine months and ten days, she gave birth to two beautiful identical girls. She called them Ngoc-Cam and Ngoc-Kho.

Someone finally recognizes the story. "Oh, it's the story of Ngoc-Cam and Ngoc-Kho." Even though people are already familiar with the story, they still want to hear it. "So what happens next?"

Uh...Ngoc-Cam and Ngoc-Kho grew up to be beautiful young ladies. When their mother died after a long illness, she left them only one set of clothes. The sisters took turns taking wood to the village to exchange for food. The one who stayed behind had to hide in the cave without clothes.

One day when it was the younger sister Ngoc-Kho's turn to go to the market, she met a mandarin's son who fell in love with her. He took her home to ask his parents for permission to marry her. The day Ngoc-Kho came back with two servants to get her sister was the same day a prince went on a hunting trip. The prince and his soldiers went after a deer and came to the cave where the sisters lived. When the soldiers set a fire to lure the deer out, Ngoc-Cam yelled out "Please stop. I am in here." The prince ordered Ngoc-Cam to appear. "Are you a ghost or a human? Come out or else you'll be burned to death." Ngoc-Cam ran out. The prince was surprised at her beauty. After hearing her story, the prince gave her clothes to wear and took her back to the palace and asked the King and Queen for permission to marry her.

Two Sisters

When Ngoc-Kho got to the cave, she saw only ashes and thought her sister was dead. She cried and asked her fiancé to let her mourn for three months and ten days before they got married. At the end of the mourning period, Ngoc-Kho came back to the cave to set up an altar for her sister and to have a ceremony to end the mourning period. At the same time, Ngoc-Cam and the prince were coming back to the mountain to look for her twin sister. It was a sweet reunion. The two couples lived happily ever after.

Ha looks up to see the top of the mountain under the moonlight clearly. She feels the presence of the twin sisters' spirits and is comforted by it. The old lady who sits across from Ha gets up to spit the areca-and-betel mixture she's been chewing into a container. Wiping her mouth with her shirt's sleeve, she praises, "My God, this girl has talent!"

Flashing a proud smile, Nana offers people cookies and tea. Women gather around Mother to seek parenting advice. They want to know how Ha knows so many fairytales. Mother says she used fairytales as bedtime stories, and admits she was not aware of her own daughter's talent of storytelling for she had never heard Ha tell stories before. Ha can tell that Mother tries her best to be modest. She is glad to see Mother, despite herself, shine with pride.

A lady pats Ha's shoulder. "Study hard in City. When ya visit again, ya can tell more stories."

Ha nods. She feels grateful that people insisted on her telling a story and listened attentively to it. They gave her confidence and boosted her ego by believing in her. She feels a bond with the villagers who allowed her an opportunity to make her imaginative world come alive. She realizes for the first time the reason she often lives under the fear of being put down, of making mistakes, of looking ridiculous with her imaginations, is because her paternal relatives look down on her. It must be the same reason she often is quiet around adults.

Thu hands her a warm bag. "I grilled rice as a reward for ya."

Ha is moved by his kindness. Knowing that Ha likes grilled rice, her cousin often makes it after he's done with his field work each day.

Vy gives Ha a big squeeze. "Tell me this story again when we get home, Sister Ha. I like it."

"Yes, I will do whatever you want. Now let's eat some grilled rice."

CHAPTER TWENTY-NINE

It is early evening when a young couple comes to the Hoang estate and the dogs bark in response. Mother shoos the dogs away and invites the couple into the little house. Ha and Vy learn that the young woman is their first cousin Tuoi, one of four children of Third Aunt, Father's sister. Tuoi has been living in Saigon with her father and siblings after her mother passed away.

Tuoi is friendly and outgoing. She takes a look at Ha and Vy and then points to Vy. "Wow, your children have grown so much. Is this Vy?" Vy crosses her arms in deference to her older cousin. Tuoi exclaims that she cannot get over how big Vy has become. Why, the last time she saw Vy, Vy was still a baby. After some time fussing over Vy, Tuoi marvels at Ha who has grown so tall. Tuoi makes Ha blush by saying Ha is about to be a young lady herself. Because Tuoi is short, Ha is almost as tall as Tuoi. Le, Tuoi's husband, is the opposite of Tuoi both in stature and in disposition. He is skinny, tall, and quiet, although no less friendly. He puts the two bags he was carrying down on the floor and smiles at Ha. Occasionally he gives a short polite "Yes" or "No" to Mother's questions. He looks rather pale and his eyes are set deep in his thin angular face, giving Ha an impression of a sick man. Tuoi apologizes to Mother for not bearing gifts from Saigon, but Mother assures her that her visit means a lot and no gifts are necessary.

For some reason, Ha is drawn to Tuoi and feels close to the older cousin as though they have known each other for a long time. Perhaps it is because they share something in common, which is the lack of wealth. Ha observes that when relatives come to visit, the rich ones come knocking at the big house, whereas the poor ones come knocking at the little house. Ha concludes that death weakens family ties, especially if disparity in wealth is involved. She finds it ironic that there is a lack of family support for poor relatives. She feels that the relatives who have lost immediate family members through death need the emotional support from their big extended family, and yet they are ignored or pushed away if they are in a lower social economic class.

At Mother's inquiry into her business in Saigon, Tuoi's face turns gloomy. "We are having a hard time. We lost our jobs and could not find work in Saigon, so we take a chance and come back here." Mother nods her approval while Tuoi expresses misgivings. "But we do not know if it is easy to find jobs in such a small city. We also do not have a place to stay—"

"Don't worry," Mother offers. "You can stay with us until you find work."

Tuoi hesitates. "I want to go say hi to Grandma and aunties before I make a decision." Then, not speaking to anyone in particular, she says, "I wonder what people are doing over at the big house. If they are having dinner, I can wait a bit."

Two Sisters

"I hope you'll stay here," Mother says. "I'll bring a mat to the altar room and sleep with the girls in there. You two can have our beds. Stay until you find work and a place to live."

"Thank you, Auntie. We'll see. It'd be nice if Grandma lets me stay at her house. If not, we'll come back." Then Tuoi tells Mother that her father is very ill but she cannot afford to take care of him. She feels bad leaving her father to the one brother who is doing well financially.

"I admire your father," Mother says. "He took care of the four of you very well after your mother died. It was to his credit that one of your brothers became a doctor."

"I think each of us has her own fate. None of my siblings is in as bad a situation as I am. I have not been successful in life and have had to move from place to place. It's good that we do not have children."

"Don't fret too much. You have a good education. You'll find a job sooner or later."

Tuoi changes the subject and asks about Vy and Ha. She learns about Ha's anemia and her staying behind one year. Mother expresses her concern that Ha is weak in math and may not pass the admission exam to the free public secondary school. If Ha does not pass, she will have to go to a private school and Mother may not be able to afford it. Mother admits she does not know enough to tutor her own daughters. Tuoi offers that Le can tutor Ha because he is good in math and he has experience tutoring students in Saigon. Le does not seem to mind that his wife offers his services; he immediately asks Ha to show him the math homework problems she needs help with and the two of them go off to a corner to work on them.

Two Sisters

Vy says she wants Tuoi and Le to stay with them so that Le can help Ha with homework and Ha will no longer cry at not being able to solve homework problems. Vy offers to share food with Tuoi, even if that means she'll go hungry. At the mention of food, Mother offers her guests a simple meal of rice and soy sauce because that is all they have in the little house, but Tuoi declines, saying she and Le already ate. Vy says she is sorry that she has eaten up all the stir-fried spinach. She would have saved some if she had known Tuoi and Le were coming. Tuoi is moved by Vy's sincerity and says she'll try to rent nearby when she can afford her own place.

Tuoi wants to take a bath before seeing Grandmother. Mother says she should bathe at the big house because the little house does not have electricity and that it will be too dark in the bathroom. Tuoi says she can use the oil lamp, but Mother says that the neighbor boys may peep if they see light. Mother sees a puzzled look on Tuoi's face. "The bathroom is at the back garden of a neighbor's house and I do not have the money to fix the holes in the outside wall. The neighbor boys often pee in their garden and they'll get curious if they see light in the bathroom."

"So how do you take a bath?"

"I bathe without light. I cover the holes with a large piece of plastic, but I can fumble around in the dark because I am familiar with my bathroom."

Tuoi reconsiders the situation and agrees that she will take a bath at the big house. Le tells his wife that he doesn't need a bath. He checks Ha's math solutions and declares that she understands the topic. He promises to help her with homework every day.

Two Sisters

Mother walks the couple to the big house because she's afraid the dogs will bother the newly arrived guests. Vy sadly says to Ha, "I don't think they'll stay with us."

"That's because our house is too small and we don't even have a bathroom."

"And there is no electricity in our house. Where do you think they'll stay?"

"With Grandma, of course."

Seeing doubt on Vy's face, Ha makes a bet even though she inwardly agrees with Vy. "I'll bet five rubber bands that they will stay at the big house."

"I don't think so. Young Aunt will chew them out and will not let them stay."

"Maybe Elder Uncle and Aunt will let them."

"No, I don't think so. I know you want them to stay so Brother Le can help you with math. But you know they won't stay here."

"I wish we have a big house like Seventh Aunt."

"We should study well so we can fix up our house when we grow up."

"We'll have money. We'll have a guest room. We'll fix the bathroom. We'll have electricity."

"Will we build another floor?"

"Of course, if we have money."

Two Sisters

"Yes, we need more rooms."

"We'll plant flowers."

"What kind of flowers?"

"Chrysanthemums, roses, and lilies."

"We'll need to water them or they'll die."

"We'll take turns watering them."

"And then Sister Tuoi and Brother Le will stay with us."

"Yes, and that's not all. We'll have other visitors. Tin, Duc, Hanh, Thanh, Trung, Phi, Phong, and Phuong will also come."

"Will we let the neighbor kids come?"

"Yes, but we'll have to build another gate so that they won't have to go through the main gate. Or they'll be scared and not come."

Mother returns and tells them to go to sleep while she takes Tuoi's bags over to Sixth Aunt's house. Ha and Vy are happy to hear that Tuoi and Le will stay with Sixth Aunt until they find a job and a place of their own.

"See, Vy, I told you," Ha crows. "From now on, I'll have a tutor."

CHAPTER THIRTY

Ha and Vy are at their newfound cousins' porch, waiting for Tuoi to come home. They nervously pace around, alternating between standing up and sitting down. They have nothing to do but watch traffic on the street and keep an eye on Le's condition. They try to ignore the heat from the harsh sun while dawdling at the door. They do not want to walk into the house where the very sick Le is lying on his bed, moaning and crying out in pain.

It is past noon and Tuoi is not yet home.

Ha and Vy have been coming here after school every day since Tuoi and Le rented the place. They come as soon as they finish eating lunch. For the past few days, Tuoi has not been home when they arrived and Le has been suffering from some kind of illness, shaking and moaning in his misery. Ha and Vy do not understand how Tuoi can leave her husband alone when he suffers so, but they do know that Le gets better when Tuoi comes home. Then he'd help Ha with math homework – and that is the reason Ha comes every day.

Two Sisters

Vy had not wanted to come today because she does not want to see Le so miserable, but Ha begged until Vy missed her nap and relented. Le's health seems to have taken a turn for the worse. His groans are louder and that scares the heck out of Ha and Vy. Ha wants to wait outside until Tuoi comes home and gives Le medicine.

Vy knits her brows in deep thoughts. "I think Brother Le should go to the doctor, don't you?"

Ha nods. "But I don't think they have money."

"What is he sick of?"

"I don't know. Maybe he was not clean when he was a little boy."

"Why do you think that?"

"Because Sister Tuoi said he doesn't like taking a bath and my teacher says being dirty causes sickness."

Ha and Vy stay outside until a cry of agony pierces the air. Vy cannot stand it any longer and makes Ha come inside with her. "I think we have to help him or else he'll die."

Ha and Vy are alarmed when they see Le's body twitch uncontrollably underneath his thin blanket. He tries to pull the blanket over himself but it gets stuck in between his thin legs and fails to cover his entire body.

Vy pulls on Ha's hands. "He looks cold. We should cover him with the blanket."

Ha is terrified at the sight of Le's convulsions. She is too scared to move. She is sure she was never this sick.

Whenever she was sick, she was always able to stay calm for Mother to check her temperature, put oil on her forehead, drape a blanket over her, and pat her until she fell asleep.

Le suddenly jerks his body up to a sitting position. With a wild look on his pale face, he curls his body into a ball and reaches the top of his head with his bony hands. He starts pulling his unkempt hair as if wanting to remove the pain he is experiencing. He grunts and groans in a tormented state, being possessed by an unknown force and suffering from unseen demons.

Vy, the braver one, walks closer to her cousin who dully looks up at her. With tears welling up in his eyes that sink deep above the shriveled cheeks, he shakes his head, indicating that he does not want her there. He seems to want to say something, but his purple lips shake and squeeze shut as if concentrating on delivering him from pain and agony.

"Oh my God, Sister Ha, how do we save him?" Vy almost screams.

Ha breaks out in sobs. "I do not know. I am so scared."

Le pays no heed to the girls. Resting his head on his knees, he wraps his arms around his waif-like body as it twitches in convulsions. When the shaking is over, Le stays in the sitting position with his eyes closed. Ha and Vy walk around his bed, whispering to each other, as though they were playing a game in which Le is "it," the one who has to figure out where the other players are without opening his eyes.

Suddenly like a tornado that comes without warning, Tuoi rushes into the house. In a dramatic and loving manner, she throws a bag of food on the floor and jumps on the bed and puts her arms around Le. "How are you doing, darling?"

Colors seem to come back to Le's face. He inquires, "Did they have it?"

Tuoi nods, searching in her pocket. Suddenly being aware of the girls' presence and seeing curious looks on their faces, Tuoi instructs them to go outside to wait. Ha does not dare to ask if Le will feel better, but from past experience she knows that he will. Ha and Vy entertain themselves while waiting outside at the door by making shadowy figures with their hands until Tuoi calls them in.

Seeing Le resting calmly on the bed, Vy's curiosity gets the better of her. "What medicine did you give him? Is he taking a nap? When will he get up?"

Tuoi smiles and asks Ha and Vy to help her fix dinner. She says they will eat when Le gets up and he will help Ha with homework afterwards. Ha is shocked to see an entirely different Le in contrast to the sickly figure of just a while ago. With a peaceful look on his face, Le appears to be in a sweet dream.

"Why is there so much food?" Vy asks.

Tuoi smiles. "Because I want to treat the two of you today."

Ha is thoughtful. "I don't know if Mother will allow us to stay."

"Why not? You'll have to stay since I already bought so much food. We have meat, vegetables, eggs, fish, and even sausage. What's up with not being allowed to eat with us?"

Two Sisters

Ha feels contrite. "I just want Brother Le to get better and help me with homework."

"So stay and eat. After dinner, he'll help you."

Ha ventures to ask a question that has been burning in her mind. "Why don't you take him to a doctor?"

• "Stay and eat. There's plenty of food."

"We'll stay, but... Is there anyway he'll be cured?"

Tuoi sets the plates on the table without looking at Ha, while calmly instructing Ha to open the sausage package and arrange the food on a plate. Tuoi gives Vy the job of washing the vegetables. Ha absentmindedly does her job. She blames herself for talking too much and not minding her own business. She is sure that Tuoi is mad at her now.

When Ha goes outside to put out the garbage, she sees neighbors indiscreetly trying to peek inside the house. She decides to stay out to stop unwanted stares. She is afraid Le will go into convulsions again and she does not care to grant the neighbors the satisfaction of witnessing it. Besides, she does not want to be in the kitchen with Tuoi at this time because she does not know what to say. She sits on the porch watching the sunlight fade from the street and sidewalk. She still blames herself for not staying out of Tuoi's business, but telling herself that there are too many unanswered questions and Tuoi should not be upset with her for being curious. She wonders why Le never goes to work, why Tuoi does not have a business like Mother, and why Tuoi goes to the market every day to sell off most of the things she owns. Once, Tuoi came to the Hoang estate very late at night to ask if anyone wanted to buy her jewelry or dresses. Ha understands that it is hard for Tuoi and Le to manage when

Two Sisters

they are so poor. She admires Le who is knowledgeable and used to wish that she will grow up to be as smart as he is so that she will have money to build a house for Mother – a house with electricity. But the reality is that Le is poor even though he is smart and educated. His intellect does not help him find a job. Ha loses faith in associating knowledge with wealth. *Is the dream of being a good student and getting a good job an unrealistic dream?* Studying her own dark and sickly-looking scrawny arms, Ha sighs and imagines she will have the same fate as Le. She will be sickly and no matter how well she does in school, she will not be able to find a job.

"Come on in for dinner."

Looking up at Tuoi's smiley face, Ha is hopeful. "Is Brother Le up?"

"He will have to be up to eat because he has not eaten since morning."

Le says, "I'll have to help you with math."

"Are you better now?" Vy asks.

"I'm much better. I gave you a scare, didn't I?"

"Ha cried, not me," Vy says.

"You cry because you want help with math," Le teases Ha, "not because you love me."

Yes, it is true that I want you to help me with math, but of course I love you. I dream of building a house for my family, and you are in it. And I'll pay the doctor to cure you, too. Seeing that Ha is deep in thoughts, Tuoi pulls on Ha's

Two Sisters

shirt sleeve. "Brother Le is just teasing you. Sit down and eat with us." At dinner, Tuoi steers the conversation to school and math. She seems apprehensive when Le says that Ha is not ready to apply concepts she has already learned to solve new problems. Ha agonizes that math homework problems are different from examples in class. Tuoi voices her concern about Ha's passing the admission test to the public secondary school, but Le dismisses her fear.

"She'll get it," Le says. "We still have a few months until the test."

"But if—"

"If what?" Le narrows his eyes. "You should eat so the children will eat. Don't talk about school right now. Let the kids enjoy the meal."

CHAPTER THIRTY-ONE

"I have lost it all! Oh God! My dowry! My money!"

Young Aunt's shrieks set a wheel of chaotic motions within the Hoang estate. Young Aunt pulls her own hair, working it into a tangled mass, while darting back and forth on the patio of the big house. "Nothing is left. All's gone!"

Elder Aunt runs out from the big house. "What did you lose?"

"Her jewelry box," Grandmother fills in.

"Where did you leave it?"

"I had it in my trunk. I hid it at the bottom of the trunk. My wallet is gone, too."

"Don't you raise your voice or else the whole neighborhood will hear you," Grandmother admonishes Young Aunt. "Who would take it? Go look again."

Two Sisters

Cuu looks nervous. Knowing it is not uncommon for people to blame the hired hands, she figures she better try to clear herself before being suspected. "I been here four years and never walked in your bedroom. Please believe me, I did not take it. I can help look."

"I did not say it was you," Young Aunt snaps. "All is gone, no need to search. They are a bunch of immoral idiots."

"Who are *they*?" Elder Aunt clears her throat.

"Who else but Tuoi and Le?" Young Aunt's eyes, fiery red from tears and fury, are like those of a wounded cornered animal.

At the mention of the names Tuoi and Le, Ha feels indignant as if her own name were mentioned. She formulates in her head a question she would like to ask Young Aunt, but Elder Aunt beats her to it, not that Ha would dare to pose the question out loud. "How do you know they took it?"

"Who else? The husband smokes weed. The wife pays for the habit. She came here just the other day to sell her gold ring. I took pity on her and bought it. She saw me get my money from the trunk. She is the only one who knows where I keep money."

"But did you see her take it?" Grandmother protests. "She came to see me for a few minutes yesterday. There was no way she could have. I'll ask her about it when I see her. Don't jump to conclusions, especially with family members."

318

Two Sisters

"I don't care if she's a family member. She's guilty, Mother. You took the lowlife under your wings and now you let them steal from me."

Grandmother's body shakes as she tries to control herself and walks away. Ha shares Grandmother's fury. She feels hot on her cheeks and it is not because of the heat from the fierce sun rays. If eyes could generate heat, she would have burned Young Aunt alive with her stare. She empathizes with Tuoi and Le because they are poor like her. Young Aunt's association of "lowlife" with "stealing" is a stereotype that is not true. Mother always holds the high standard of being "pure and clean in poverty," and Ha appreciates Mother's teaching at this moment. She feels as though her own honor has been violated. She wants to state firmly and loudly for all to hear "Not every poor person steals." But just as other times, the words occur only in her mind, and do not materialize into actions.

Grandmother comes back to ask Ha and Vy to go fetch Tuoi. "Tell her to come as soon as possible." Ha and Vy take off in a flash. Ha has her own motive for being in a hurry. She is sure of Tuoi's innocence and wants Tuoi to know about this as soon as possible so that Tuoi can prepare her defense. Perhaps because Ha wants to reach Tuoi so badly, the distance from the Hoang estate to Tuoi's place seems to have lengthened. When they finally get to Tuoi's house, they find the door shut. Ha has a sensation of being watched as she pounds on the door. She calls out Tuoi's and Le's names in vain.

"They moved away. Don't you see the lock?" the lady next door says.

"Where did they go?" Ha asks.

Two Sisters

"I think they moved away for good."

A man, who must be the lady's husband, snaps, "How do you know if they moved away for good? We should keep out of people's business. Let's go inside and close the door."

"I just told the girls what I saw so they will not keep pounding at that door," the wife protests. Even so, she closes the door and disappears inside after her husband.

Ha and Vy walk to the back of the house and see no one. Ha wants to wait, hoping Tuoi and Le will come back from an errand, but Vy wants to go home to drink a glass of water because she is dry and thirsty from the heat. On the way home, Vy asks Ha what "weed" is. Ha explains that it is marijuana and says she does not believe that Le smokes weed. Ha thinks the reason people suspect that Le smokes it is because he's so thin. That's what Sixth Aunt and Young Aunt say, that marijuana users are skinny. Ha shudders when she looks at her skinny arms and wonders what people think of her.

"You're right. We came to his house many times and never saw him smoke, but where did he go? He knows we're coming. Why didn't he wait for us?" Vy's question is like a bell that suddenly rings after a long period of dormancy and it awakens a seed of doubt in Ha's mind. It is true that Tuoi and Le have never closed their door before. Ha recalls the time Le went to the general store to buy cigarettes. He had left the door open then, saying he did not want Ha and Vy to have to wait outside in the heat. Tuoi also said she wanted to leave the door open so they could come in any time. Tuoi was true to her words even when Le's illness was at its worst and the neighbors could look in. Being dizzy with many questions tumbling in her mind, Ha walks to the general store to look for Le. The proprietor says she has not seen Le

Two Sisters

that day, but Tuoi had come the previous day to pay off debts.

Ha walks away in disappointment. She slows down to catch words from a conversation concerning the two people that are so dear to her.

"I heard they moved away."

"These girls are their cousins. Why on earth didn't they tell their relatives that they moved?"

When Ha and Vy get home, they are bombarded with questions from their grandmother and aunts who have been waiting impatiently for their return. Upon hearing the news from Ha and Vy, Young Aunt breaks down in loud sobs and accuses Grandmother, "See, I told you. They fled after stealing from me. Do you still want to defend them?"

Seventh Aunt tries to comfort Young Aunt, but the latter is inconsolable. She utters phrases such as "ungrateful lot" and "mean as a devil" while babbling about her loss. In tears, she lists the precious things that were stolen which include a necklace with a cross pendant that was a souvenir and never worn, a gold plaque, jade and gold bracelets, pearl strings, and gold rings.

Grandmother seems lost in her own world. She slowly chews her areca-and-betel paste while avoiding looking at Young Aunt, as though ruminating about her own worries.

Young Aunt suddenly stops crying and looks sternly at Ha and Vy. "Why are you two still here? What do you want to stand under the sun for?"

Two Sisters

Ha and Vy start to scurry away but when they see Cuu hurry back from the errand Grandmother sent her on, they turn around and follow Cuu back to the patio. Cuu dutifully reports to Grandmother before even taking off her hat. "Ma'am, her landlady got busy with a commemoration at her house and couldn't come, but she said the couple already returned the house key. She also said everything was paid up and you do not have to worry about paying the rent."

Young Aunt bursts out in sobs again. "They are gone with all my things! There is no way I can get them back."

Ha freezes. *Was it not just yesterday when I had dinner with Sister Tuoi and Brother Le? How could it be?* Ha attentively listens to every word being said, as if the words carried life-and-death importance. Sixth Aunt fires several questions in rapid succession. "Did they leave things behind? Did the landlady say where they went? Does she know they did not tell us that they were leaving?"

"Landlady said the couple gave her all the pots and pans because they left in a hurry. Miss Tuoi's father is ill in Saigon."

Grandmother is at once relieved and worried at the same time. "They didn't tell me about her father being sick. I wonder how sick he is."

Seventh Aunt jeers, "That is just an excuse. Don't you worry about it." Turning to Cuu, she asks, "Did the landlady say anything else?"

Cuu hesitates, but eventually blurts out, "She said everyone knew he was addicted to marijuana and she worried the couple would not pay the rent."

Two Sisters

Young Aunt repeatedly bangs her head on her knee, moaning. "I've labored and saved for many years and in one day, they took it all." Looking up at Grandmother, she bitterly says, "It's all because of you. If you did not contact them, this would not have happened. Are you pleased, Mother?"

Sixth Aunt disappears for a while and comes back with an engraved box and gives it to Young Aunt. "Here, you can have all my jewelry. Don't be mean to Mother. Let her be."

Seventh Aunt opens her wallet and takes out a thick wad of bills. "This is to cover your loss. If it's not enough, I'll give you more."

Young Aunt accepts the offerings. In between whimpers, she says, "If they did not steal from me, I'd have double this amount."

Ha feels wet and hot on her cheeks. Not wanting people to know she cries, she walks away to the star apple tree. Vy follows. "You are sad because there is no one to help you with math, right?"

"Uh huh, I do not have Brother Le any more. No one will help me with math."

Vy is not sure how to comfort Ha. "I wish he's still here."

The big house resumes its regular rhythm after Sixth Aunt and Seventh Aunt leave to visit their grandparents' grave. Ha takes it as the sign that Young Aunt is satisfied with her compensation. She finds she does not care that much about Young Aunt's loss. But she is more keenly aware of the feelings she has toward Tuoi and Le. Their leaving has affected her deeply. She finds it hard to control her emotions.

Ha closes her eyes and envisions Tuoi and Le's rental house with herself in it. She sees Le lying on his bed next to the wall with a table and a chair at its side. She hears Le's gentle Saigon accent. The images of her being there yesterday and two days before and three days before come together, blur, and blend into one image – an image Ha is sure will stay with her for a long, long time.

CHAPTER THIRTY-TWO

Ha taps the ruler on the table, watching Vy's face. "Do you understand?"

"Yes, Teacher," Vy replies.

Ha points the ruler at the board, full of her own writing. She has set the board on the floor leaning against a chair. "Now that you understand, copy this to your notebook. Do good work."

"Yes, Teacher."

"Good."

Vy bends down, transcribing words from the board to her notebook. Ha feels important as if being a real teacher. She crosses her arms behind her back, walking to and fro and around her student Vy. She is immersed in her new role and does not notice Elder Uncle standing at the door at first. When she sees him, she stops in mid-stride while feeling ridiculous and nervous. She is not sure if he brings good or bad news. She manages a weak greeting. "Hello, Uncle."

Two Sisters

Elder Uncle nods at her. "Come with me." He walks away as quickly as he has appeared. Ha wastes no time in slipping her feet into a pair of plastic flip-flops and following him, leaving Vy alone in the little house. Elder Uncle walks into the big house, stops at his room, and motions Ha to come in. This is the first time Ha is invited into Elder Uncle's private world. She has butterflies in her stomach, not knowing what to expect. She figures she's going to get a lecture in either morality or academics and formulates a plan in her head to be agreeable to whatever he says so that she can be dismissed from this uncomfortable situation as quickly as possible. Elder Uncle motions her to sit down on a shiny black wood chair in the middle of the room. Ha tentatively lowers herself edgewise on the chair corner. From there, she observes the largest quantity of books she has ever seen contained in one single room. They are neatly arranged on bookshelves, in glass cabinets, and on his large desk. She glances at an open book on the desk. It is filled with foreign words she does not understand. Perhaps Elder Uncle is about to give her a lesson in a foreign language. If so, that would not be so bad. Ha relaxes a bit, pushing herself backward until her back is against the chair, and waits patiently.

Elder Uncle reappears from behind the bookshelf. He approaches Ha with a pair of scissors, a comb, and a towel in his hands. Ha looks at him with wide-opened eyes. He says, "I'm going to give you a haircut before you start school tomorrow."

Ha is immediately sorry for obediently uttering "Yes, Uncle," without considering if this is something she wants. Ha loves her long thick black hair, which is just like Mother's. Mother wants Ha to braid her own hair or tie it into a ponytail so that the hair does not cover up her thin face and, in Mother's opinion, darken it. Ha has known how to braid her own hair since she was in third grade when Mother began to go to the market early in the morning and Ha had to get Vy and herself ready for school. When Ha parts her hair to self-braid, Vy would gush that Ha does a great job because the part would be so straight as though Ha had eyes in the back of her head. Ha does not mind to be teased often by classmates who call her "Chinese" because she wears two braids. One time when Ha's hair was still loose after being washed, her cousin Nghia gave her a compliment on the smooth and beautiful hair. Nghia said if she had hair like Ha's, she would not ruin it by braiding it or tying it with a rubber band, but would display its beauty by leaving it loose and spreading it over her back. Ha said that she did not mind braiding it because it looked neat to both her mother and teacher and she wanted to please them. Thinking of Mother, Ha turns around to tell Elder Uncle she would need to ask for Mother's permission to have her hair cut, but Elder Uncle grasps her head and turns it back. "Sit straight so I can put a towel around you."

Ha gets a shiver when Elder Uncle's fingers touch her neck. He carefully pushes the edge of the towel under Ha's collar and unties the rubber bands that hold the braids together. Ha sits straight and still, feeling the teeth of a comb gently against her skull from the top of her head to the lower part of the nape. After combing Ha's hair, Elder Uncle moves her head this way and that with the precision of an engineer. He puts the comb down on the desk, picks up the pair of scissors, and begins to methodically cut Ha's hair. Watching lock after lock of hair falling down like water cascading from a high mountain above, Ha shudders and feels naked without the familiar feel of hair touching her skin on the neck.

As if reading Ha's thoughts, Elder Uncle gives her an upbeat assessment. "I'm giving you a 'demi-garçon' cut. It is the style most becoming for you."

Two Sisters

Ha is quiet in acquiescence even though she has no idea what a "demi-garçon" cut should look like. As more and more hair falls down, she feels lighter and lighter at the top. She is mournful for the loss of something she had been nurturing for years. Elder Uncle seems to take more time styling than cutting the hair. Watching sweat beading on his forehead, Ha figures that it must be a labor of love since it takes a lot out of Elder Uncle to execute a haircut.

Elder Uncle is still focused on his task when there is a knock on the door. When his niece[18] Chau announces her presence, he simply tells her to come in. Without turning to look at Chau, he curtly asks what she wants. As soon as Chau absorbs what is going on, she does not answer his question but gasps, "You cut her hair that short?"

When Chau tells Elder Uncle that she brings him mail, he dryly commands, "Just leave it on my desk."

Chau slowly approaches the desk while keeping an eye on Ha, looking concerned. Even as she leaves the room, she turns around to throw one last look at Ha. Seeing Chau's long hair, Ha cries inside for the loss of her hair even more; she wishes Elder Uncle were not too liberal with the scissors. If he had left the hair at shoulder length, she'd look more grown up. Ha is apprehensive, especially with the way Chau looked at her. She wants so badly to run home to look in a mirror to see how much damage has been done.

As if he could again read her thoughts, Elder Uncle hands Ha a tiny mirror. With butterflies in her stomach, Ha takes a look. But all she sees are her two big, anxious brown

---

[18] She is considered his niece in the Vietnamese culture, but technically she is his first cousin once removed.

eyes looking back at herself. She does not see her whole face, much less the hair on her head. Bending her head this way and that, she still cannot see the entire head.

Removing the towel from Ha's shoulders, Elder Uncle dismisses Ha and says he will take care of the mess on the floor. Ha tries to catch one more look in the mirror without success, before giving it back to her uncle. Elder Uncle reminds her to have everything ready for school and wait for him at the carport the next morning. He says he has already talked to Mother about taking her to school in his car.

Ha crosses her arms and says thank you to Elder Uncle as she leaves. As soon as she is out of his sight, she skips across the hall to run out of the big house as quickly as she can. Before she reaches the little house, Vy jumps out from underneath the star apple tree, takes a look at Ha, and laughs her head off. "Oh my God, you look so funny."

Ha brushes past Vy to run into the little house, retrieves a small rectangular mirror from the dresser, and stares at it. Her head is crowned with an up-side-down soot-covered cooking pot. The imaginary black pot frames her round face perfectly. Ha searches in vain for the Western beauty of the so-called "demi-garçon" cut. She is sure there is an implied promise of beauty which she fails to find – despite turning her head up and down, twisting it left and right, squinting her eyes, pursing her lips, smiling, pouting, and contorting her facial muscles in a multitude of ways.

Vy wants to know with a hint of worry. "Is he going to cut my hair, too?"

Ha shakes her head, dropping the mirror, and giving up on looking pretty. "No."

Vy heaves a sigh of relief. "Oh good, I like my long hair, but now we do not match."

"He says this style is...something French... Oh yes, something like 'deme gar song.'" Ha sadly runs her fingers along the short hairdo. "It sounds cool, but it doesn't look so cool."

"Are you sure he will not cut my hair?"

"He did not say anything about cutting your hair, but I think he will if you go to his school."

"I'll try to go to the public school. I don't want to go to his private school. Why did you let him cut your hair?"

"I don't know. I did not dare say no to him. I thought he would just cut it a little shorter. He said he already spoke to Mom about cutting my hair and giving me a ride to school."

"So you get to ride in his nice car. But do you know the results of your admission exam yet?"

"Mom thinks I flunked the exam for public school. That's why she wants me to go to Elder Uncle's school. If we wait until we know the results, it may be too late for me to register. But I don't know how Mom can afford the private school tuition."

They hear the dogs bark and know Mother is home. Mother looks happy as she puts the carrying pole against a coconut tree. "So I see Elder Uncle gave you a haircut."

Ha pouts. "Why didn't you tell me about it?"

"About what?"

Two Sisters

"I didn't want a haircut."

"You should be grateful that Uncle spent his precious time cutting your hair and not complain."

"But I don't like this style. It is even shorter than a doll's hair."

Mother tries to appease Ha. "It opens up your face and you look smart." When Mother sees that Ha still pouts, she snaps, "Why didn't you tell him you don't want a haircut then?"

Ha has no good reply. She realizes Mother and she are in the same situation. They are not in the position to decline offers from higher-ranking relatives. Mother tries to soothe Ha again. "Elder Uncle is not a skilled hairdresser, but you should feel lucky he wants to help. He is a smart and successful educator. You'll get his luck since he cuts your hair." Ha closes her eyes and shakes her head in disbelief. Mother is too superstitious for her taste. Mother continues with comforting words. "A bad haircut is not as permanent as being ugly. In a few months, your hair will grow and you can keep it long if you want." Then as if wanting to cheer Ha up, Mother pulls out two dresses from her shopping bag and gives them to Ha. "Go try these on."

"I have to wear these dresses to school?"

"You can wear anything you want. There is no uniform."

•

"You didn't get any for Vy?"

"You start school tomorrow. Vy does not start for a while. When I have money, I'll buy her dresses too."

Two Sisters

"I don't like to wear dresses with too many colors."

Vy chimes in, "Mom, buy me white dresses. I don't like colorful dresses either. I'll try to be accepted to public school so that I can wear a white Vietnamese dress as my uniform."

"It will save me money if you go to public school. But no matter what, I'll make sure the two of you finish your high school education."

Ha puts on a dress and asks Vy, "What do you think? How do I look?"

Vy giggles. "You look like one of those foreign girls on Elder Uncle's television."

"What does that mean? Am I pretty?"

"No. I don't like Western dresses. I just like white Vietnamese dresses."

"What do you know? Sometimes you say you hate Vietnamese dresses, and then sometimes you say you like them."

"Well, now I see how you look in a Western dress, I decide that I like Vietnamese dresses."

Ha silently puts the dresses away and walks to the window. The sun has gone down. Chau and Yen are watering the flower pots in front of the big house. The flowers have looked much better now since Chau and Yen came to live with Elder Aunt and Uncle. They are daughters of one of Father's cousins. They were sent here to attend the private school where Elder Uncle teaches. They came just

Two Sisters

after Cuu resigned and were willing to do the chores that Cuu used to do.

Ha feels comforted to know that Chau and Yen will also ride in Elder Uncle's car, but when she remembers the bus ride to Mother's village, she worries about getting carsick. She plans to bring plastic bags just in case. Ha does not relish the thought of having to behave in the presence of Elder Uncle, but what can she do? The new school is at least three times as far from home as her old elementary school. Furthermore, she does not know the way to the new school.

Running her hand over her short hair, Ha muses that her six years in elementary school will soon be only a memory. She knows that her long-term goal is to finish high school, attain a higher education, and be successful in life so she can help Mother. She does not have short-term wishes besides not having to behave in the presence of Elder Uncle. Since both the private and public secondary schools are far from home, no matter which school she goes to, she will probably still need to get a ride from Elder Uncle and thus, is still far from being free.

Two Sisters

CHAPTER THIRTY-THREE

•

It is an important event for residents of the city of Nha-Trang when the two public secondary schools, a boys' school and a girls' school, announce their admission results. Speculation ran rife for several days preceding the event, and the day itself generates excitement and gossip. It is a happy day for the lucky students who are admitted to the public schools, for they not only save their parents money, but they also bring honor and pride to their families.

The results have been posted at the school grounds since morning, but Ha was not aware of the special day until her neighbor Hong invited her to go to check their status. Ha and Vy walk with Hong and her younger sister Hoa to Nha-Trang Secondary Girls' School. A wall of people has already formed in front of the fence behind which names are posted on several lists. Ha stands on tiptoe, trying to look over the heads of people in front of her, and silently prays for her name to be on one of the lists. She moves forward after a few girls in front of her squeal in happiness upon seeing their names and leave together in noisy chit-chat. Looking up and down the list in front of her and not finding her name, Ha is

Two Sisters

disappointed. She perks up when Vy yells out, "I see your name!"

Ha immediately runs over to Vy. "Where do you see it?"

"Here. Your number is 113."

"Oh my God, it *IS* my name," Ha squeals just as those who have found their names.

After confirming that her own name is indeed posted, Ha helps Hong look for Hong's name. They run their fingers down all the lists and do not see it, although Ha sees the name of her cousin Tin, daughter of Seventh Aunt. Hoa reminds Hong that she can try again the year after. Hong says she should have stayed in the exam preparation class instead of dropping out when she felt she was being punished unfairly by the teacher. She was slapped in front of the whole class for asking a classmate to repeat the teacher's instructions because the class was too noisy for her to hear. She faults the teacher for not keeping order in the classroom and not acting professionally. She did not tell her mother about this because it would always be her fault no matter what happened. Her mother was too busy working to notice that Hong no longer went to class. Hong worries that her mother will find out if she discusses the effectiveness of the preparation class with the teacher.

Ha says that luck plays a big part in her passing the exam. On the day of the exam, Chau took her to school early and bought her a bowl of mung-bean pudding for good luck. Chau says that mung beans and red beans bring good luck, whereas black beans bring bad luck. Ha was not the only one who went to school early to eat mung-bean pudding; she saw many other students do the same thing. Ha does not normally eat sweets for breakfast, but she did her best to finish the

Two Sisters

sweet pudding that day. Besides the mung-bean diet, Ha followed Chau's instructions carefully. She went to bed early the night before. At the exam, she read everything carefully before giving an answer and did not omit any questions. She credits Le for tutoring her in math. Thinking of Le, Ha chokes up. "I wish I could tell Brother Le that I passed the exam, but he is no longer here. I will never forget him and I will always be grateful to him. He helped me understand math and pass the exam."

CHAPTER THIRTY-FOUR

It is early evening when Ha and Vy get back home. While Ha is still latching the gate, Vy runs in and calls out to Mother. "Mom, Mom, Sister Ha passed the exam!"

Mother comes to the door. "You are already nine years old and yet you still act like a small child. Didn't I teach you properly? Do you have to scream for the whole neighborhood to hear?"

"Mom, I'm so happy for Sister Ha. She passed the exam to go to Nha-Trang Secondary Girls' School."

Mother smiles. "I already knew. I am also very happy. What took you two so long?"

Feeling deflated like a balloon that has lost its air, Vy lowers her voice. "How did you find out, Mom?"

"From Seventh Uncle and Aunt. They came to inform Grandma that Tin passed the exam. They told us that they saw Ha's name as well."

Two Sisters

"Are they still here, Mom?" Ha asks while removing her flip-flops.

"Yes, they are. Put your flip-flops back on. Let's go say hi and tell your relatives the good news."

"Why do we need to tell them?"

"So they will be happy for you."

"They will be happy for me?"

"Yes."

Mother promptly takes Vy's hands and heads toward the big house. Ha follows behind, not exactly sure why Mother feels the need to inform the paternal relatives about her being admitted to the public school. *Has it not always been just the three of us who share happiness or commiserate misfortunes together?* Ha has never thought of sharing news, good or bad, with the whole Hoang extended family. With the good news, Mother seems to exude a newfound confidence with each step she takes. She waltzes into the big house without waiting to be invited. She happily calls on Ha to announce to Grandmother the good news in front of everyone who has gathered in Grandmother's private guest room. Ha is shocked to see, for the first time, the ease and confidence Mother displays. At first, she is not sure how to proceed, but quickly follows Mother's cue. She walks with chin up to face Grandmother, crosses her arms, and says, "Grandma, I announce to you that I passed the admission exam to Nha-Trang Secondary Girls' School."

"Very good, my granddaughter." Grandmother smiles and motions Ha to come closer. "I already received the good news."

Two Sisters

Seeing her cousin Tin already standing to the left of Grandmother's inlaid chair, Ha timidly walks over to the right side. Grandmother puts Ha's and Tin's hands on her stomach, looks to her left and then to her right, and says, "This year I have two granddaughters being accepted to Nha-Trang Secondary Girls' School. I am happier than if I had received gold and pearls. I am so proud of both of you."

"There are many more candidates this year than other years," Seventh Aunt gushes. "Mrs. Tai spent a lot of money on prep classes for her daughter and the girl did not pass. The same is true with Mrs. Thuc's daughter who crammed day and night. Daughters of women I know from my business all failed. We are so blessed that we have two family members who passed the exam."

Young Aunt repeats an adage: *"Learn by wits, compete by luck."* She adds, "No surprise here. There are many smart students who failed."

"Where is the luck in this?" Elder Aunt protests, her face red with indignation. "If their answers were not correct, would they have passed?"

Ha thinks Elder Aunt must be very proud of her grandsons who had previously passed the admission exams to the Nha-Trang Secondary Boys' School.

Mother softly says, "Ha is lucky to pass. She's been sick and is not as smart as others. Perhaps the repeat of fourth grade gave her a good foundation."

Elder Aunt looks straight at Mother with a raised voice. "Ha passed because she is smart. Fourth grade is not the same as fifth grade. Anyone with the Hoang blood in their veins must be smart."

Two Sisters

Elder Aunt stuns the relatives into silence. They are shocked to hear her promote blood connection and praise the lineage of her husband's side for she is generally known to be selfish and cold. They are moved and appreciative of her gesture. When Ha looks up, Elder Aunt's eyes lock with hers. Ha sees a direct and honest look of respect for her in Elder Aunt's eyes. Ha's heart wells up with unnamed emotions that are hard to control. Her lips quiver as she is about to muster a thank-you to Elder Aunt. But conflicting thoughts emerge and crowd out her voice. She shudders to think about the scorn and belittling that would surely follow if she had not passed. The imaginary words are shrill and clear in her mind. *"It's no surprise. You know the Giu children, a dirty and lazy bunch."* Ha recalls the nights she stayed up to study under the dim oil lamp, her desperation for a tutor, and the countless times she had cried under the star apple tree. The more she remembers, the more bitter she feels. *Should success by any member of the extended family be ascribed to his or her efforts alone, and not to the support and love given by other members as a whole? Should poverty of any one member not be a concern for all? Does a member's success bring pride to all, but his or her failure should be suffered by him or her alone?* Ha has seen gifts and parties lavished on the relatives who passed exams, but no one ever gave emotional support or encouragement to those who failed. She wants to obtain answers to questions that can resolve her conflicting thoughts, but knowing she is only a twelve-year-old girl who would not be taken seriously, she dares not open her mouth. Besides, she does not wish to destroy the ambiance of honor and pride that rarely happens within the four walls of the Hoang estate.

Elder Aunt happily announces the news to her husband when he walks in. "Dear, Ha is admitted to Nha-Trang Secondary Girls' School. You should give her something as a reward."

Two Sisters

"Really?" Elder Uncle raises his spectacles and appears impressed. "Very good, Ha. So now you won't have to attend my private school."

"I passed the exam, too," Tin says.

Elder Uncle nods in understanding. "Yes, of course. You passed because of your ability, whereas Ha passed because her father gave her a blessing."

Ha cannot believe what she has just heard. She looks at Elder Uncle in astonishment. *He also believes in Dad's spirit as I do? So he does not think I am smart as Elder Aunt does.* She now understands why he has arranged with Mother for her to attend the private school where he teaches before they learned of the admission results, but never bothered to talk to Seventh Uncle and Aunt about Tin. He had been sure of Tin's admission but not hers. Ha stares at her uncle, knowing that she does not see him often and she can count on the fingers of one hand the number of times the two of them had any meaningful interaction, and is not sure of her feelings toward him.

Elder Uncle's voice booms across the room. "It's good that Ha was admitted to the public school," he says to Mother, "but you should see what you can do to assure her success and a passing grade each year. It is not easy to maintain good grades at this level."

"Yes, I will do my best," Mother concurs.

"Why don't you and the girls come live with us?" Seventh Uncle proposes to Mother. "You can help us in our business and Ha and Tin can go to school together. I'll hire a tutor to help the girls in the evening."

343

Two Sisters

Seventh Aunt shakes her head. "But Ha doesn't want to live with us. If she runs home and gets sick because she has nothing to eat like she did before, we'll be blamed."

Mother says, "I've expanded my business and I am doing much better than before. But I should stay home to take care of the girls. I don't think I should go far again. Ha is a sickly girl."

Seventh Aunt opens her crocodile wallet and hands Ha some money. "I give you this to celebrate your admission to the public school. You can spend it on anything you like."

"Thank you, Auntie. I'll ask Mom to buy me white uniform materials."

Seventh Aunt nods as she bids goodbye. She announces an upcoming party for Tin to which everyone will be invited, but the date is not yet set. As Seventh Aunt's family is leaving, Chau and Yen arrive on their bicycles. They also have a gift for Ha. "Here is a gift from the two of us," Yen says as she hands a small box to Ha. Ha is happy to see it is a pencil box with a lid kept closed with a magnet. Chau and Yen know exactly what Ha wants because Ha has always admired Chau's pencil box.

Elder Uncle walks away and comes back with a thick book. "I give you this French-Vietnamese dictionary as a practical gift that will help you with your studies."

Young Aunt and Sixth Aunt each gives Ha money, telling her she should save for a bicycle. Grandmother says to Ha, "I give you more money than Tin because Tin's mother is well off. Study well so you'll get a high school diploma." Wiping tears from her face, Grandmother

Two Sisters

continues, "Too bad your father is not alive to see you today."

Ha is again filled with emotions. She cries inside for the loss of Father. As they walk back to their little house, Vy whispers softly, "You have so many gifts. Why do you cry?"

"I am very happy that I passed the exam, but I wish Dad were here with us."

"I will study hard so I'll pass the exam and go to the same school with you."

"And we will finish high school and get high school diplomas."

"Yes, we will pass the exam for the high school diploma."

Looking up at the power lines that are tangled in the coconut leaves, Ha says, "And we will have money to bring electricity to our house. We will have our own power lines. If we depend on our relatives, the little house will stay dark forever."

CHAPTER THIRTY-FIVE

Ha and Vy do not know what to think when Mother brings home a stranger and tells them to call this person "Sixth Aunt." Mother includes the supposed Sixth Aunt in the family dinner. Sixth Aunt, wiping tears off her eyes, chokes up. "Thank you for your kindness. Without you, I do not know where to turn. I likely would die. I do not know when my wallet was stolen. It's hard to manage as a woman."

Mother says, "Please eat and don't worry about anything. There is no way to know when bad luck comes. Make yourself at home. You can stay with us tonight before taking a bus home tomorrow."

"But I have no money for a bus ticket. My ma is very sick and waits each minute to see me."

Mother looks at Sixth Aunt with compassion. "Don't worry. I'll give you the bus money."

Ha and Vy glance at each other. They can tell they share the same uneasy feeling. This Sixth Aunt looks suspicious to them. Why, the woman darts her eyes here and there, watching Mother's every movement, seemingly searching for something. Ha and Vy dare not tell Mother how they feel, since children are to be seen and not heard – and besides, what if they are wrong?

Sixth Aunt's eyes brighten up at the promise of money. "I am very much grateful," she says, a little too eagerly.

"Nonsense. It's normal to help others. I was in hard times before, so I am ready to help those in need."

"You do good things and will not have hard times," Sixth Aunt predicts.

"I hope to pass the blessings to my daughters so they won't have to suffer as I did. It does not matter much if I have to suffer some more."

Sixth Aunt quickly surveys the house. "Why do you say that? You've done well to own a city house like this, much bigger than my country house."

"I am a country girl, too. I followed my husband to the city but I am not wealthy. My husband died, leaving me with two daughters since they were babies. Now they are this big."

Sensing that they are being observed, Ha and Vy look down at their rice bowls, avoiding eye contact with the woman who has not gained their trust. Mother is oblivious to their reaction and continues her saga. "I had to work hard to raise my daughters all by myself. I was so poor that when my father died, I did not have money to buy a bus ticket to attend the funeral. People talked. That's why I feel for you. Tonight you sleep on my bed with me and I'll tell you all about my life."

Two Sisters

Sixth Aunt accepts Mother's help readily and assimilates herself easily to the new environment as though she were a close friend or relative of the family. After dinner, Mother lights the oil lamp and takes out a square handkerchief from the plastic basket that she takes to the market with her each day. With Sixth Aunt next to her, Mother opens the handkerchief to reveal a pad of bills which springs open from the folded position. Mother must have taken great care in folding the bills because they are lined up neatly with no loose edge and they are put in the order of their values. The smaller bills are inside of the larger ones, so that when they open up, the top bill is of the smallest denomination. Pulling out a few of the top bills, Mother gives them to her newfound friend. "This is for your bus fare. You should hurry home to look after your ma. I feel for her. It is tough to be elderly and sick."

Sixth Aunt trembles. "This is more than enough. I do not know how to repay you."

"Oh, forget about it. I'm happy to help. When your ma gets better, come back to visit us. Who knows? Maybe my business will take me to your village and I'll see you then."

"Oh yes, I'll come back to invite you and your girls to my country house."

"You must be tired. Let's get ready for bed."

Mother admonishes Sixth Aunt for casually putting the money in her small leather bag. "No wonder you got your money stolen. You have to hide your bills like I do, so no one will see."

"Right, I'll hide the money under my clothes."

Two Sisters

Ha and Vy leave the adults to themselves and push their conversation out of their mind. After washing dishes and finishing their homework, they are ready for bed. Mother puts a little oil lamp on the chair next to the bed in case Sixth Aunt needs to go to the bathroom during the night. Perhaps because they are not used to having any kind of light in the bedroom – or because they have so much to talk about to each other, especially the doubt they have about the strange woman – Ha and Vy have a hard time falling asleep, but they stay quiet because they share the same space with the adults whose whispered conversation soon lulls them to sleep.

Before daybreak, Ha is awakened by Mother's frantic calling. "Sixth, Sixth, where are you?"

Ha pokes her head through the mosquito net. "Did she go to the bathroom?"

"I woke up and saw the front door open. I already looked for her in the kitchen and bathroom."

Ha climbs out of bed. "I'll go look."

"Why don't you walk in the garden to see if she's there? But it's four in the morning, be quiet so you won't wake up the big house."

Ha walks out and looks all over the garden, but sees no one. Mother jerks open her plastic basket and throws its content on the floor. Even after turning the basket up-side-down to completely empty it, Mother still does not find what she looks for. She gets more and more agitated. "I am doomed! Oh God, my handkerchief is not here."

Two Sisters

Ha walks over to the altar room to light the large oil lamp and brings it to Mother. "I think Sixth Aunt took your money."

Mother turns pale. "How could I be so stupid as to allow a stranger into my house, dear God?" Running her hands through every item on the floor as though wishing them to turn into the money she has lost, Mother says, "Ha, please look through everything again and recheck my bag. It is a sin to accuse someone before we know the truth."

Ha inspects each item on the floor as Mother instructs and feels the need to tell Mother her fear. "Mom, I think that Sixth Aunt is gone. Otherwise we would have already found her. She can hear us if she is in the garden."

Mother looks Ha in the eye. "So did you have a bad feeling about this person from the beginning?" When Ha nods, Mother waves her hands at Ha. "Why didn't you say anything to me?"

Ha immediately gives Mother a spiel as though it is a memorized piece of speech that has been lying dormant and now has an outlet to bubble to the surface. "You did not ask me. You told us not to interrupt the adults. You told us not to judge a book by its cover. I didn't know if I was right." Ha lowers her voice when she sees dark shadows in the garden. She becomes unsure of herself. "What if she's still here? Do you think we'd hear the dogs if she walked out through the garden?"

Mother picks up the oil lamp and extends it toward the bedroom to confirm Sixth Aunt's absence. "I looked everywhere for her before you woke up. I'm sure I put the handkerchief with the money back in the basket before going to bed last night. When this woman gave the dogs bread yesterday, I thought she did not want to waste food; but now it is clear that she planned ahead and wanted the dogs to be familiar with her scent."

Mother puts her elbows on her knees while holding her head in her hands and begins to cry. Ha puts everything back into the basket. "Did you lose the business principal?"

"I still have some merchandise left and that will give us some money when I sell, but I won't have enough money to stock more merchandise."

Ha brings up the courage to ask, "Do you have anything to sell?"

At that, Mother jumps and runs to the dresser. "Please God, let it be that she did not know about this." The look on Mother's face bodes bad news. "Oh my God, everything is gone!" Turning over rags and worn-out shirts used to hide her "treasure" in the dresser, Mother mumbles to herself. "Just the other day I added five ounces of gold and hid it here. How did she know where to find it?" Mother's body sways and she looks like a lunatic from an asylum. She suddenly lets out a piercing scream as though a sword just slashed through her body. "What an ungrateful and immoral woman! Devil with no soul! I gave her shelter, food, and money. How could she steal everything from me?"

Ha is shaking herself and has to lean against the dresser for support. She feels her brain freeze as she stands there with her mouth open. There is nothing she can do or say to help the situation and alleviate Mother's grief. Mother flings the old shirts in all directions and bangs her head on the floor. "I have lost everything, oh God. Let me die. What do I live for? I worked hard and all the sweat and labor were in vain."

Two Sisters

Ha jerks her body into a walking frenzy, trying to pull Mother up by the arm. "Mom, don't die and leave us alone. Please think of your daughters and have pity on us."

Ha's shout wakes up Vy who has been asleep and oblivious to the drama of the little house. Seeing Mother struggle on the floor and hearing "suicide," Vy jumps on top of Mother, holding her as to dear life, crying. "I am so scared, Mom. Please stop."

Mother's face stays glued to the floor. Her voice is now a desperate whimper. "The immoral woman deceived me and already killed me. She took everything we had."

Ha feels the need to fill Vy in. "Sixth Aunt stole money from Mom and is gone."

Mother's face is drained of color. "Not just money, she stole our gold, too."

As the reality of the loss sinks in, hopelessness fills Ha's being. "What about the gold you keep for our dowry? Is that also gone?"

"Yes, Daughter. Everything is gone."

"This Sixth Aunt is so evil," Ha manages to say.

"Do you know where she lives, Mom?" Vy asks.

- Mother shakes her head. "She said she lived in Suoi-Dau Village, but it's a lie. Even if she lives there, there is no way I can find her without an address." Mother slaps her head with her hand. "God, why didn't you warn me about this woman? I denied my children food and clothes, just so that everything I worked so hard for was gone in a minute. Why am I so stupid, God?"

Ha is the first to regain her composure. "Mom, let's not cry about it anymore. When I grow up, I'll give you back what you lost."

"And when will it be, Daughter? How do we survive right now? Where do I find money to do business and pay Vy's tuition?"

Vy lowers her eyes. She feels bad that she did not pass the admission exam to be accepted to the secondary public school. Even though Mother gets a fifty-percent discount to the private school where Elder Uncle teaches, the tuition still creates a hardship for Mother. It is painful for Vy each morning when she walks to school with Ha. When they get to Nha-Trang Secondary Girls' School, Ha goes in while Vy continues to walk alone to her private Le-Quy-Don Secondary School.

Ha sighs and looks out at the empty garden while sensing Vy's guilt hanging in the air. The sun has come up. The sunlight spreads over the flowers that sway gently in the dawn breeze, welcoming the warmth of the day. Suddenly, the flower stems are pushed to the sides and a path opens up like the parting of the Red Sea and the woman called Sixth Aunt appears. She walks toward the little house with a smiling face. The smiling face grows bigger and bigger until it pops at Ha's face.

Mother breaks the silence. "Help me put these away and get ready for school."

Ha blinks with a start. The smiling face disappears. In its place, she sees Mother's reddened eyes on a haggard face.

CHAPTER THIRTY-SIX

Mother places the shopping bags on the floor when she returns from her shopping trip. "Help me bring food inside. I'll clean and set up the altars."

• Ha and Vy are excited to see so much food in the bags. "What day is it? Do we have a commemoration?"

"No," Mother says. "It's been a while since we did anything to remember and pay respect to the ancestors. I don't want to leave the altars empty for so long."

Vy pulls out the food from one shopping bag. "Look, there are all sorts of cakes and meats. Wow, you bought so much, Mom."

"Don't put the meat near the Buddha's altar," Mother reminds Vy.

Vy's mouth is agape when she sees shiny red apples, juicy pears, large oranges with stem and leaves still attached, and saliva-inducing yellow papayas. Vy swallows hard.

Two Sisters

"Why do we have fancy fruit, Mom? And even special flowers, too!"

Ha happily goes through the three shopping bags. She is relieved to see Mother smile for the first time since the woman called Sixth Aunt left. Today, Ha tells herself, she will not have to hear Mother's laments or look at Mother's sad face. She figures Mother has found Sixth Aunt and was able to reclaim everything Sixth Aunt had taken from them. She cheerfully takes part in helping Mother set up the altars in anticipation of the good food they are going to enjoy.

At dinner, Mother pushes her daughters to eat. "Eat more, girls. I feel bad that I haven't been able to give you a proper meal in a long while."

"You eat with us, Mom."

"I am so happy that I don't feel hungry," Mother says.

"I know that Sixth Aunt gave back the money and gold she took. Right, Mom?" Ha inquires.

Mother's face darkens at the mention of the supposed Sixth Aunt. "That woman deceived us and is long gone. Don't mention her any more or I'll get a headache."

Ha's brow furrows. "Then how can you afford this?"

"Keep eating. I'll tell you everything."

Seeing Ha's questioning eyes, Mother reassures her, "I didn't do anything wrong. Don't worry." Then she beams. "I just won a lottery."

Two Sisters

Ha blushes with shame and guilt for doubting Mother. "I did not think that. It's just that this morning you were still complaining about Sixth Aunt and now we have all this food."

"How much did you win, Mom?" Vy asks.

"I won fourteen hundreds dongs."

"Wow, that's a lot, Mom," Vy gushes. "Does that mean you can buy a few ounces of gold?"

"Mom, you're so lucky to win the lottery," Ha says. "But Mom, why did you spend the money? Why didn't you use it for your business?"

"Don't worry, I still have some money," Mother says. "And...from now on, I will not be so thrifty anymore. I saved and deprived the two of you and then lost it all. I want you two to enjoy what we have at the moment."

Ha's thoughts turn to the lottery cart near the street corner she passes each day on the way to and from school. It is in front of the Tan-Quang theater. Once a week, colorful pieces of torn lottery tickets are scattered all over the ground. One day, out of curiosity, she stopped to pick up a few to look at and learned how much each ticket costs. She says to Mother, "Each lottery ticket costs only two dongs. You are so lucky to win fourteen hundred."

"I didn't win a National lottery ticket."

"So what did you win?"

"I win the 'De' lottery."

"What is it, Mom?"

"It is not legal. The police would put the De lottery seller in jail."

"Mom, why do you play the De lottery when you have to hide from the police?"

"The De lottery is much easier to win than the National lottery. You bet on numbers that are called heads and tails."

"I don't understand."

"That's okay. You should not learn about gambling."

"What about you, Mom? Why do you gamble?"

"My business friends play, so I thought I'd try just once. I couldn't believe I won the first time I played."

"I know the results of the National lottery came out this evening. Does it have anything to do with heads and tails?"

"Yes, the first two digits of the winning lottery ticket make the head and the last two digits make the tail."

"How do you play?"

"You can bet any head or tail numbers you want, from 00 to 99."

"So which numbers did you bet?"

"I picked 19 for both head and tail. I bet twenty dongs for head and ten dongs for tail."

Two Sisters

"Mom, you spent thirty dongs? That's a lot to lose if you don't win."

"I planned to play only once and I wanted to try my luck. I played high so that if I won, it'd be big. Losing another thirty dongs is nothing compared to what I've already lost."

"But thirty is a lot for us, Mom. If you work hard and save again, we'll get it back."

Mother sighs. "When will it be, Daughter? I do not have much profit each day, and yet there are so many expenses. My labor for the past several years was in vain." Looking at Ha's worried face, Mother adds, "Don't worry. I just tried it once and I won't play again."

Vy is interested in the lottery and not ready to drop the fascinating subject. "Did you win with the head or the tail, Mom?"

Mother looks pleased as if Vy had scratched an itchy part of her body. She smiles pleasantly. "I knew it would be the head and bet more money there and I was right."

"How did you know?"

"A butterfly landed on my head. My friends told me nineteen is the number for butterflies, so that's the number I played."

Vy laughs as if being tickled. "Ha ha. The butterfly on your head becomes the head number nineteen. That's so funny that butterflies have a number. And you're so smart. No wonder you won. Does each animal have a number, Mom?"

Two Sisters

"Yes."

"So what's the number for dogs?"

"Eleven."

"And goats?"

"Thirty-five."

"Ha ha. That's the same number for old men who run after much younger women."

Ha is mortified. She is sure Mother is going to sternly scold or punish Vy since the subject of old men chasing young ladies is certainly not appropriate for a girl of Vy's age. Ha quickly glances at Mother but to her surprise, Mother laughs with Vy. Vy is encouraged "What's the number for lizards?"

"Ninety-nine, the last number."

"Does the Kitchen God have a number, Mom?"

"Of course, it's thirty-nine or forty.'

Ha frowns and puts down her chopsticks. "How do you know so much about lottery numbers, Mom? I thought you only learned about the lottery today."

"I have a list. When I collected my winnings, I saw the same list posted there, too. I just remember a few of them."

Vy does calculations in her head. "Mom, you played twenty dongs for the head and won fourteen hundred dongs.

Two Sisters

That means the payout is seventy to one. Right, Mom?" Vy gets excited. "I want to play with my breakfast money."

Mother turns serious. "No, you may not. It would be a bad habit that would follow you the rest of your life."

Vy does not seem upset. "Okay. But after we clean up, can I see the list of animals and their numbers? I just want to know."

Ha is confused and does not like what is going on. Mother is clearly contradictory in her actions and words. Ha thinks gambling is wrong, but is it wrong to bring food to the table? Recalling the hungry days when there was nothing to eat but old rice and fish sauce, Ha feels comforted. She is also happy to see Mother and Vy laugh, a rare event indeed. A small part of Ha hopes that Mother will continue to play and win the lottery.

Later that night, when it is dark and quiet, the people in the little house resume their daily activities under the dim oil lamp. The silence is broken by Vy's reciting her lesson in a regular and monotone voice, which sounds to Ha like a monk's chanting.

CHAPTER THIRTY-SEVEN

The sunlight is fading. Sitting cross-legged next to a basket of yarn and knitting materials on the doorstep of the little house, Vy moves her hands back and forth in quick motions and in sync with the clacking sounds of the knitting needles in her hands. She is no less active with her mouth as with her hands. "Today is Tuesday. I'm sure Mom will win. She is so good at the lottery. She comes up with the right animal each time. The other day when she won, I thought 99 was a number for lizards, but she said it was for giant butterflies. Did you know butterflies have a series of numbers: 19, 59, and 99, Sister Ha?"

"I know," Ha replies from the kitchen, over the sizzling sound of sand roasting. "Didn't Mom also win with 91 when she saw a small butterfly up-side-down on a flower bush? I don't know what animal she picked today, but she can't keep winning."

"Mom likes the number 19. She says she sees butterflies all the time and she thinks they're fairies."

Two Sisters

Ha's voice has a hint of disapproval and irony. "I don't understand Mom. She said she wanted to play only once."

"But she's so good. It will be a waste of her talent if she doesn't play. Besides, she wins so many times, it does not matter if she loses once."

"I worry because Mom's bets get bigger and bigger. If she loses even once, it will wipe out all the gains."

Vy concentrates to make sure she has exactly twenty knit stitches before asking Ha for instructions to make an increase, which Ha is happy to do. "Pull the yarn over the needle and make another knit stitch. Do that twice before going to another row. Then do purl stitches."

After giving Vy some time to complete her task, Ha asks, "How did it go?"

"I don't know yet."

Ha's voice is less than gentle. "You already made a sock. How can you not remember?"

"What are you so grumpy for?"

Ha raises her voice. "What do you mean? I just say you should pay attention when you knit. Otherwise, your socks will not look good."

"You get to learn how to knit at school and practice with your friends. I only learn from you and can't be as fast. If I knew it was this hard, I would not knit."

Ha feels contrite. "I'm sorry. Go on and you'll have a pair of socks. Don't be mad at me."

Two Sisters

"I just finished the knit row and have holes on both sides as I want," Vy exclaims happily. "Now I remember what to do, you don't have to remind me anymore."

Ha carries a heavy pot out of the kitchen. She spreads a piece of newspaper on the ground and dumps the pot's content on it.

"Did you roast sand?" Vy asks.

"Yes."

"Why is the color so strange?"

"This is the color of Kiki's fur. I worked very hard to make this color."

Vy puts down her knitting materials and squats down next to Ha. "Wow. You are so good in matching Kiki's fur color."

Ha rakes the fur-colored sand with a pair of chopsticks. "Yes, I mixed brown and orange and a few other colors. I wanted to paint a picture of Kiki."

"Where did you learn how to do this?"

"From my art teacher. I learned to mix different colors to create a unique color. I'll teach you." Picking up the sand and letting it run down her fingers, Ha says, "The sand is cool now. Do you want to see the picture I drew of Kiki?"

Ha brings the sand inside their house and shows Vy a large piece of drawing paper. "What do you think?"

"It looks just like Kiki, the way he sits. You're very good. Now what do you do with the sand?"

"I'll put glue on the picture and pour sand over it. When it dries, I'll turn it upside down to let the loose sand fall out. Then I'll color Kiki's eyes and the background."

Vy attentively watches Ha work on the picture. "You still miss Kiki?"

"I loved Kiki more than Yellow because Kiki watched the house and was easy to take care of," Ha says while shaking loose sand off the drawing. When she is satisfied with the result, she starts coloring the background. "Yellow acts like a Japanese prince. He just wants to sleep and eat fancy food. It was my fault that Kiki died."

"No, it was not your fault."

"I know what I did. Since I fell on Kiki from the star apple tree while he was sleeping, he stopped eating and then died."

"But Young Aunt and Sixth Aunt said Kiki died of old age."

"They didn't know what happened."

"They know everything because they are adults."

Ha stops coloring to look straight at Vy and speaks in an authoritative tone. "Did you imply I don't know anything? Of course I know what I did. You were not there when I fell on Kiki. Don't talk back to your older sister. That's rude."

Two Sisters

"I only talk back when you're wrong. I know that you fell on Kiki, but he was okay after that. You just want to say it's your fault to be important."

"Don't talk back to me when you do not make sense. Shut up."

"No."

Ha puts her brush down. "You dare to be rude to me?"

"I'm not rude. I'm just telling the truth."

Ha cups her hands around her ears. "I'm not listening."

"Kiki died because he was old."

Ha's eyes widen as she points her finger at Vy's forehead, looking ferocious. "Go away. Don't look at my picture."

"I'm not going anywhere. This is my house, too."

Ha stands up, arms akimbo. Vy does the same. They glare at each other with fiery red eyes. Just then Mother walks in. Mother is angry at their quarreling. She looks even more ferocious than her daughters. "What are you two doing? You have nothing else to do but fight?"

Ha and Vy jump. They separate from each other and go to opposite sides of the table while continuing to glare at each other. Mother points to the floor. "Look around you. The house is a mess with paper, sand, and yarn. It looks just like a market." Mother walks outside and goes berserk. "And you left a black pot right at the front door! No wonder I had bad luck." Going into the kitchen, Mother's voice rises. "Oh

Two Sisters

my God, look at all this, you left colors all over the place. You even colored our rice bowls. I can't believe this."

Coming back into the little house, Mother points her finger at her daughters. "Is this how you take care of the house? Go lie down on the bed. You are not helpful as any daughter should be." Mother then goes to the garden where she snatches a few star apple branches and starts stripping off their leaves.

Ha and Vy know the routine and exactly what they are about to get as they climb on the bed. Mother moves swiftly as though in a hurry. She does not even take off her flip-flops at the door. Upon entering the bedroom, she sits down on her bed and immediately strikes Ha's bottom with the star apple branch she holds in her hand. "This is for leaving the house a mess and not being an example for your little sister."

Ha's body jerks in pain. The sudden lash stuns her. She rubs her bottom while bursting out in sobs. "Remove your hand or I'll break it," Mother commands. Ha removes her hand, but has a hard time recovering from the shock of being struck without having a lecture first as usual. She did not have time to prepare herself mentally. Moreover, she feels that she is being punished without a good cause. She whimpers in bitterness.

"Who put the black pot in front of the house?" Mother interrogates.

Ha looks up, intending to explain to Mother that she used the pot to roast the sand to create colors for a very important art contest at school. But when she sees fury in Mother's eyes, she simply says, "I did."

Two Sisters

Ha frantically raises her arm to block the rod that comes down repeatedly. Mother is in a frenzy and continues to strike Ha's bottom and right arm, as though that would relieve her disappointment in losing the lottery. "So you left the black pot in front of the house to bring me bad luck, huh? What kind of daughter are you to bring harm to your own mother?"

Ha has never seen Mother this angry before. When her arm gets tired from blocking the blows, Ha lowers it and resigns to bury her head in the pillow, hoping the striking will stop. When Ha finally gets a relief from the rod, she hears Vy's scream.

"Here's for fighting with your sister and for crying to bring me bad luck."

The little house is filled with sobs. Mother makes Ha and Vy stand up to apologize.

"Mom, I apologize. I will not leave the house a mess from now on," Ha says.

"Mom, I will not fight with my sister anymore. You can hit me even more if I do again," Vy says.

Mother speaks in an even, unemotional tone. "Fine. Now go clean up before dinner. Let's see if there is anything to eat today after you brought bad luck to the house."

While cleaning up, Ha pulls Mother's shopping bag aside and notices lottery tickets scattered among other things. She knows for sure then that Mother had bet on many numbers and had lost. Ha feels a sharp stab at her heart as she mentally adds up the costs of these tickets. Ha painfully understands the reason for the "punishment" she and Vy just received.

As Ha prepares for dinner and pours fish sauce on a little bowl, she sighs with the newfound realization that superstition has gotten the better of Mother. Mother must truly believe that her daughters had brought bad luck to the house by leaving a black pot on the doorstep.

CHAPTER THIRTY-EIGHT

Vy runs breathlessly toward Ha who sits beneath their star apple tree and appears to be listening attentively to something. "Mom lost again, Sister Ha."

"Can you be quiet so I can listen to the radio?" Ha scolds.

Vy stops to listen. A female voice with a Saigon accent comes from the Chinese neighbor's radio across the street. *"I repeat. The number of the one-million-dong winning ticket is 172096."*

"The tail is 96 and the head is 17," Vy says. "So Mom lost. I wish the numbers were 99 and 19."

Ha gets up, her face turns somber. "Well, let's go home and clean up. Else we'll get a whipping for sure."

The radio continues its broadcast of the lottery. Music for its advertisement blares in the air. *"The National Lottery helps build houses and enrich our citizens in a flash. The National Lottery..."*

Ha mocks the announcement by singing in her own words. *"The National Lottery helps destroy houses and impoverish our citizens in a flash."*

Vy protests, "What are you singing? Those are not the right words."

"Well, the lottery hurts people."

"How?"

"It can make a person lose all her money."

"Who?"

"Well, Mom, for one."

"But she's not buying the National lottery."

"Can't you think for yourself? Without the National lottery, is there a De lottery for Mom to play? So isn't it true that the National lottery hurts people?" After a moment of silence, Ha continues, "We get a beating every Tuesday because of it. I don't like any form of lottery, whether it is head, tail, or national. I hate them all."

To minimize the chance of being "punished" after Mother loses money, Ha and Vy work hard cleaning up the house. After the house is in order and the water barrel is filled, Mother is still not home. Ha and Vy decide to walk to the lottery stand to confirm the winning number. If by chance they had the number wrong, they might have good things to eat instead of being beaten. They have no such luck. The winning number posted at the lottery stand confirms the radio announcement.

Two Sisters

Ha reminds Vy not to fight each other that day. "Also make sure to do whatever Mom asks right away. That's the only way to avoid being whipped."

When Mother comes home, she seems lethargic and oblivious to the clean and neat house. She does not bother to look for reasons to fault Ha and Vy with. It seems as though they have escaped the worst. Feeling "safe," Vy starts to sing the lottery advertisement song, but substitutes Ha's words for the real ones. *"The National Lottery helps destroy houses and impoverish our citizens in a flash—"*

Ha quickly throws a warning look at Vy, but it is too late. Mother abruptly stops arranging things in her shopping bag and looks up. "What did you just sing, Vy?"

"I... I sang the lottery song."

"Let me hear it again."

Vy slowly states rather than sing the original words, but Mother says, "That's not what you sang. Do you want to deceive me?"

Vy nervously repeats the song with Ha's words. Mother furrows her brows. "Who taught you that?"

Vy cannot bring herself to answer Mother, so Ha says, "I did."

Mother narrows her eyes. "You did? What do you imply? So you insinuate that I play the lottery and destroy our home? Did you not think about the hard work I did to raise the two of you? Now you think you have feathers and wings and can talk back to your parent, huh?" The more Ha remains silent, the angrier Mother becomes. "You are in sixth and seventh grades and you think you know better than your mother. Let's see how much better. Go lie down on the bed."

In no time, Mother is already picking branches from the star apple tree. Vy quickly pulls a shirt from the dresser, crumbles it up, and stuffs it inside her pants to pad her behind. She twists around to look at her padded bottom to check its adequacy and is not pleased with the first attempt. Removing the shirt and folding it more carefully the second time, she pulls down both pants and underwear and puts the shirt neatly on her behind before pulling the underwear and pants up again. Then she lies down on the bed, as far away from the outer edge as possible. Ha follows and lies down next to Vy, feeling empty inside just like any other Tuesday. A twang of anguish tears at Ha's heart when she hears Vy whisper a prayer. "I pray that Mom does not know about the padding. I pray to Dad that Mom will not hit too hard or too long."

Ha feels detached from time and space. The sounds of Mother's yelling and her footsteps approaching from the garden are all too familiar. Ha automatically cuts herself off from reality and does not register what happens next. She is not aware of what Mother says or how long the so-called punishment lasts. The only reaction she has is reflexive in nature. She raises a hand to block the rod.

At one point, the familiar rhythm of the striking rod is broken by Vy's stammering. "I... I...was afraid of being hurt, that is why...I put the shirt there...not because I want to deceive you, Mom." Upon hearing this, as if waking up from a stupor, Mother lets go of the rod and tells Ha and Vy to go clean up and get ready for dinner. Mother's anger seems to dissipate. This time she does not make Ha and Vy recite promises to not repeat mistakes.

Two Sisters

After dinner, they go to bed earlier than usual. Vy has no trouble falling asleep. Ha rubs Vy's back for a while, and then she touches her own body to feel the welts on her arms, thighs, and bottom, while brewing in anger and bitterness. Mother is not fair. Mother is a hypocrite who gambles while declaring gambling is a sin. Ha extends her hatred toward the people who run the De lottery for destroying families. Ha thinks of Father and feels a deep pain inside, much deeper than the physical pain inflicted on her body. She whispers in the dark, "Dad, why did you leave us so soon? Don't you know we are miserable without you?"

Ha keeps on swallowing to contain her sobs; her tears are a steady stream of salt that she keeps licking from her lips. In the dark, a shadow moves. Ha closes her eyes, pretending to be asleep. She hears Mother's cry and feels the warmth of Mother's touch. She tries not to move her body to appear to be sleeping, but keeps it supple enough so she can subtly move in the direction that Mother's hand turns it. She feels Mother's hands searching for the welts on her body. Her skin is rubbed with something soothing. Mother's cry continues. Ha's feelings soften at each touch and rub. Gradually her hatred subsides. She finally decides to open her eyes to talk to Mother, but before she has a chance to tell Mother to stop crying, Mother walks away – with a little bowl in her hand. Ha wants to tell Mother that she forgives her for the unjust treatment, but she stays silent and does not get up. Ha's body feels as stiff as a corpse, and tears continue to roll down her cheeks.

•

Ha touches a welt where the salve was rubbed in and puts her finger in her mouth to taste it. It is as salty as the tears on her lips. Mother has gone outside to sit on the doorstep, crying by her lonely self. Mother's cries and the insect calls seem to last the whole night long.

CHAPTER THIRTY-NINE

Laying down the white chalk, the teacher says, "Of all the seventh grade classes, your class has the most A's. Many get 19 or 20 out of 20. Very good work."

Students of the seventh grade class, including Ha, get excited. They talk over each other and implore the teacher to let them see their papers right away until the teacher puts a finger on his lips. "I will read your name and deliver your paper to your seat. Please be quiet and raise your hand when I call your name."

Ha smiles when she imagines a big red twenty on her paper. She listens attentively to what the teacher is saying. "Some of you earned fewer points on an item that required a higher level of thinking. If you have questions about your work, raise your hand."

Ha likes this Social Studies teacher and considers him a living model of his own preaching. Although Mr. Bao is young, Ha respects him and thinks he must be as wise as Father was. Mr. Bao teaches her right from wrong and guides her to become a good citizen. She likes the subject because she feels it is important to apply what she learns in class to everyday life. She always pays attention in class and therefore, it is natural for her to believe she is one of those who got the high grade.

Ha's thoughts are interrupted when her name is announced. Mr. Bao comes over and places her paper upside-down on her desk. Ha slowly turns it over, expecting a twenty, and is both shocked and disappointed to see a twelve. *Twelve out of twenty?* She cannot believe her eyes. Although she meant to talk only to herself, she was loud enough for others to hear and discern her dismay. Myle, her best friend sitting at the desk next to hers, looks over. "You got twelve? Check to see if Mr. Bao added up the score correctly."

Ha reviews her paper and informs Myle that item number five is the cause for the low score. Scrutinizing Ha's paper, Myle says, "You're right. His note says that your analysis is flawed. Well, don't feel bad. This quiz does not count much and besides, it is an average score."

"But most of you get 19 or 20. That means I have the worst grade."

Mr. Bao does not like to have his students talk in class. He frowns, walking back toward Ha's seat. "You know you're not supposed to talk among yourselves. Why didn't you raise your hand if you had a question?"

"I... We just wondered why Ha got a low score for item number five," Myle stammers a reply.

Mr. Bao readjusts his glasses. "Let me see." Myle gives Ha's paper to Mr. Bao, holding it with both hands as a gesture of respect. Mr. Bao squints at the small letters to read

Two Sisters

Ha's answer. "Ah, I see... The question was 'What do you have to do to choose good books that are beneficial and appropriate to your age. Explain your reasons.'...and your answer was... 'To have good books that are appropriate to my age, I have to do my own research. When I go to a bookstore, I need to go to the children's section. I will pick picture books or fairytales. I will not pick novels or books in the adult section. That is because I know adults and children do not like the same thing and they read different kinds of books. Adults read adult books and children read children books...'" Mr. Bao stops reading. "You have your own reasoning, but your reasons are not sound. They do not fully and appropriately answer the question. You did not address the 'beneficial' aspect."

Seeing that Ha is not satisfied with his analysis of her answer, Mr. Bao walks to the front and reads question number five aloud to the whole class. He asks for volunteers to provide answers. He calls on Loc who says, "Sir, I think to find out what books are beneficial and appropriate for my age, I have to seek opinions and advice from my parents, teachers, older siblings, or people who have read many books. The people who are well-read will know what books are good and what books should not be read and they will be able to help me choose a book that is beneficial to me."

Another student raises her hand and says, "I think that if I want to read good books, I have to ask people who have the experience reading books such as teachers, parents, aunts, or uncles. That is because these people are trustworthy and they have read many books. They can guide me to choose the appropriate books. If I pick books by myself, I may read books that are not good for me and are not appropriate for my age."

Two Sisters

Mr. Bao asks the class if they agree with the two answers. When the other students concur, Mr. Bao says, "That is right. When you want to read books that are beneficial, you have to ask opinions of well-read adults. A book's language and ideas could either be good or bad medicine for your innocent minds. If you read a bad book, you will be influenced by bad ideas. That is why you should not choose books on your own. I see many books supposedly written for adolescents but contain slang, bad grammar, and inappropriate graphics for your age. So you have to be very careful."

After a moment of silence, Mr. Bao continues to elaborate on his teaching. "And some of you who think that long books without pictures are novels written only for adults will not seek to read them and will therefore miss out on good ideas, fine literature, and famous works. In summary, you should ask adults' advice for books that are beneficial and beware of those that are not."

Ha's mind comes alive with the image of Elder Uncle's book cases that are full of beautiful books. Envisioning his solemn and humorless face, Ha twists her mouth in an ironic smirk. It would be unthinkable for her to walk into the big house to seek Elder Uncle's advice and ask him which books she should read. *And my own parents? Dad is no longer on this earth and Mom never reads. So how am I going to ask for advice from adults?* Ha thinks of past mistakes of not touching long novels because she thought they were for adults and of the few times she bought books that indeed turned out to contain inappropriate language or graphics. She decides that Mr. Bao imparts good wisdom and knowledge. She feels better when Mr. Bao says, "The score on this quiz is not important. The important thing is for you to ask when you are not sure about something and to apply what you learned to your everyday living."

Two Sisters

Mr. Bao walks back to Ha's seat to return her paper. As Ha reaches out both hands to receive it, her right sleeve rolls back to reveal the swollen and bruised skin. Ha becomes flustered and awkwardly moves her right arm under her left to hide it. Her action is clumsy at best. Mr. Bao looks stunned and appears about to say something, but perhaps sensing Ha's discomfort, he turns and walks away. However, Ha's right arm does not escape Myle's inquisitive eyes.

"What happened to you?" Myle asks.

Ha's face turns red. "Oh, I was just shaking because I was nervous."

"No, what I mean is what happened to your arm."

Ha lowers her voice. "I got a beating for climbing the guava tree."

Ha is amazed at herself for coming up with a lie so quickly. However, she is not sure if Myle really believes her. Her heart skips a beat when she reads doubt in Myle's eyes and sees Mr. Bao look back with questioning eyes. Ha decides to think ahead of what to say if other people happen to ask the same question. She will not be able to deny the reason for the bruises and have to come up with the reason for the beating. *I don't know why I can't stop climbing the guava tree although it is forbidden. My mother thinks it is dangerous and only punishes me for my own good. There was a time I fell from the high branch onto a sleeping dog. Later the dog got sick and died. I should stop climbing, but I can't help myself. I deserve the punishment.*

Ha is relieved when Mr. Bao and Myle go about their businesses and seem to forget about her arm. Mr. Bao gets busy and Myle stops asking questions. But the subject does not leave Myle's mind. Later, she leans over and whispers in Ha's ear, "Listen to your mother. Don't climb trees anymore."

Ha nods, but she avoids looking at Myle. She pretends to pay attention to the lesson on the blackboard. Myle does the same, but she does not drop the subject. Again she whispers, "Don't let other students see your arm. They'll laugh at you for being flogged now that you're already in secondary school."

Ha looks at Myle this time and nods in appreciation. She is silently thankful that the long Vietnamese dress is able to hide her bruised skin. The welts on her body probably will not go away in a week – and depending on whether or not Mother wins the lottery, she may get more welts the following Tuesday. Ha tries to erase the image of star apple branches and Tuesdays from her mind. She tries to focus on the blackboard and Mr. Bao's lecture. His words flow in a regular rhythm and are somehow comforting. For a brief time, she is able to not think about what may lie ahead.

CHAPTER FORTY

Today, like other Tuesdays, Ha and Vy are anxious before Mother gets home. They do not know if Mother will come home sad or happy, if she will possess the fury of a cornered animal or bring home a basketful of food. This Tuesday, unlike other Tuesdays, the sun has already faded when Mother comes home as if it were part of a conspiracy to soften Mother's haggard look. The disheveled hair and sunken eyes on Mother's bony face do not bode well for Ha and Vy. Ha signals for Vy to set the table for dinner. Mother seems to be in another world. There is no reaction from her when dinner is served. Ha is the first to speak. "Dinner is ready, Mom. Fourth Uncle and Aunt are visiting. After we eat, let's go over to Grandma's to say hello to them."

Mother brightens up. "They are here?"

"Yes, Sister Chau and Sister Yen told me Fourth Uncle and Aunt are having dinner at Grandma's place today."

"Eat then, and don't wait for me," Mother says. "I'll wash my hands and eat later."

Two Sisters

As Mother walks out to the garden, the dogs begin to bark at two strange women who ignore them. The women walk toward Mother with purpose and determination. Mother's face pales at the sight of these two women. She falters, "Oh, Sister Lien and Fourth Sister, so you know where I live!"

"Of course we had to find out where you live because you owe us money," one of the women speaks. She is the larger of the two. Despite the size differences, the women dress and act similarly. They both have an aggressive look, as if daring anyone to cross them. The larger woman speaks again. "You disappeared from us after promising to pay."

The smaller woman is as loud and forceful as the first one. "What time did you say you'd pay us today? We've been waiting since three thirty. You're losing credibility with us, you know."

Mother acts as a guilty person who is caught red-handed. She stammers a compromise. "Please come in and we'll talk. No need to be so loud out here."

"We only want to have what you owe us. Otherwise we won't be able to do business anymore. We gave you merchandise before payment because we trusted you. Let's not abuse the trust."

The two women walk in and totally ignore Ha and Vy. Their tone is threatening. "Do you want the whole neighborhood to hear us? No matter what, you'll pay us today. We're not going anywhere until you do."

"Please give me a few more days. I promise I'll pay you next Tuesday at three thirty."

Two Sisters

The larger woman moves forward until her body brushes Mother's. She snarls, "Tuesday, huh? Every time you open your mouth, it's Tuesday. Do you remember how many Tuesdays ago you promised to pay?"

Wiping tears from her eyes, Mother pulls money out of her pocket. "I was able to borrow some money for my daughter's school tuition. The tuition is due tomorrow. If you have pity on me, please give me another seven days and I'll pay back every cent."

The larger woman snatches the bills from Mother's hand and counts them. "Seven hundred. Fine. We'll take this much for now. Tomorrow I'll go over to your market stand. If you don't pay us then, I'll confiscate all of your merchandise."

"You can do whatever you want tomorrow, but this is tuition money. Please have pity on me just this one time. I had to jump through hoops to be able to borrow this amount. Please, please."

The smaller woman looks as heartless as the larger woman. She walks toward the door. "We have pity on you and who will have pity on us? Let's go, Sister Lien. We'll figure out what to do tomorrow."

The two women leave amid loud sobs from Mother. Vy stops eating, throws her chopsticks down, and runs to the dresser where she bursts out crying. "I will have to go to the principal's office again tomorrow," she wails.

The food Ha is chewing suddenly becomes tasteless. She is surprised to find herself tearless. Her brain must be on vacation. Everything appears to be in slow motion. Her thoughts freeze and float. In a dreamlike state, Ha sees

Two Sisters

herself in the middle of a forest. She has discovered a treasure chest hidden in a cave. She is not alone. Aladdin and a genie are there. Aladdin is asking the genie to give Ha a large sum of money. Then Ha is at a bank. Father is in disguise. He robs the bank. Father and Ha are back home in the altar room. Father puts a stack of money on his own altar. Ha starts from her daydreams and shakes her head in amazement. So childlike illusions still occupy her mind and she cannot help herself. Each of the paternal relatives in the big house reaches out and contributes to a monetary fund for Mother. Ha shakes her head again to force herself back to reality, knowing in her mind that in the real world, Mother does not ask for help and her paternal relatives are indifferent to their plight. Numbers are floating in front of her eyes. She sees eleven and ninety-one. Her mind registers eleven as the first two digits and ninety-one as the last two digits of today's winning lottery number. Vaguely she recalls that numbers 11, 51, and 91 are numbers for dogs. Didn't she see Mino and Yellow at the gate this morning before going to school? Mino is a pup so eleven must be her number. Yellow is a small Japanese dog, but he is old, so both eleven and ninety-one must be his numbers. Ha hits her forehead hard. *Why didn't I think of this? I should have used the breakfast money that I've been saving to buy these numbers for the De lottery. I'd have won both head and tail and there would be enough money to help Mother pay her debt, and perhaps even to pay Vy's tuition.* Ha starts with the realization that she is daydreaming about the lottery. She begins to understand what she thought was Mother's hypocrisy. Perhaps it is not hypocrisy, but an irony – the irony of a person's knowledge that gambling is a destructive force and yet not being able to pull herself away from it.

Deep in her thoughts and daydreams, Ha does not see Fourth Uncle and Aunt approach and walk into the little house. She only becomes aware of them when they are right

Two Sisters

in the middle of the room. Ha is so surprised to see the presence of elegant clothing in her humble dwelling that she forgets to utter a greeting. Mother must feel the same way. She looks at the couple in stunned silence.

Fourth Aunt clicks her tongue. "It is so dark in here. How can you see?"

Mother stammers a greeting and walks to the altar room to light the large oil lamp. Fourth Uncle looks at Ha. "You are eating alone? Where's Vy?"

Ha remembers her manners. "Please come in and have a seat. Vy has finished her dinner." Then she turns toward the bedroom. "Vy, come out to say hello to Fourth Uncle and Aunt."

Fourth Uncle sits down on a chair at the lone table in the altar room and looks around. He is surprised and incredulous when he spots a light fixture on the ceiling. "Why don't you turn the light on? Why are you using an oil lamp?"

"We do not have power," Mother says. "Elder Sister says the power lines are tangled with the coconut leaves and do not work."

Fourth Uncle knits his brows. "All we have to do is hire someone to fix the lines. How can the girls study without a good light?"

Vy suddenly blurts out in pitiful sobs. "I can't go to school anymore. Mom has no tuition money." She looks just as pitiful as she sounds.

"What are you saying?" Fourth Uncle says in shock. Everyone is stunned into silence.

Two Sisters

"Mom cannot pay the tuition so I won't be going to school anymore," Vy wails.

Mother is caught in a difficult situation. She clumsily stammers an explanation. "That's because...because...my business is not doing well lately. Tomorrow is the deadline to pay tuition and I have no money."

"I thought Elder Brother would be able to get her free tuition."

"No, he could only arrange for a fifty-percent discount. I still have to pay fifty percent."

Fourth Aunt pulls Vy to her and strokes her hair. "Don't worry. I will pay the tuition for you. If your mother cannot afford to send you to school, you can come live with us and we will take care of you."

Vy calms down in Fourth Aunt's embrace. Ha throws Vy an accusing look. She is hurt by Vy's action. Her heart aches even more when Fourth Aunt hands Mother a stack of bills. Ha remembers what Mother used to say: "Be content with what you have. Do not covet, beg, or accept pity and handouts. We do not want people to feel they have to do charity each time they see us." Ha wonders when Mother's business will be completely stable and she will be truly financially independent and free of handouts from rich people. She feels as if her heart is being cut with a knife when she thinks of the incident between Mother and the two women earlier. And on top of all this, she is losing her only sister to Fourth Aunt's sweet promises. She feels utterly alone. A bitter pain is wedged and lodged at the bottom of her heart. She has an inkling that the calmness and peacefulness of better times will never return to the little house from this point forward. What she holds dear in her heart is slipping away from her and she is losing control. She is grateful for the dimness cast by the feeble oil lamp so that she can hide the stream of tears that starts falling down her cheeks.

•

CHAPTER FORTY-ONE

The rain has not stopped since Ha and Vy left for school, and it picks up as the day goes on. The garden is darkened with thick sheets of rain. At the bushes, the flowers and leaves are beaten down to the ground and sprawl over the walkway. At the well where there are no trees to block the sunlight overhead, the raindrops shine like clear diamonds that shatter when hitting the well and water barrel, before scattering to the ground and mixing with the steady flow of water that would disappear into cracks and trenches if not for the fact that the ground is nearly saturated and water is not draining fast enough. Flooding is imminent.

Ha and Vy sit at the table in the altar room. They are not in a playful mood today. They do not bother to close the window but leave it ajar, allowing raindrops to hit the window slats and splash on the tabletop. Closing the window would bring darkness and they want to look out. The rain registers regular and melancholy sounds. Rainy days remind Ha and Vy what they lack in material comfort. Without looking, they know exactly where the holes in the roof are and exactly where to place the pots on the floor to catch the rain water. Often they make origami boats and let them float on the flooded stoop. In the past, they left the front door open and squatted down on their haunches to watch the teetering paper boats that would eventually sink under heavy raindrops. But today they just sit at the window, lost in their own thoughts, watching the rain.

They stay silent until Vy pouts. "I don't want to anymore."

"You don't want to go to Saigon?" Ha asks.

"No."

"Why not? What would Mom say to Fourth Uncle and Aunt?"

"My friends cried when I said goodbye to them this morning. Now I don't want to be far away from my friends." After a brief silence, Vy adds, "I don't want to be far away from Mom and you either."

"So why didn't you say that when Fourth Aunt asked you? Why didn't you say anything when Mom asked Seventh Uncle to give you a ride to Saigon?"

"Well... I wanted to go then. I didn't want to stay home when I thought about Tuesdays."

"Aren't you afraid of Tuesdays anymore?"

"You're staying home. If you're not afraid, I'm not afraid."

"I can stay home because Mom doesn't have to pay tuition for me. If you stay home, you will not be able to finish high school."

Two Sisters

Vy's eyes brim with tears. "So do I have to leave for Saigon tomorrow?"

"Yes. You'll get to see the elephants."

"Are you sure there are elephants in the zoo?"

"Yes."

"How do you know?"

"My friend told me there are big elephant in the Saigon zoo. I'm sure you'll get a chance to go to the zoo to see them. I won't have that chance."

"But... I still don't want to go."

"Why not?"

"I'm afraid to be all by myself in a strange place."

"Fourth Uncle and Aunt are our relatives. You'll get used to living with them."

"But Sister Lily didn't want to talk to us or play with us. What if no one wants to play with me?"

"Fourth Uncle and Aunt also have a son, Brother Duy."

"We never met him. He probably does not want to play with me either."

Ha sighs. "Same here. I won't have you to play with. I don't have any friends who want to come to our house to play with me."

Two Sisters

"So why do you want me to leave?"

"If Mom loses the lottery again, she will keep asking us questions until we blame each other and then fight, and we'll both get a whipping."

"I promise I won't fight with you and we won't get a whipping."

"But you know we'll get whipped anyway. Besides, you need to go so Fourth Uncle and Aunt can help you finish high school."

Vy breaks down in sobs. "So there is no way I can stay home?"

"You'll be better off because Mom won't hit you anymore."

"What about you?"

"I think Mom may not hit me when you're not here. Don't worry."

"How do you know?"

"Mom will miss you and won't hit me. And she may not play the lottery anymore because she won't need the money to pay tuition."

"But she still needs to buy clothes and food and school supplies for you."

"She'll manage."

"So she can only take care of one of us?"

Two Sisters

"Don't be sad anymore because you'll be better off."

"Who will you play with?"

"I don't need to play with anyone. I will knit things and ask Sixth Aunt to sell them at the market for me. I'll make money to help Mom out and I will study hard to get a high school diploma."

Vy brightens at the idea of a high school diploma. "Me too."

"After high school, we'll go to school some more before we get jobs."

"We'll make money and will not need to play the lottery, right?"

"Right."

"Then we'll build a house for Mom, right?"

"Right. We already crossed our fingers about that long ago."

"Yes, and don't forget we'll plant beautiful flowers, too."

"I won't forget."

Hearing the dogs bark outside, Vy asks, "Will we have dogs?"

"No. If we do, people may not want to visit us."

Two Sisters

Vy pouts. "But I want to have a Japanese dog like Mino or Yellow. Rich people have them."

Before Ha could reply, the front door opens and Mother comes in, soaked to the bone. Wet clothes cling tightly to Mother's shivering body. She asks, "Have you set out the pots to catch the rain?"

Ha runs to the door to greet Mother. "Yes, we did. You should change right away, Mom."

Mother looks with concern at Vy who wears a long sad face. "What's wrong, Vy? Are you upset that I am sending you to Saigon?"

Vy's tears readily fall at the question. Mother sits down on the floor and her voice catches. "Please understand. I do not want to send you away, but there is nothing else I can do. You'll get a high school education if you go live with Fourth Uncle and Aunt."

Ha runs over to Vy and shakes her hands. "Vy, Vy, tell Mom you're not sad so she will go change her clothes."

Ha is not sure if Vy heard her. As if she has lost her senses, Vy sits immobile, staring straight ahead without speaking or focusing on anything. Her face is covered with a stream of tears.

It is late, but rain drops are still thundering down as though being in a race with each other. These are tears from heaven, Ha tells herself, mourning the impending separation of her little family. Thick sheets of rain darken the air and blur the images in the garden. Ha can see flickers of light from the big house. It must be warm and cozy in there, Ha

Two Sisters

muses. The relatives in the big house are probably gathering in the living room to chat and laugh together.

Ha starts when Vy suddenly springs to life and jumps up from her chair to run to Mother and puts her arms around Mother. "I am not sad any more, Mom. I'm not mad at you. Go change. I'll go to Saigon tomorrow. I will."

"Forgive me," Mother sobs. "I did not fulfill my responsibilities to you. Please understand and know that I love you and want you to succeed in academics."

Vy puts her head on Mother's chest, nodding and crying with her. "I promise I will study hard until I get my high school diploma. Can you promise not to beat Sister Ha after I'm gone. She is so skinny, I don't want her to be hurt."

Ha is totally taken by surprise at Vy's words. In a daze, she slowly sinks her body down on the chair left vacant by Vy. She had no idea Vy felt that way about her. Ha always thought of Vy as being on the selfish side, who worried about no one else but herself. She recalls the Tuesdays when Vy and she fought and threw blames at each other to avoid being whipped by Mother and when Vy padded her behind with something to ease the pain. Ha did not think Vy cared about her then. Now she feels guilty about misreading Vy. Two days ago when Vy was still debating whether or not to go to Saigon, Ha encouraged her to go by telling her about the elephants. Ha realizes that she is the selfish one who wants Vy to go because she figures she will not get flogged after Vy is gone. Ha does not know for sure if there are elephants in the Saigon zoo, and yet she spoke as if she knew. Ha feels so bad. Her stomach churns as though there were thousands of marching ants inside.

Two Sisters

The rain is still going strong. Its rhythmic sound hitting the rooftop makes Ha feel sleepy. She decides she would rather sleep than ponder unpleasant thoughts. In the familiar darkness, she gets up to walk to the bedroom. She can make out the shapes of Mother and Vy hugging each other on the floor as she passes them. Lying alone on the bed, Ha cannot find sleep for a long time. Tears fall down her cheeks as raindrops continue to fall.

CHAPTER FORTY-TWO

After Vy leaves for Saigon, Mother works only in the morning and stays home in the afternoon. Ha misses Vy very much even though Mother is there when she gets home from school. Without Vy, the little house suddenly appears large, empty, and cold. Silence reigns in place of familiar chatter and laughter. Ha's life becomes boring and lonely.

Ha doodles on a piece of paper as she sits at the table by the window. She crumbles it up and throws it away. In Vy's absence, even the sunlight has lost its luster. The light it casts on the leaves looks pale and ordinary. Ha wants Vy home so much. She looks out, yearning for the familiar sound and sight of the mailman at the gate, for she has been waiting for a letter from Vy. Instead, she sees her second cousin Yen standing outside looking in through the window bars.

"Are you doing homework, Ha?"

"No, I want to write a letter to Vy."

"Are you done?"

Two Sisters

"No, I did not start because I don't have her address. I'm waiting to get her letter first."

"Do you want to come play cards with me, Chau, and Young Aunt?"

Ha quickly declines when she hears Mother, sitting at the door, clear her throat.

"Why not?" Yen insists. "We taught you how to play just the other day and you did so well."

Ha cringes at Yen's words. She hears Mother clear her throat again, and again she declines Yen's request. She wants dearly to say out loud "*My mother does not let me play*," but she dares not.

"You promised that you'd play today," Yen says. "Young Aunt sent me over here to get you. If you have nothing else to do, please come."

Ha shakes her head. To her chagrin, Mother now knows about her learning to play cards. When she got Mother's permission to go over to the big house before, she never mentioned card playing; she had said she wanted to spend time with Yen and Chau. Ha silently blames Yen for not being sharp enough to understand that Mother's throat clearing is a warning, intending to tell Ha not do participate in something Mother disapproves of. Mother clears her throat at times when she is not pleased with her children's behavior or activities, but it is too inconvenient for her to issue a scolding. Clearing her throat is the way Mother tells Ha and Vy to stop what they are doing and think of the consequences before acting. Unfortunately, Yen does not understand this peculiar way that Mother communicates with her children.

Two Sisters

After cajoling Ha for a while without success, Yen gets upset and leaves. Ha feels the need to immediately clarify things to Mother. "The other day when you let me go over to the big house, I learned how to play cards with the cousins and Young Aunt, but we did not play with money. The winner got to be the dealer, that's all."

But Mother is not appeased. "I don't want you to play anymore. From now on, you're not allowed to go *there*. You should not play even without money. You should concentrate on studying and if you have spare time, you can knit. I want you to remember what I say and mind me."

Just then, Young Aunt's voice can be heard from the outside. "Ha, come. Quick. I have something to tell you."

Seeing Mother's disapproval look, Ha hesitates. "Young Aunt is calling me. May I go?"

Mother does not reply while Young Aunt continues to call. "Hurry, Ha. I have something to give to you."

Ha stands up. "Young Aunt is calling me. I think I should go, okay?"

Mother avoids speaking and looking at Ha as she folds and stacks paper bags; her face turns downward toward the floor. Ha patiently waits for a while before she slips her feet into her flip-flops and walks out. She goes through the garden without encountering anyone. When she enters the big house through the back door, she sees Grandmother, Young Aunt, and her two cousins already sitting around the card table.

"Grandma and Young Aunt, here I am," Ha says.

Two Sisters

Grandmother states the obvious while arranging cards in her hand. "Your mother does not let you play cards, right?"

Ha shakes her head. "No, she does not. I come to let you know I'm not allowed to play."

Ha is about to leave when Young Aunt stops her. "Wait. I didn't call you here to play."

"What do you need, Young Aunt?"

"Nothing," Young Aunt says while keeping her eyes on the cards in her hand. "Sit down and wait until I finish this. There is something for you."

Ha pulls out a chair to sit next to Young Aunt and watches her play. Ha does not agree with Young Aunt's card playing strategy. Ha wishes she had the cards in her own hand so she could arrange them to her liking. She thinks she has a knack for card playing. She feels sorry that Yen came at an unfortunate time when Mother was home. If Yen did not talk about card playing, Mother probably would have let her walk over here and she could then play all she wants without worrying about anything.

Grandmother knocks on the table with her knuckle. "Whose turn is it? Go!"

Yen frowns. "Mine, but I am not ready. Give me a few seconds."

Yen hesitates while holding some cards in her right hand and wavers about what cards to put down on the table. She cannot make up her mind and keeps looking at the remaining cards that are spread out as a fan in a semi-circle in her left hand. She mumbles to herself. "Not sure what is best."

Two Sisters

Impatiently waiting for Yen's play, Grandmother crosses her arms. "I have to wait until my bones crack, playing with you girls. For a young and healthy girl, you're as slow as a turtle. I'd be better off taking an afternoon nap."

"You're quick because you have experience," Yen chirps. "I'm done now. I'll play these cards although I'm not so sure. I have no good cards."

Young Aunt says, "Wait for me at my turn. I'll go get Vy's letter for Ha."

Ha brightens up. "A letter from Vy? That's great. I thought you wanted me to come here to play cards."

Retrieving a thick blue envelope from Young Aunt, Ha is anxious to run home to gobble up every word in it, but Young Aunt stops her. "You can read the letter any time. The ink will not fade away if you wait. Vy probably just says she misses you and there's nothing too important." Spreading her cards out for Ha to see, Young Aunt implores, "Show me what you'd do."

Ha happily obliges. She quickly puts the blue envelope away in her pocket and leans over to look at Young Aunt's cards against what was already played on the table. Mumbling the suits of the cards to herself, Ha turns on her thinking cap to figure out the best configuration of singles, doubles, or triples to maximize the chance of winning. "*General, Student, Elephant, Carriage, Canon, Knight, Soldier.*"

Ha is immersed in pointing out possibilities to Young Aunt and does not notice anything unusual until she hears a stern voice from behind. She jumps when she realizes it is Mother's. "Ha, come home right now. I have something to

Two Sisters

tell you." Ha is floored that she does not know how long Mother has been standing at the door watching her. She breaks out in sweat when she looks up at Mother and sees only harshness on her face. Mother's cold-as-ice face matches the dry voice that is devoid of emotions. Ha has a foreboding of bad happenings. She wonders why she did not hear Mother's greeting to Grandmother and why no one warned her of Mother's presence.

Ha quietly follows Mother home. When they reach their front door, Mother orders Ha to go lie down on the bed. Ha meekly does what Mother orders. She lowers her body to the same spot where she used to lie with Vy on Tuesdays. She feels utterly alone on the enormous bed, missing hearing Vy's prayer and the sound of Vy's twisting and turning against the mat. She feels overwhelmed with the loneliness that descends upon her. Her mind slowly disengages from her body. She is oblivious to Mother's voice and the sound of the stripping of leaves from a star apple branch.

Ha only becomes aware of Mother's presence when she feels a sting on her bottom. Mother sits on her own bed as she gives Ha the first lash. "Ha, who gave you permission to play cards?"

Ha jumps, but she does not answer Mother. She acknowledges to herself that she left for the big house before obtaining Mother's permission. She is indeed guilty of not respecting Mother.

"Ha, what do you say?"

Again, Ha remains silent. Another lash comes down. "Here's for your stubbornness. So you decide to be disrespectful, huh?"

Two Sisters

Ha refuses to speak or cry out. She tries to ignore the pain from the rod that repeatedly comes down in a fury at her insistence of being silent. She stops herself from jumping after the first lash and presses her body as flatly and as closely as possible against the mat. She deliberately presses her lips together so that no cry comes out.

Mother is driven crazy. "Are you going to answer me? Here's for your rudeness, for not respecting your mother."

Ha's lips stay pressed together. She is determined not to raise her hand to block the rod and not to utter a sound. Once in a while, her body involuntarily jumps as a reaction to a particularly hard blow. Ha feels hatred and anger fill her body. As though being hypnotized, she eventually no longer feels anything and no cry ever comes.

When Mother is exhausted and gives up, she slumps down next to the dresser like a soldier who has run out of ammunition and cries like a miserable child. "I raised her up to be this big just so that she refuses to listen to me. She does not answer me or mind me. It is unfortunate for me that I have children who behave this way. My daughter who is not yet an adult and does not have strong enough wings and feathers already treats me this way, much less..."

Ha tunes Mother out. Ignoring Mother's cry and feeling no remorse, Ha stays on the bed until she wordlessly gets up and slips out to the garden.

CHAPTER FORTY-THREE

Sitting under the star apple tree, Ha feels excruciatingly lonely. The sunlight sneaks through the branches above to shine on the dry leaves scattered on the ground. Ha misses Vy even more as she sits there. It has been a long while since the ground under their tree was animated with footsteps or imprinted with stick figures or piled into dirt mounds. A sound that could be mistaken for Vy's laugh comes from a distance. Ha listens attentively and realizes it is the laughter of Elder Aunt's grandchildren from the big house.

Ha picks up a stick and scribbles all over the dirt with it. She misses the games of hopscotch, jump-rope, housekeeping, or man-eating crocodiles that she played with Vy. She misses the days they shared a sweet carambola, a juicy sapoche, a half-eaten soursop, or a stolen wax jambu. She misses the times they were hungry with nothing to eat. She misses the confidence they shared, especially about losing their father at an early age. She remembers the time she told Vy that Father was invisible and that he could eat anything in the garden and would know everything they do. She ponders the two opposite worlds of the living and the dead. She wonders if her own living world could actually be worse than hell. Although Mother has told her that those who do not do the right things will be punished and go to hell, she does not entirely believe that the dead world is full of sadness and misery. There is a possibility that Father's world is a calm and peaceful one where the invisible souls have no worries or cares. She thinks she would welcome death as a release from the dark and depressed world she is in. She dreams of seeing Father again and of the two of them floating all over the universe side by side. They would have nice adventures as they travel together, invisible to the living world. Her face twists in anguish when unpleasant images of what might happen if she died come to mind. She sees Mother violently thrash her body against the coffin, asking to join the dead daughter. She sees Vy come back from Saigon, standing confused and alone with hands gripping the luggage and feet glued to the bus station floor. She sees Vy's crying in front of the altars for Father, Mother, and sister. Ha shakes her head and tries to push the images out of her mind. She decides that death is not the answer to life's problems. Death may bring eternal peace to the dead, but would bring pain and havoc to the living. She cannot seek solace at the expense of misery and sorrow descending upon her loved ones. Tears stream down her face.

She is startled by Young Aunt's voice. "You got another beating, didn't you, Ha?"

Ha bends her head as she utters a barely audible "Yes." Young Aunt clears out a space under the tree to sit next to Ha. "So she thought you were playing cards?"

Ha nods. After sitting in silence for a while, it feels right to confide in Young Aunt. "I think Vy is luckier than I am. She won't get any more flogging."

Two Sisters

"But she may not be that happy living in Saigon," Young Aunt says.

Ha turns to Young Aunt. "Why not? She lives with Fourth Uncle and Aunt who are rich and will take care of her."

Young Aunt shakes her head. "Being rich does not always bring happiness."

Ha is bewildered at Young Aunt's words. She does not know Young Aunt's philosophy of life because the two of them do not sit down and talk to each other on a regular basis. As far as Ha remembers, Young Aunt has never shared her thoughts and feelings with Ha. Ha is chagrined that she does not know this side of Young Aunt. She hardly knows her own aunt who lives at the same address. Ha feels the door of opportunity to get to know her aunt is wide open and she wants to take advantage of it before it shuts closed again. In a quickened breath, she asks, "Tell me why Vy should not be happy. Fourth Uncle has money. Fourth Aunt is generous and loving. Whatever Vy wants, she'll have."

"Sometimes people do nice things to cover for their past mistakes."

"What past mistakes? I don't understand."

Young Aunt looks straight into Ha's eyes. "Do you know why your father died?"

"Mom said something about his liver. That's why she doesn't want me to eat lots of eggs."

"That's right, but do you know where he died?"

Two Sisters

"In Saigon? I think I heard that he was in Grant Hospital."

"I came to see him the day before he died."

Ha is dying to hear more about Father's last days. "Was I there? What did he say?"

Young Aunt wraps her knees in her arms and rocks her body back and forth, eyes searching far away. "That evening, your grandmother, your mother, the two of you, and I went to Saigon to see your father. When we got to Fourth Uncle's house, your mother fanned herself with her cone hat, saying that Saigon was too hot, much hotter than Nha-Trang. Your cousin Lily got mad when she heard that. She came over, pointed her finger at your mother, and said, 'How dare you complain that my house is hot? If you like Nha-Trang so much, go back there.' At that moment, Fourth Uncle came home from work. He slapped Lily and ordered her to apologize to your mother. But when Fourth Aunt cried and defended Lily, saying that it was your mother's fault for being rude, your Fourth Uncle threw your mother's bags out on the street and told her to go look for another place to stay."

Ha's heart thumps loudly in her chest as Young Aunt pours out a family secret. Not wanting it to end, she quickly throws out another question. "What happened next? Where did Mother stay?"

"Your mother cried her heart out. She took the two of you with her to the street to gather her belongings, while your grandmother banged her head on the ground, saying she wanted to die right there."

Two Sisters

Ha cannot believe her ears. Her eyes fly open wide. "Why did Grandma want to die, Young Aunt?"

"What a dumb question! Your grandmother loved your mother and felt for her. That's why."

"So did Grandma try to kill herself?"

Young Aunt shakes her head. "The maid pulled your grandmother up. Your grandmother continued to cry and scream at Fourth Uncle for sending your mother away."

Ha feels her cheeks hot with fresh tears. "So what happened to Grandma and Mom?"

"Your grandmother said she'd follow your mother."

"And then?"

"I also cried. I wanted to run after your grandmother and mother, but Fourth Uncle convinced me to stay behind."

Ha looks at Young Aunt in confusion. Remembering the disparaging words and despising actions that Young Aunt reserved for Mother in the past several years, Ha cannot reconcile the difference between the Young Aunt then and the Young Aunt sitting next to her now. Ha wants to ask Young Aunt to explain the reason she wanted to go after Mother and if she had sympathy for Mother, but Ha does not want to interrupt the story. Instead, she urges Young Aunt to continue.

"Eventually Fourth Uncle relented and let your mother stay at his house. The next day when your mother went to the hospital, your father passed away. Fourth Uncle felt guilty for kicking your mother out of his house the day before your father died. So he arranged for your father's body to be transported back to Nha-Trang by railroad and buried there at his expense."

Ha is reeling with this new information. She sadly shakes her head. "I don't remember any of this. I feel bad that Mother said things that hurt the feelings of the rich and sophisticated relatives." Ha begins to pour out the feelings she has been suppressing, oblivious to any discomfort Young Aunt may have. "Now I understand how hard Mom had to work to raise us. We receive only pity from the relatives, not real love and compassion. I feel sad for Mom who has to endure poverty and loneliness as a widow with two children to take care of."

Ha hears no words of acknowledgement or opinion from Young Aunt, but she does not turn to look at Young Aunt for approval. She continues on without taking her eyes off the straight path ahead to the flower bushes at the big house. "I don't know why no one in the extended family likes Mom and her simple ways. Mom did not have a chance to go to school. Why do we dislike what is different from us? What kind of crime did the uneducated, the unsophisticated, and the poor commit? Don't you think they should be helped and loved, rather than despised and hated?"

Ha's eyes have a dreamy appearance of being beyond space and time, without focusing on anything in particular. Like an open dam, her feelings are poured forth with no restraint. "I also wonder where hatred begins. What is the cause of hatred? Is it because we do not speak the same dialect, do not dress the same way, do not have the same style, and do not have the same education that we do not understand each other? And is it true that we cannot love each other if we don't understand each other? What do you think? My teacher says that prejudice causes hatred, do you agree?"

When Ha finally turns to face Young Aunt, Young Aunt is no longer there. Ha has no idea how long she has been talking to herself. Ha feels more and more for Mother, thinking of the many burdens Mother has had to bear. Vy's words suddenly come to Ha's mind. *"I don't want to go to Saigon. I'm scared. I'm afraid to be all by myself in a strange place. Sister Lily didn't want to talk to us or play with us. She didn't come to our little house. I will have no one to play with and I will not get used to living there."* Ha feels guilty that she has pressured Vy to go to Saigon for her own selfish reasons. She covers her face with her hands and cries out in anguish. "Oh no, Vy, I am so sorry I pushed you to do the wrong thing."

Pulling Vy's unread letter from her pocket, Ha tears the blue envelope open and hungrily reads the purple-ink words.

My dearest sister Ha,

I promised to write you as soon as I got to Saigon, but I did not write until today. You've been waiting and are not pleased with me, right? I apologize a thousand times. I have been very busy. Fourth Aunt took me places to try to find a private school for me. After a week of looking, she enrolled me at Quoc-Anh School. Of all the private schools we looked at, this school is the farthest away from her house, but she likes that it has the best reputation both in education and discipline. This school requires a uniform, unlike my school Le-Quy-Don in Nha-Trang. Fourth Aunt took me to the tailor to have my uniform made, white blouses and navy skirts. I am having a good time. The students here are very nice and they like talking to people from Nha-Trang. I made friends with a girl in our neighborhood. Her name is Nguyen. She

Two Sisters

showed me around and helped me buy stamps and mail this letter to you. I got used to living here more quickly than I thought. Sister Lily went to college overseas. I am living on the third floor, in a large room, with two maids, Sister An and Fifth Sister. They are very nice and take care of me very well. Brother Duy often gives me money and buys me ice cream. Saigon ice cream is really good, Sister Ha. Every time I eat ice cream or sleep on a nice mattress or study under the bright electric light, I wish you were here with me to enjoy the same things I have.

How are you at home? Do you miss me? Does Mom still beat you? I often pray to Dad that Mom will not hurt you. I love you very much, Sister Ha. Although I am homesick for you and Mom, I will study hard so that I will finish high school and have a high school diploma, so that we can do what we promised each other. I just want to ask that when we build a house for Mom, we will also build a shower in the bathroom. Fourth Aunt's house has a shower. It is really nice. It's like standing under the rain when you wash yourself. If you see the shower, you'll love it, too. So please promise to have a shower, Sister Ha. What time do you bathe at home? Make sure you do it in the evening when no one can peek in. This weekend, Fourth Aunt will take me to the zoo to see the elephants. I want to thank you for encouraging me to go to Saigon because I get to see the elephants and have everything I need.

I hope you and Mom will be healthy and peaceful. Give my love and greeting to Mom and tell her I love her very much. I will ask Fourth Aunt to let me go back to visit Mom and you in the summer.

Your little sister,

Vy

Two Sisters

Ha puts the letter back into her pocket and returns to the little house. Mother still sits forlornly next to the dresser. Handing Vy's letter to Mother, Ha says, "I went into the big house to get this letter, not to play cards. Don't worry. I will not get addicted to card playing or gambling. I promise I will not play cards *over there*. I will study hard and finish high school and I will not let you down. I will live in honor of Dad's name and his memories, and will not give anyone reasons to criticize the Hoang daughters."

Mother looks up. Her face is wet with tears of surprise and happiness.

Ha walks out to the well to wash her face. It is early evening, but the sun is still bright. In the garden, under the golden sunlight, the orange yellow lucuma fruit glisten among the glowing green branches.

About The Author

Cung Thi Lan is originally from Nha-Trang, Vietnam. She has been a teacher, a Girl Scout leader, and a social worker. She currently resides in Maryland with her family.

Two Sisters is a story of two sisters growing up in poverty in Central Vietnam. It is written from the perspective of the big sister who is little girl herself. It is a story of struggling for survival, of sisterly and family bonds, of the devastating effect of poverty on people, and of the problem with social classes. Via vivid imagination and invented games, the two sisters live through indifference, injustice, contradiction, and poverty and soar above them.

List of published books by the author:

Nha Trang Memoir (2004)
Two Sisters (2005)
Sorrowful Love (2006)
Distance of Eternal Separation (2009)
Unforgettable Kindness (2011)
A Great Legend of Love (2012)
Forever Apart (2014)

About the Translator

Diem-Tran Kratzke was born in Saigon, Vietnam. She has been living in the United States since 1975. She currently resides in Northern Virginia with her husband. She works as a mathematical statistician for the Department of Labor. She is a member of the Fairfax Public School Improv Troupe. She met the author Lan Cung through volunteering and working for the Girl Scouts Council of the Nation's Capital. She encouraged Lan Cung to start writing books in the Vietnamese language. *Two Sisters* is the second published work in Vietnamese by Lan Cung and is the second book that has been translated into English by the translator. Kratzke also has translated *Unforgettable Kindness* into English.